MW01097435

The Green Wave

*Environmentalism
and Its Consequences*

Bonner R. Cohen

Capital Research Center

About the Author

BONNER R. COHEN serves as senior fellow at the National Center for Public Policy Research and as senior policy analyst for the Committee for a Constructive Tomorrow. He has written widely on environmental issues for over 15 years. His articles have appeared in the *Wall Street Journal, Forbes, Investor's Business Daily, National Review, Philadelphia Inquirer, Miami Herald, Milwaukee Journal-Sentinel, Atlanta Journal-Constitution, Washington Times,* and dozens of other newspapers around the country. He has been interviewed on FoxNews, CNN, BBC, National Public Radio, and scores of radio talk shows in the U.S. As a correspondent, he has covered international conferences on environmental issues in Japan, Australia, Germany, Switzerland, the Netherlands, Morocco, Turkey, Bangladesh, Italy and South Africa. He also has testified before the U.S. Senate Environment and Public Works Committee and before subcommittees of the Senate Energy and Natural Resources Committee, House Resources Committee and House Judiciary Committee.

Cohen received a Ph. D. summa cum laude from the University of Munich and a B.A. from the University of Georgia.

ISBN 1-892934-11-6

Acknowledgements

I would like to thank The Capital Research Center for making this book possible. The support and patience shown by Terrence Scanlon, David Hogberg, and CRC's fine editor, Bob Huberty, went far beyond the call of duty. My special thanks also go to Karl Eiselsberg and Lori Reid who provided invaluable assistance in conducting research for this book.

Over the years, I have benefited greatly from the knowledge and insights of many experts in the field of environmental policy. I owe a special debt of gratitude to Ron Arnold (Center for the Defense of Free Enterprise), Angela Logomasini (Competitive Enterprise Institute), Myron Ebell (Competitive Enterprise Institute), R.J. Smith (National Center for Public Policy Research), Henry Miller (Hoover Institution), Steve Milloy (Free Enterprise Action Fund), Paul Driessen (Atlas Economic Research Foundation), Dennis and Alex Avery (Hudson Institute for Global Food Issues), Michael Hardiman (Hardiman Consulting), Elizabeth Whelan (American Council on Science and Health), Chuck Cushman (American Land Rights Association), Tom Randall (Winninggreen), Fred Smith (Competitive Enterprise Institute), and Kathy Benedetto (formerly with the National Wilderness Institute).

Bonner R. Cohen
Arlington, Virginia
May 2006

Contents

Appendix
THE KEY PLAYERS

Introduction

[W]hen the search for truth is confused with political advocacy, the pursuit of knowledge is reduced to the quest for power.[1]

ALSTON CHASE

"We have become convinced that modern environmentalism, with all its unexamined assumptions, outdated concepts and exhausted strategies, must die so that something new can live."[2]

As the year 2004 drew to a close, an intriguing essay on the state of the modern environmental movement appeared on the Internet. Provocatively titled "The Death of Environmentalism," the 25-page document is the work of two relatively obscure environmental activists, Michael Shellenberger and Ted Nordhaus, both in their thirties.

The essay is based in large part on interviews Shellenberger and Nordhaus conducted with over 25 leading environmentalists, including some of the movement's most generous donors. Originally released at the October 2004 meeting of the Environmental Grantmakers Association, a well-heeled foundation that underwrites a host of environmental groups, the essay is an analysis of what the authors believe is an alarming decline in the power and influence of environmentalism, particularly in the United States.

"From battles over higher fuel efficiency for cars and trucks to attempts to reduce carbon emissions through international treaties, environmental groups have repeatedly tried and failed to win national legislation that would reduce the threat of global warming," they wrote. "As a result, people in the environmental movement today find themselves less politically powerful than we were one and a half decades ago." The authors point out, for example, that, over the last 15 years, environmental foundations and organizations have invested hundreds of millions of dollars into global warming. "We have strikingly little to show for it," they note.

1

To buttress their case, the activists cite data obtained by Environics, a Canadian polling company, showing Americans distancing themselves from environmentalists on several key issues. According to Environics, the number of Americans who agree with the statement, "To preserve people's jobs in this country, we must accept higher levels of pollution in the future," increased from 17 percent in 1996 to 26 percent in 2000. Even more troubling for the movement was Environics' finding that the number of Americans who agreed that, "Most of the people actively involved in environmental groups are extremists, not reasonable people," leaped from 32 percent in 1996 to 41 percent in 2000.[3]

The pair readily acknowledge that leading environmental organizations "boast large professional staffs and receive tens of millions of dollars in donations every year from foundations and individuals." But for all its wealth, the authors contend that "the environmental movement's fundamental concepts, its method for framing legislative proposals, and its *very institutions* are outmoded. Today environmentalism is just another special interest." (emphasis in the original).

It comes as no surprise that such apostate thoughts have not been universally welcomed by the authors' fellow activists. Carl Pope, executive director of the Sierra Club, issued a scathing 6,000-word denunciation of the paper, saying the essay "is unfair, unclear and divisive [and] has actually muddied the water and made the task of figuring out a comprehensive and effective set of strategies more difficult." Pope even questioned the pair's motives. "Given the chosen audience of the paper was the funders," he wrote, "it will be hard for many readers to avoid suspicion that the not-so-hidden message was 'Fund us instead.'"[4]

Equally critical of Shellenberger's and Nordhaus's remarks, albeit from an entirely different perspective, was Angela Logomasini, director of risk studies at the Washington-based Competitive Enterprise Institute (CEI). "They may well be facing new challenges and even be in some kind of transition, but they are still...dangerously powerful," she wrote in early February 2005. "They have become institutionalized...they are in the agencies, the courts, our educational system and they get most [of] the good press," she noted. "They cry that they have not enacted national legislation on global warming, yet they have all of Europe and much of the rest of the world actually working on this issue even when it is clear that their policies won't solve a thing."[5]

The lively debate spawned by "The Death of Environmentalism" came at a pivotal time for the nation's major environmental organizations. In the November 2004 election, groups like Pope's

Sierra Club and the League of Conservation Voters spent at least $15 million, much of it in a vain effort to prevent the re-election of President George W. Bush.

A setback of a different kind, and from an unexpected source, came about at the end of 2004 with the release of Michael Crichton's book *State of Fear*. Like *Jurassic Park, The Andromeda Strain, The Lost World* and many other Crichton books, *State of Fear* is a work of fiction, albeit one with an interesting twist. The novel's villains are eco-terrorists who use modern technology to induce natural disasters that can be blamed on global warming. They also engage in elaborate fundraising schemes and cynically skew the facts so as to manipulate public opinion and the media into believing that human-induced global warming poses a serious threat to the world.

In Crichton's thriller, the plotters are eventually undone thanks to tireless efforts by an intrepid counter-terrorist, John Kenner, and to the eco-terrorists' hubris. Ultimately, *State of Fear* is about the politicization of science and its disastrous consequences. Indeed, a unique aspect of *State of Fear* is Crichton's repeated citation of the scientific literature that contradicts the alleged "consensus" on the dangers of global warming.

Within weeks of its release, the Crichton book became a worldwide best-seller, and therein lies its potential to affect public discourse on climate change and other environmental issues.[6] The author's enormous popularity guarantees that his unflattering portrait of environmental true-believers, and his systematic debunking of key tenets of modern environmentalism, will reach a far wider audience than those who customarily participate in environmental policy debate. But does this mean we are experiencing "the death of environmentalism?" The answer is most assuredly "no." Rifts within political organizations and movements have existed since antiquity. The ebb and flow of political fortunes—and the environmental movement is nothing if not intensely political—will always produce its share of finger-pointing when things appear to go badly. Shellenberger, Nordhaus, Pope, and their colleagues are simply carrying on a long tradition of internecine conflict. Furthermore, CEI's Logomasini is certainly correct in pointing to the environmentalists' impressive and ongoing success in burrowing into institutions and transforming them into instruments that further their political agenda. Like any other interest group, the environmental movement has had its share of defeats, many of them self-inflicted, but, as we shall see, "death" is nowhere on the horizon.

This book will take stock of the environmental movement in the U.S. as it stands three-and-one-half decades after the first Earth Day was celebrated in 1970. The environmental movement is one of thousands of interest groups that vie for power, influence, profile, support, and money in the United States. While they exhibit traits common to other interest groups, environmental organizations also employ strategies and tactics that are unique to their movement. From traditional scare campaigns aimed at denigrating targeted technologies or industries, to innovative schemes for raising money and influencing corporate and government policies, environmental activists have, over the years, refined the ways they seek to achieve their ends. What we see today is not necessarily what was there just a few years ago.

Of the roughly 8,000 environmental organizations currently operating in the U.S., only a few dozen of the most influential groups can be dealt with in this narrative. This is not to say that smaller groups, whose financial resources are a pittance when compared to the likes of the Nature Conservancy, Sierra Club or the Wilderness Society, are only marginal players. On the contrary, smaller groups that know what they want and how to get it often have a profound influence on such matters as local zoning and land-use decisions. Considerations of space, however, will keep most of our focus on the rich and powerful among the nation's green advocacy groups.

The important point to keep in mind is that today's environmental activists, though guided by roughly the same view of the world, go about their tasks in manifold ways and from many directions. It is this division of labor that has enabled the movement to confront adversity and remain a formidable force in American society.

Chapter 1

INTO THE BOARDROOM

"We must consider changes in the rules of society by challenging the unchallenged politics of corporations."[1]

TOM HAYDEN

Traversing Manhattan's busy sidewalks can be a daunting task, particularly in the last hectic shopping days leading up to Christmas. As if New York's much-jostled pedestrians didn't have enough to slow them down, a demonstration in December 2004 before the corporate headquarters of banking giant J.P. Morgan Chase further impeded their progress.

There was something about this demonstration, however, that set it apart from picket lines, marches, rallies, and other outdoor political events the city had witnessed so many times before. This one featured second-graders from Fairfield County, Conn. who had been brought to Manhattan courtesy of the Rainforest Action Network (RAN). Having been lured to the Big Apple under the pretext of participating in an environmental poster-drawing contest, the seven-year-olds instead found themselves being used by RAN activists as demonstrators to protest JP Morgan's lending practices in developing countries.

More accustomed to traditional field trips to the zoo or a museum, the children were now enlisted in RAN's campaign to "stop lending money to projects that destroy endangered forests and cause global warming." One youngster held up a poster urging J.P. Morgan's CEO William Harrison to "protect the rain forest instead of hurting the Earth for oil." The whole exercise was, as Terence Corcoran of Canada's *National Post* aptly put it, "ideological child abuse."[2]

It would be easy to dismiss RAN's stunt with the second-graders as mere street theater, worthy at best of a couple of minutes of coverage on the local evening news. But there is much more going on here. The attack on J.P. Morgan was but the latest salvo in RAN's Global Finance Campaign aimed at pressuring banks to align their lending practices in developing countries with RAN's environmental agenda. That agenda, as the demonstration in Manhattan shows, includes fierce opposition to logging and the use of fossil fuels in poor countries, and enthusiastic support for the theory of human-induced global warming.

By any measure, RAN's campaign has been a spectacular success. The San Francisco-based group scored two impressive victories in 2004 when Citigroup and Bank of America capitulated to the environmentalists' demands, after putting up only token resistance.

RAN's tactics, and the subsequent surrender of both financial service institutions, are instructive. RAN activists targeted Citigroup by stalking its former CEO Sandy Weill around the world. This harassment was augmented by a RAN-sponsored TV ad in which Hollywood luminaries Susan Sarandon, Daryl Hannah and Ed Asner cut up their Citi credit cards to protest the bank's lending practices. Schoolchildren also played a prominent role in the attack on Citigroup, with letters to Weill posted on the RAN Web site from outraged pupils. One read:

"My name is Aekta, and I am in the 4th grade at Canyon Elementary. I am studying about the rainforest...I guarantee you that all my relatives will find some other bank, unless you stop lending money to rainforest destroyers."

Duly intimidated, Citigroup surrendered. In a joint announcement with RAN, it adopted a new set of environmental standards to guide its lending decisions in poor countries.

Bank of America was next. Unable, or unwilling, to withstand RAN's heat on the issue of global warming, Bank of America went beyond the concessions made by Citigroup and set an explicit goal of reducing greenhouse-gas emission by 7 percent "within our energy and utilities portfolio."

Commenting on RAN's intimidation of the banks, *Wall Street Journal* columnist Alan Murray pointed out that the "politization of bank lending," which is what RAN's campaign is all about, not only undermines financial institutions, but also has serious economic implications for the developing world as well. In fact, the assault on the financial service industry is only the latest manifestation of a much larger effort by leftist activists—one decades in the making—to redirect global financial assets to causes of their own choosing.

Their goal, according to George Washington University professor Jarol B. Manheim is to "build an alternative power structure—and a new set of strategies to achieve it." The alternative power structure, which Manheim calls "the Out-of-Power Elite," is based on the Left's understanding of the old power structure and how it should be undermined and transformed to serve the activists' purposes. "Much of the activism we see today," he explains, "is designed for one of two purposes—either to undermine confidence in the political and economic establishment or to replicate portions of the current system but under new management and with a new purpose."

Manheim claims this approach would transform capitalism by co-opting its institutions, and he dates its origins to the *Port Huron Statement* of 1962. Drafted by prominent New Left activist Tom Hayden, then with the radical Students for a Democratic Society (SDS), the statement is largely devoid of the shop-worn ideological jargon that pervades more traditional socialist or marxist texts. In one pivotal passage in the statement, Hayden postulated a strategic vision that— decades later—would inspire groups like the Rainforest Action Network in mounting their offensive against the established economic order:

It is not possible to believe that true democracy can exist where a minority utterly controls enormous wealth and power...We can no longer rely on the competition of the many to assure that business enterprise is responsible to social needs...Nor can we trust the corporate bureaucracy to be socially responsible or to develop a 'corporate conscience' that is democratic....We must consider changes in the rules of society by challenging the unchallenged politics of American corporations.[3]

While Hayden went on to make a name for himself as one of the most vocal opponents of the Vietnam War, his thoughts on the social responsibility of corporations would far outlive the conflict in Southeast Asia. Indeed, Hayden's ideas were fine-tuned a few years later in an obscure document with the improbable title of *Research Methodology Guide*. Drafted in 1970 in part by two SDS alumni, Michael Locker and Paul Booth, the guide is actually a how-to manual on attacking corporations written to support the activities of the decidedly left-of-center North American Congress on Latin America (NACLA). The manual laid out guidelines for what it called "power structure research," the objective of which was:

Identifying the people and institutions that make our lives and the lives of others intolerable...locating weak points in the system... suggesting a strategy for resistance...[and] propelling ourselves and others into a high state of consciousness of where the modes of power lie and how they function.

Knowledge of such points gives us the leverage to challenge the system effectively with the means at our disposal. Sometimes even an apparently insignificant weakness can be effectively exploited. The public image of a corporation, for instance, can be important to its continued prosperity—investment, government contracts, employee recruiting, etc., can all be affected by a change in this image."[4]

George Washington University's Manheim describes this passage as the first clearly delineated doctrine of what he has termed "Biz-War"—"the waging of reputational warfare on the corporation as a means of changing corporation policy company by company and in the process of redirecting public policy through the aggregation of these individual-level changes."

There is little reason to believe that the authors of the *Research Methodology Guide* were thinking of environmental policy when they developed their strategy to attack corporations. More likely, they saw corporations as epitomizing an economic system they thoroughly detested and deemed responsible for many of the ills in the world.

But the manual did appear the same year, 1970, as the first Earth Day, which was proclaimed just eight years after the publication of Rachel Carson's *Silent Spring*. Carson's best-selling book, in which she claimed that man-made chemicals were harming humans and the environment, helped give rise to the environmental movement we know today. In other words, the new anti-capitalist strategy now had a green context in which it could unfold. Alongside more traditional goals like redistributing income to secure "equality," activists seized on the environment as an issue with enormous potential to influence young educated urbanites who felt guilty about their affluence. Their aim: to bring about the reordering of national and global priorities.

The rise of environmentalism would open up new avenues for activists to demand changes in the status quo. Their professions of concern for clean air, clean water and the state of the natural world would resonate far beyond the narrow ideological confines of what was then known as the New Left. Within a few years, those engaged in environmental issues would range from government officials (federal, state and local), international agencies, the business community, and global non-governmental organizations (NGOs) to scientists, engineers, journalists and academics. As John McCormick has put it: "The concerns of a few scientists, administrators and conservation groups blossomed into a fervent mass movement that swept the industrialized world."[5]

The fusion of two strands of thought—one focused on economic

8

development, the other on concern for the environment—created a potent concoction, particularly when infused by their proponents with a sense of urgency bordering on alarmism. David Henderson, former head of the economics and statistics department for the Paris-based Organization for Economic Cooperation and Development (OECD), has unearthed a quotation buried in a 1975 report by the Club of Rome that captures perfectly the spirit of the times. Henderson sees the quotation as representative of the kind of "global salvationism" prevalent in much of today's environmentalist literature.

Two gaps, steadily widening, appear to be at the heart of mankind's present crises: the gap between man and nature, and the gap between 'North' and South,' rich and poor. Both gaps must be narrowed if world-shattering catastrophes are to be avoided; but they can be narrowed only if global 'unity' and Earth's 'fitness' are explicitly recognized.[6]

With the decision at the UN-sponsored Stockholm Conference on the Human Environment in 1972 to create the United Nations Environmental Programme (UNEP), environmentalism now had a powerful global sponsor. UN Secretary-General U Thant commissioned an unofficial report for the conference. The report was published that same year with the revealing title: *Only One Earth: The Care and Maintenance of a Small Planet*. In the coming decades, the UN would provide a useful, high-profile platform for airing environmental issues. It would also lend its support to a host of causes pushed by environmental activists, including efforts to influence corporate conduct.

Underlying those efforts are two separate but related concepts that are at the core of global environmental activism: they are *sustainable development* and *corporate social responsibility*. Sustainable development will be dealt with more thoroughly elsewhere in this book. However, it is important to understand how the concept relates to environmental activists' attacks on corporations. In the words of former Norwegian prime minister Gro Harlem Brundtland, sustainable development means that "humanity must ensure that meeting present needs does not compromise the ability of future generations to meet their own needs."[7]

Brundtland's definition may appear to be no more than the standard boiler-plate served up in otherwise forgettable UN publications—in this case a report called *Our Common Future*, released in 1987 by the UN-sponsored World Commission on Environment and Development. But Brundtland's little definition deserves closer scrutiny. We are first told that "humanity must ensure...," which raises the intriguing question of who will act in the name of "humanity"? The other tricky word in the definition is "needs." Who determines what constitutes humanity's "needs"—both present and future? Far more than just a fashionable phrase to be tossed around at international gatherings, sustainable development, if pursued relentlessly on a broad front, can be a potent vehicle for putting considerable power in the hands of its proponents.

Furthermore, sustainable development, the concept's supporters argue, "will require the greatest changes in the wealthiest nations, which consume the most resources, release the most pollution, and have the greatest capacity to make the necessary changes."[8] And what better way to provide for those "necessary changes" than through sustainable development's constant companion, corporate social responsibility (CSR).

At first glance, corporate social responsibility seems like little more than another way of expressing the conventional idea of "corporate governance." The latter customarily refers to a company's efforts not only to conduct its business in accordance with the highest ethical and legal standards, but also to be a good neighbor by donating to charities, funding scholarships or performing other good works not directly tied to its immediate business interests. But "social responsibility" suggests something far more ambitious.

Attempts by activists to affect corporate policies in matters outside the traditional sphere of business—wages, pensions health care etc.—are nothing new. They range from the efforts of civil rights demonstrators to integrate Woolworth lunch counters in the South in the late 1950s and early 1960s, to nationwide campaigns in the 1970s and 1980s to pressure corporations to cease investments in South Africa as a way to put an end to the Apartheid regime. "The idea in each instance," Manheim notes, "was that, if they lacked the resources to force governments to change *public* policy directly, the advocates of these causes nevertheless could achieve their objectives by motivating private institutions to change their *private* policies on such a large scale as to constitute a de facto change in public policy. The target of choice: corporations."[9]

By recognizing the decisive role a redirected private sector can play in altering public policy, today's proponents of CSR have further refined tactics activists employed decades ago. In their view, according to Sir Geoffrey Owen of the London School of Economics, "the activities of companies—especially large, multinational companies—impinge in a variety of ways on the health of the societies in which they operate, and on the environment. In return for the freedom they enjoy in pursuing their commercial objectives, companies must recognize these externalities and adjust their behavior accordingly."[10]

Just as Brundtland's brief definition of sustainable development leaves much to the imagination, precise definitions of CSR have been hard to come by. Yet because both terms have a superficial appeal—at least to the politically uninitiated—uncertainty over their meaning is a source of strength. Those who take the trouble to search the literature can unearth enough information about CSR to disabuse them of any uncertainty about the concept's true meaning.

'The Internet source Wikipedia, for example, currently defines CSR as "a company's obligation to be accountable to all of its stakeholders in all its operations and activities with the aim of achieving sustainable development not only in the economical dimension but also in the social and environmental dimensions."[11]

David Henderson sheds further light on the subject by noting that advocates of CSR "view enterprise profitability not as a *criterion* which can be improved as such, but as the happy outcome of virtuous conduct. They believe that enterprises can best contribute to the general welfare by consciously adopting sustainable development as their objective, and pursuing in consequence a range of self-chosen social and environmental goals, with higher expected profits as a likely reward. They assume uncritically that the notion of sustainable development, and with it these new goals, is well defined and generally agreed: the path of virtue is supposedly clear for all to follow."[12]

Note how forceful and far-reaching the Wikipedia definition is. It speaks of *"a company's obligation to be accountable to all of its stakeholders in all its operations and activities..."* (emphasis added). And just who are these "stakeholders" to whom a company is obligated to be accountable? Webster's defines a stakeholder as a gambling term. But consult Wikipedia and you discover a new acquired meaning, one rife with political implications. It defines stakeholder as "everyone with an interest in what an entity does...[including] not only its vendors, employees, and customers, but even members of a community where its offices or factory may affect the local economy or environment."[13]

The idea of a stakeholder is thus far removed from the traditional shareholder of a corporation. Stakeholders are those who use corporate social responsibility to prod companies down the "path of virtue" to achieve sustainable development. In this view, RAN is a self-appointed stakeholder of Citigroup, Bank of America and J.P. Morgan Chase as well as any other company its activists choose to target.

Acting in the name of CSR, activists push businesses to meet the "triple bottom line," which is economic, environmental and social, as opposed to focusing on profitability and shareholder value. Only in this way can they meet "society's expectations."[14]

And CSR's swift rise to almost unquestioned acceptance by the public and private sector shows that "society" is expecting a lot. Henderson has tracked CSR's triumphs in recent years, which include its having been formally commended by the European Commission, with the approval of the EU Council of Ministers. In the recently revised version of the OECD's *Guidelines for Multinational Enterprises*, the new text is presented as "a tool for promoting corporate social responsibility." Similarly, in the agreed "outcome" document of the 2002 UN conference in Monterrey, Mexico on "financing for development," the participating governments said: "We urge businesses not only to take into account the economic and financial but also the development, social, gender and environmental implications of their undertakings." The United Kingdom even has a minister charged with the responsibility of promoting CSR.[15]

Indeed, CSR has gained such currency that over 150 multinational corporations from over 30 countries have formed the World Business Council on Sustainable Development (WBCSD). Its current membership currently includes such corporate giants as ABB, BP Amoco, Deloitte Touche Tomatsu, Ford, General Motors, Mitsubishi, Monsanto, Procter & Gamble, Rio Tinto, Shell International, Sony, Time Warner, Toyota, Unilever and Volkswagen.[16]

The WBCSD has even provided the most direct link between sustainable development and CSR. In 1998, it created a working group composed of representatives of 65 member-companies to launch an inquiry into sustainable development/CSR. Two years later, and after a series of "global stakeholder dialogues," the WBCSD issued a report: *Corporate Social Responsibility: Making Good Business Sense*. It defined CSR as follows:

Corporate social responsibility is the commitment of business to contribute to sustainable development, working with their employees, their families, their community and society at large to improve their quality of life.[17]

To many companies, no doubt, embracing sustainable development and CSR may seem like little more than making vague but sweet-sounding commitments that put them in good stead with activists and regulators in key global markets. They do not seem to appreciate the extent to which they are being used as agents of social change—a change not necessarily in their interest. As Sir Geoffrey Owen points out, many advocates of CSR have little understanding of, and in some cases a deep distaste for, the capitalist system. "Their interest is not in making the system work better," he says, "but in altering it in a way that suits their idea of what companies are for."[18]

That "deep distaste" for the capitalist system is rarely very far from the surface. If cajoling and other forms of friendly persuasion don't work, there are always ways to make reluctant companies see the light. After months of relentless pressure expertly applied by the Rainforest Action Network, J.P. Morgan Chase capitulated to the activist group in late April 2005. The company agreed to sweeping changes in its lending and underwriting practices for projects likely to have an environmental effect.

In a far-reaching, 10-page policy statement, the bank—whose assets are the third largest in the U.S.—pledged to take an aggressive stance on global warming, including tying carbon-dioxide emissions to its loan-review process for power plants and other major emitters of greenhouse gases. *The Wall Street Journal* also reported that the bank "plans to calculate in loan reviews the financial cost of greenhouse-gas emissions, such as the risk of a company losing business to a competitor with lower emissions because it has a better public standing." Alongside its commitments on global warming, J.P. Morgan pledged to set up "No Go Zones," or "sensitive" regions where it won't finance commercial logging or underwrite projects that pose an environmental "threat."[19]

Shareholder Activism: Another Way to Skin the Cat

J.P. Morgan's decision was met with great approval by Steve Lippman, vice president of social research at Trillium Asset Management, a socially oriented investment firm based in Boston. "This is increasingly becoming the way all banks operate," he commented. "J.P. Morgan is now raising the bar for the sector." Lippman's firm is not a disinterested party to the outcome of the RAN-J.P. Morgan conflict. Together with the Christian Brothers Investment Services, Inc., it lobbied J.P. Morgan to change its lending practices, and had extracted a pledge from the bank to issue a new environmental policy statement, even before RAN's demonstrations got underway.[20]

The involvement of Trillium and Christian Brothers in the attack on J.P. Morgan points to another way activists can influence corporate behavior. Both companies exemplify the growing role of socially responsible shareholder groups in shaping corporate policies on the environment and other issues. In 2004, 25 shareholder resolutions on global warming were filed against U.S. companies, and the number is expected to grow in the years to come.

We have already discussed the distinction between traditional shareholders and today's self-appointed stakeholders. That distinction, however, can become blurred. The collaboration between Trillium and RAN in the case of J.P. Morgan shows that, under certain circumstances, shareholders and activists can join forces to pursue a common goal. Those circumstances come into play when an investment firm like Trillium makes common cause with outside activist groups like RAN.

While the origins of socially responsible investing (SRI) date from the late 1970s, momentum didn't really develop until after the election of Ronald Reagan to the White House in November 1980. "In disaster lies opportunity," an old saying goes, and to the activist Left, Reagan's election was a calamity that changed the political landscape and demanded innovative counter-measures. One of those innovations was the founding of America's first socially responsible investment fund, the Calvert Social Investment Fund in 1982. It was the creation of the Calvert Group, a Washington, D.C.-based investment management fund founded by Wayne Silby and John Guffey Jr.

Silby is of particular interest. Together with Joshua Mailman, a leading fund-raiser for the Left in the aftermath of Reagan's election, he helped establish the Social Venture Network (SVN).[21] SVN is a membership organization designed to mobilize small and mid-size businesses committed, in the organization's words, "to the use of business as a vehicle to create a more just, humane and environmentally sustainable society."

In a few short years, the Calvert Social Investment Fund (CSIF) went from being the brain-child of Silby and Guffey to become the vanguard of corporate social investing. Only companies that pass CSIF's strict criteria on such issues as the environment, product safety and impact and human rights are considered for investment by the fund's managers. To assist fund managers in making these evaluations, CSIF avails itself of expertise drawn from such groups as Greenpeace, the Wilderness Society, World Resources Institute and Amnesty International. In 1986, CSIF became the first mutual fund to sponsor a shareholder resolution on social issues.

The trail CSIF blazed has been followed by a host of other like-minded firms, of which Trillium, a key player in RAN's successful campaign against J.P. Morgan, is one of the more prominent. Today, there are over 200 socially responsible funds in the United States. Some have criteria, similar to those used by CSIF, to screen companies

14

to see if they are suitable candidates for investment. Others engage in what Steven Milloy calls "exclusionary investing"—e.g., "avoidance of companies in particular industries or companies otherwise in disfavor of social activists."[22] SRI funds reportedly controlled over $2 trillion in assets (1 in 9 dollars invested) in 2003. Though most SRI is not currently activist-oriented, Milloy points out that an estimated $448 billion in assets was reportedly controlled in 2003 by shareholder activists.[45]

Yet there is something far more important than the amount of money involved and that is the political uses to which it can be applied as part of a well-coordinated strategy to change corporate behavior. By bowing to the demands of environmental activists and committing themselves to revise their lending practices, J.P. Morgan Chase, Citigroup and BankAmerica, in effect, were adopting a code of conduct to which they can be held accountable. This point was expressed most vividly— and cynically—by community organizer Saul Alinsky. In his *Rules for Radicals* (1971), he wrote:

Make the enemy live up to their own book of rules. You can kill them with this, for they can no more obey their own rules than the Christian Church can live up to Christianity.[23]

As noted, Trillium Asset Management played a significant behind-the-scenes role in RAN's defeat of J.P. Morgan. Trillium's president, Joan Bavaria, was the founding chair of the Coalition for environmentally Responsible Economies (CERES), which wrote the rulebook that has been used against corporate America. Founded in 1989, CERES is a coalition of environmental groups, labor unions, activist public pension funds, socially responsible investors, and more than 200 Protestant denominations and Catholic orders. Manheim describes CERES's objective as "to supplement governmental efforts at environmental protection by changing private corporate policies and behaviors." "The means to that end," he explains, "has been through the shareholder resolutions intended to impose on corporate management a code of environmental conduct known as the 'CERES Principles.'"[24]

The CERES Principles have been adopted by over 70 companies, including American Airlines, Ford, General Motors, Polaroid and Sunoco. In committing to these principles, companies pledge to do such seemingly benign things as reduce their discharges into the environment, conserve nonrenewable resources, practice recycling, save energy and use "environmentally sound" technologies and processes.

With the adoption of the CERES Principles, the notion of agreeing to an environmental code of conduct gained a degree of acceptance in the business community. Once the idea is accepted, codes of conduct can be broadened to include issues that are far more important than recycling. What's more, the voluntary nature of the CERES Principles can be replaced by codes of conduct into which companies can be pushed by activist-led public campaigns. As Alinsky shrewdly observed, a company's failure to abide by the code—at least to the satisfaction of anti-business activists—can become a weapon to force the firm to mend its ways.

All these elements were present in the activist-driven campaigns against the three financial institutions. Not only were the banks' pledges to change their lending policies anything but voluntary, but activists didn't hesitate to express their disapproval when a bank's performance failed to meet their expectations. On the very day J.P. Morgan Chase unveiled its new environmental policies, RAN officials criticized Bank of America, saying it "needs to do more" to carry out the environmental guidelines it announced in May 2004. Alinsky knew what he was talking about.

And there's more to come. RAN's strategy is to target the leaders in each business sector, brow-beat them into submission, and use their extracted environmental pledges as the standard to be followed by other companies in that sector. "We call it 'Rank 'em and spank 'em,'" said Mike Brune, RAN's executive director. In 2003, the group got Home Depot, Inc., the nation's leader in the housewares sector, to use its considerable purchasing power to get loggers in Chile to quit buying land RAN said was being deforested. In April 2005, Brune told the *Wall Street Journal* that RAN's next target would be U.S. auto manufacturers.[25]

Given the prominent role global warming plays in the current environmental debate, businesses of all sorts—banks, manufacturers, utilities, transportation providers, etc.—should expect to be asked to explain what they, as "socially responsible corporations," are doing to curtail their greenhouse-gas emissions. "We now see a significant trend among a range of companies to address climate change. If we're not at the tipping point, we're coming close to it," commented Timothy Smith of Walden Asset Management in Boston, a fund manager specializing in social investing.[26]

Smith may be engaging in far more than just wishful thinking. Walden Asset Management is part of a major initiative on global warming, the Carbon Disclosure Project (CDP), that was launched in 2003 with the goal of pushing companies to that "tipping point." The CDP is a group of CSR-minded institutional investors who send out annual questionnaires to the CEOs of large companies, inquiring into how they stand on the subject of global warming and what they are doing to combat this alleged menace. "As institutional investors representing $20 trillion in funds under management, we are continually examining our portfolios in order to assess the potential risks and opportunities relating to climate change for companies in which we invest," the 2005 survey ominously states.[27] The intimidating tone of the surveys sent to the CEOs is not lost on the recipients. In 2003, 245 companies completed the survey, and 300 companies filled it out in 2004.

The CDP survey is one example of how environmental activists use the private sector to alter public policy. While the administration of George W. Bush rejected the Kyoto Protocol, the Clinton administration, which negotiated and signed the global warming treaty, refused to submit it to the U.S. Senate, knowing it stood no chance of receiving the two-thirds vote necessary for ratification. Unable to get the U.S. government to go along with the Kyoto Protocol's restrictions on greenhouse-gas emissions, activists, including the signatories of the CDP survey, are seeking to pressure companies to implement the treaty on their own.

As Steven Milloy has suggested, the people behind the CDP may have more on their minds than just the future of the planet. Among the 143 signatories of the 2005 CDP survey, he notes, are companies that stand to benefit financially from global warming hysteria. They include socially responsible investment managers such as the Calvert Group, Domini Social Advisers, and Walden Asset Management. "Global warming is a significant part of their strategy to attract new investors," he points out. Milloy, whose CSRwatch.com website monitors these developments, notes that politicized state pension funds, such as CDP signatories Connecticut Retirement Plans and Trust Funds and New York State Common Retirement Fund, have petitioned the Securities and Exchange Commission to require the financial disclosure of global-warming liabilities—"setting the stage for class action litigation— even though no one knows whether any damage giving rise to any liability will ever occur."

"Disclosing greenhouse gas emission levels to environmentalists and their political allies—who happen to be well-connected to trial lawyers— can only serve as a basis for proving and appropriating global warming liability," he warns.[28]

"Fateful Choices"

Implicit in the demands of CSR-inspired environmental activists, and in the acceptance of those demands by elements of the business community, is the belief that nothing short of urgent action can save the world, or the "planet," as environmentalists prefer to call it. This conviction lies at the heart of the "global salvationism" referred to by Henderson. CSR advocates, both in the business world and outside it, he explains, accept "alarmist views on the state of the environment and the damage done to it by business-related activities, a belief that fateful choices now have to be made on behalf of humanity and the planet, and a distorted view of globalization and its effects."[29]

Business leaders who go along with the alarmist view are, no doubt, guided by a variety or combination of motives. Some might actually believe the alarmist rhetoric, or at least some of it. Others might just want to spare themselves the RAN-style harassment that has been dished out to other companies. Still others might want to profit by replacing technologies or products condemned by activists with their own offerings, which they can present to the public and regulators as environmentally superior. Some combination of all these motives is possible. Whatever their thoughts or interests, the business community gives victory to the environmental movement when it allows them to set the terms of the environmental debate.

Besides appealing to social responsibility, CSR activists attract the business community by appealing to their bottom line. In a 2002 study, for example, noted CSR advocate and Boston College management professor Sandra Waddock wrote: "There is significant evidence from a large and growing body of academic research that there is at minimum a neutral, and quite likely a positive relationship between responsible corporate practices and financial performance."[30] Similarly, a 1997 meta-analysis appearing in *Business and Society* reviewed 51 analyses that claimed to have tested the relationship between financial performance of companies and adherence to CSR principles. It found that in a majority of these studies there was a positive relationship between CSR and corporate profitability.

These findings were challenged in a 2004 study by economist Arthur Laffer. Laffer's paper, *Does Corporate Social Responsibility Enhance Business Profitability?*, examined 28 companies selected from a list of the "Top 100 Corporate Citizens" appearing in *Business Ethics* magazine. The companies were chosen based on consistently "high" CSR performance, as defined by their inclusion in the *Business Ethics* list for the last five years. Company financial performances were compared with those of their chief competitors. In terms of compound annual net income growth, net profit margins and stock price appreciation, Laffer and his research team found that only a minority of the CSR companies outperformed their competitors in each category. Laffer and his researchers acknowledge that their findings do not prove conclusively that CSR initiatives have a negative impact on a business's financial performance. "They are, however, strong evidence against the claim that CSR initiatives have universal or systematic positive financial impacts on companies. Perhaps the most that can be said at this point is that research in this area should continue," they caution.[31]

In the wake of the scandals that shook the corporate world in the late 1990s and early 2000s, business leaders, in what is sometimes called the "post-Enron world," have had an additional reason to present a positive image of their enterprises to the public. It has become fashionable in business circles to issue assurances that "corporate governance" is uppermost in the minds of boardroom decision-makers. This is a perfectly understandable reaction by businesspeople who don't want to see their company's reputation sullied by the misdeeds of a small group of corporate bad actors. But they will commit another corporate misdeed if their desire to exhibit compassion and accountability leads them into the waiting arms of corporate social responsibility activists, without knowing the ideology that stands behind CSR.

At the very least, businesspeople should be aware of the level of political sophistication employed by activists determined to use the business community for their own purposes. Jarol Manheim, whose ground-breaking study of the Progressive Left's attack on corporations should be required reading for today's CEOs, has described the activists' grand strategy:

> Rather then overthrowing, figuratively speaking, the interlocked, networked structure by which power was effectively exercised to the disadvantage of the Left, capture that structure or, in the alternative, mimic it with a parallel network to produce what is to the Left a more salubrious set of outcomes.[32]

From the Left's perspective, one could hardly imagine a more "salubrious set of outcomes" than the success that RAN and its allies have enjoyed over three of the world's most powerful financial services institutions. At the time of its victory, RAN had a staff of 27 and an annual budget of about $2 million—small potatoes compared with the vast resources of its vanquished foes.[33] The political and economic implications of what these groups can achieve should be lost on no one.

Chapter 2

THE GLOBAL GREENS

"How can we speak to those who live in the villages and slums about keeping the oceans, the rivers and air clean when their own lives are contaminated at the source? The environment cannot be improved in conditions of poverty. Nor can poverty be eradicated without the use of science and technology."[1]

INDIRA GANDHI

In his 2005 book, *The March of Unreason: Science, Democracy, and the New Fundamentalism*, British House of Lords member Sir Dick Taverne notes that "in the practice of medicine, popular approaches to farming and food, policies to reduce hunger and disease and many other practical issues, there is an undercurrent of irrationality that threatens the progress that depends on science and even [threatens] the civilized basis of our democracy."[2]

Lord Taverne lays the blame for this "undercurrent of irrationality" squarely at the feet of those he calls "eco-fundamentalists," whose incessant environmental campaigns, he argues, are undermining scientific creativity and technological innovation. His warning comes nearly three-and-one-half decades after India's Prime Minister Gandhi, in the above quotation, underscored the decisive role science and technology play in eradicating poverty and disease. The very things she saw then as holding the key to alleviating the afflictions that plague the world's downtrodden, he now sees as under siege in rich and poor nations alike.

Something happened in the years between Indira Gandhi's remarks and the release of Lord Taverne's book. That "something" was the emergence of the modern environmental movement.

From today's vantage point, the world of the late 1960s—with its hippies, psychedelic music, urban riots in the U.S., and body counts in

Vietnam—may seem like some long-bygone age—known only to our distant ancestors. Yet the counter-culture of that era gave rise to profound societal changes that are still very much with us today. Among other things, the tumultuous era proved to be a fertile breeding ground for the nascent environmental movement in the United States and elsewhere in the non-communist industrialized world. Philip Shabecoff, the former chief environmental correspondent for the *New York Times*, described the cross-currents swirling around the founding generation of environmentalism as follows:

[The green movement] has tap roots in the Vietnam era peace movement, the antinuclear protests, ecofeminism, Gaian principles of an holistic earth, the ethical insistence on the rights of nature of the deep ecologists, and the E.F. Schumacher *Small Is Beautiful* approach to economics and technology, the successes of the environmental activists in the United States, and the inchoate but widely shared sense of dread that late-twentieth century civilization was on a collision course with ecological catastrophe.[3]

Rachel Carson's 1962 best-seller, *Silent Spring*, set the stage on which environmentalism would perform over the coming decades. Her belief that man-made chemicals used in pesticides and other products were not only killing birds and other wildlife, creating a "silent spring," but also were causing cancer in humans fit well into the emerging *Zeitgeist* as described by Shabecoff. Quite apart from Carson's views on chemicals, which have not withstood the test of time, there was nonetheless growing awareness, particularly in the wealthier industrialized world, that more could and should be done to provide for cleaner air and water and to protect wildlife.

In keeping with the spirit of the time, the first Earth Day was celebrated by newly-minted environmental activists on April 22 (Lenin's birthday), 1970, and later that year President Richard Nixon, through an executive order, created the U.S. Environmental Protection Agency (EPA). In short order environmental ministries sprang up in governments around the world, a clear indication that the environment was now deemed a subject worthy of official attention.

But could a subject whose primary focus is on man's interaction with nature be adequately addressed on a purely national basis? After all, isn't the "environment" something that by definition transcends political boundaries? The answer from environmental activists, the United Nations, and officials at the growing number of environmental ministries and agencies was a resounding "no." And so the movement made its global debut at the UN Conference on the Human Environment in

Stockholm, Sweden in 1972. Chaired by Maurice Strong, a wealthy Canadian businessman who would play a pivotal role in global environmental affairs in the decades to come, the conference served as a forum at which delegates could give voice to the then fashionable idea that limiting economic growth was the best way to protect the planet from further environmental degradation. To ensure that the United Nations would have a voice in the emerging domain of environmental policy, delegates to the conference also created a new UN agency, the United Nation Environmental Programme (UNEP). Strong would serve as UNEP's first executive director.

The Stockholm conference also gave the world its first exposure to "non-governmental organizations" (NGOs). While official delegates to the Stockholm proceedings hammered out positions the conference would later adopt, there was a parallel gathering of activists that came to be known as the "Hog Farm." It was a forum where environmental activists from around the world could deliver speeches, organize demonstrations, and issue demands they hoped the official delegates would adopt. From these humble beginnings as little more than camp followers holed up at the Hog Farm in Stockholm, NGOs have become a ubiquitous presence at UN-sponsored conferences from Rio de Janeiro and Kyoto to The Hague and Johannesburg. Organizations that want to obtain official NGO status now can be accredited to the UN by filing the proper paperwork in advance of the UN-sponsored event they want to attend. That paperwork includes providing proof to the UN Department of Public Information that the would-be NGO meets certain requirements. Groups must:

- Share the ideals of the UN;
- Operate solely on a not-for-profit basis;
- Have a demonstrated interest in United Nations issues and proven ability to reach large or specialized audiences, such as educators, media representatives, policy makers and the business community;
- Have the commitment and means to conduct effective information programs about United Nations activities through publication of newsletters, bulletins, backgrounders and pamphlets; organization of conferences, seminars and round tables; and enlisting the cooperation of print and broadcast media.[4]

Though barred from participating directly in the negotiations, NGOs endeavor to influence the outcome of the talks in a variety of ways. According to James Sheehan and Jeremy Rabkin:

They design and propose texts for international treaties, conventions and other international law instruments. They monitor governments and private businesses to determine if they are in compliance with national and international rules. Their attorneys file suits in U.S. and other courts against public and private bodies they consider to be out of compliance with [the] law. NGOs sponsor consumer boycotts and launch media campaigns against policies, companies and governments they oppose. Indeed, the most enterprising NGOs help governments enforce environmental legislation their own lobbyists helped write in response to 'public' protests their own activists organized.[5]

There are over 4,000 environmentally active NGOs currently registered with the UN. They range from small farmers cooperatives, women's groups, and labor unions to well-known environmental organizations like Greenpeace, Friends of the Earth, Environmental Defense, Natural Resources Defense Council, Worldwatch Institute, World Resources Institute, Union of Concerned Scientists and the World Wildlife Fund for Nature.

The large number of groups involved, however, does not mean that they hold a diversity of views on how best to approach environmental issues. On the contrary, the predominant voice of the NGOs is one that speaks in terms of approaching global environmental disaster. And because the disaster will be global, the measures to combat it must also be global in scope. This is where NGOs put to good use the public-relations skills the UN requires of them in order to be accredited to it. These organizations, especially the larger, well-funded ones, are superbly equipped to convince the public, government officials, and the media that global action is urgently needed on whatever environmental issue the NGOs select. In this way, NGOs are not only advocates of certain policies but they are also partners of international bodies intent upon writing those policies into global agreements.

"Far from taking 'non-governmental' roles," observes Sheehan, "they [NGOs] aspire to be extensions of a global governance they helped create."[6]

It is doubtful that even the most optimistic of activists attending that first UN environmental conference in Stockholm could have imagined how the descendants of the "Hog Farmers" would come to occupy such a powerful position on the world stage. At the time, however, their eyes were fixed on more immediate concerns such as getting international bodies to act on environmental issues near and dear to the NGOs' hearts. Taking his cue from the assembled activists at the Hog Farm who demanded an international ban on whaling, Maurice Strong flew from Stockholm to London. There, at a meeting of the International Whaling

Commission (IWC), he prevailed on the delegates to give the activists what they wanted. It is significant that, to this day, Strong attributes the action of the IWC to the demands of the NGOs in Stockholm. The global environmental movement had scored its first success. It was only getting started.

The Ban on DDT

Thousands of miles from Stockholm, another environmental decision was pondered in 1972, one whose tragic outcome would come to epitomize the "undercurrent of irrationality" referred to by Lord Taverne. In Washington, D.C. EPA Administrator William Ruckelshaus was in the midst of deciding whether his agency, not yet two years old, should ban the widely used pesticide DDT. The push to do something about DDT, dichloro-diphenyl-trichloroethane, had been underway ever since Rachel Carson, ten years earlier, identified the insecticide as one of the man-made chemicals posing a threat to human health and the environment. At the time Ruckelshaus was mulling his decision, DDT in the U.S. was being used primarily to protect cotton from boll weevils. Previously, DDT had been used for other agricultural purposes, and there were claims that the massive spraying of the chemical from crop dusters was having its effect on the environment, namely, the thinning of eggshells and the declining populations of various raptors, including bald eagles.[7] In the wake of the uproar over Carson's book, DDT was linked to breast cancer and other illnesses, although data substantiating such links were, and still are, completely lacking.[8]

In the spirit of Carson's book, DDT was coming to symbolize all the harm that modern technology was said to be doing to the earth and its inhabitants. The Environmental Defense Fund (EDF), for example, was created in 1967 for the exclusive purpose of getting DDT banned, and the group spent the next several years in a relentless pursuit of that goal.[9] (EDF is now known as Environmental Defense.) Conspicuously absent from most of the harangues over the supposed ill-effects of DDT, however, was any acknowledgement of the role the chemical played in performing an extraordinary service—saving lives, millions of them.

"In the early 1940s, when the world's population was half of what it is today," writes Indur Goklany, "it was estimated that malaria, a mosquito-borne disease suspected to have plagued humanity since prehistoric times, afflicted at least 300 million people worldwide, causing 3 million deaths annually, including 1 million in India alone." With the help of DDT, he notes, the global malaria death rate—which had been

1,740 deaths per million in 1930—dropped over 70 percent to 480 per million in 1950. In recognition of DDT's remarkable contribution to combating this ancient dreaded disease, Paul Mueller, the Swiss chemist who discovered the substance's insecticidal properties, was awarded the Nobel Prize for Physiology and Medicine in 1948. (Such was the esteem the medical community had for DDT's ability to kill disease-carrying insects that it was used against scourges other than malaria. Viewers of "The History Channel" may have seen its segment on the last days of World War II in which the liberation of the concentration camp at Dachau, Germany, is shown in full color. The segment contains moving footage of emaciated newly-freed prisoners undergoing de-lousing by U.S. Army medics. The prisoners' heads are being sprayed heavily with a substance the announcer identifies as—DDT.)

By 1970, two years before EPA's ban, the death rate from malaria had dropped another two-thirds to 160 per million. Malaria had all but disappeared in the developed world and was close to being eradicated in the rest of the world, except for impoverished Sub-Saharan Africa.

DDT's success in controlling malaria, Goklany points out, was due to malariaologists' recognition of the insecticide's unique mechanisms— it repels, irritates and poisons mosquitoes.[10] Far from being dumped on fields from an airplane, DDT, in combating malaria, was sprayed in huts where its presence posed no threat to humans but was deadly to mosquitoes. In 1970 the National Academy of Sciences stated: "To only a few chemicals does man owe as great a debt as to DDT. In little more than two decades DDT has prevented 500 million human deaths due to malaria that would have otherwise have been inevitable."[11]

"Nowhere in *Silent Spring* did Carson acknowledge that the chemical she was excoriating as a menace had, in the previous two decades, been used by malariaologists to save somewhere in the vicinity of ten million lives," commented Malcolm Gladwell. "Nor did she make it clear how judiciously the public health community was using the chemical."[12]

What was not made clear by Carson, was made perfectly clear by Judge Edmund Sweeney, who chaired an EPA panel convened by the agency to decide whether to ban DDT. Judge Sweeney's panel held hearings over a seven-month period and took over 9,300 pages of testimony. The final, 113-page report was issued on April 25, 1972. In it Sweeney wrote: "DDT is not a carcinogenic, mutagenic, or teratogenic hazard to man. The uses under regulations involved here do not have a deleterious effect on fresh water fish, estuarine organisms, wild birds or other wildlife...and...there is a present need for essential uses of DDT."[13]

That was not, however, how Administrator Ruckelshaus saw it. On June 2, 1972, Ruckelshaus, who had attended none of EPA's hearings on the chemical, overturned Judge Sweeney's decision and, to the delight of environmentalists, banned the use of DDT in the U.S., except for certain emergencies. Thirty-two years later, long after the unintended, but completely predictable, consequences of his decision had made their presence felt, Ruckelshaus offered this explanation to Tina Rosenberg of the *New York Times Magazine*:

> But if I were a decision maker in Sri Lanka, where the benefits from use outweigh the risks, I would decide differently. It's not up to us to balance risks and benefits for other people. There's arrogance in the idea that everybody's going to do what we do. We're not making these decisions for the rest of the world, are we?[14]

Sri Lanka would seem an odd example for Ruckelshaus to cite. In the years before *Silent Spring* cast its long, deadly shadow, the island nation off the southeast coast of India had been a poster child for DDT's success in combatting malaria. In Sri Lanka there were only 31 cases of malaria in 1962 and 17 in 1963, but more than a million cases in 1968 after the use of DDT there was banned.[15] The resurgence of malaria in Sri Lanka was an unmistakable sign of what would happen if the global campaign against DDT led to the product's being banned elsewhere. Ruckelshaus was now an integral part of that campaign. As administrator of the U.S. Environmental Protection Agency, he legitimized the activist-led campaign against DDT by putting Washington's considerable prestige behind his decision on the chemical. To imply, as he did in his interview with Rosenberg, that the U.S. doesn't "make these decisions for the rest of the world," is to ignore the global influence the United States has on matters relating to public health and the environment. Malaria may not have posed a threat to the U.S., in part thanks to prior use of DDT there, but, as the example of Sri Lanka showed, the scourge could wreak havoc elsewhere in the world if given a chance. Ruckelshaus, Carson, EDF, the World Wildlife Fund for Nature (WWF), and others demanding an end to DDT's use gave malaria that chance.

According to a study sponsored by the Institute of Medicine, the National Research Council, and the National Academy of Sciences:

> The declining availability and use of DDT was not without its cost in human health, but those who promoted the ban were not those who suffered the consequences...The removal of this cheap and effective antimalaria weapon

from the U.S. marketplace had a negative impact on malaria control efforts worldwide.[16]

Separately, Tina Rosenberg and Paul Driessen have put human faces on what those scientific bodies refer to as "a negative impact of malaria control worldwide." Rosenberg notes:

Independent malariologists believe it [malaria] kills two million people a year, mainly children under 5 and 90 percent of them in Africa. Until it was overtaken by AIDS in 1999, it was Africa's leading killer. One in 20 African children dies of malaria, and many of those who survive are brain-damaged. Each year, 300 to 500 million people worldwide get malaria. During the rainy season in some parts of Africa, entire villages of people lie in bed, shivering with fever, too weak to stand or eat. Many spend a good part of the year incapacitated, which cripples African economies. A commission of the World Health Organization found that malaria alone shrinks the economy in countries where it is most endemic by 20 percent over 15 years.[17]

Driessen, senior policy advisor for the Congress for Racial Equality, adds:

In 2000, say the World Health Organization and other studies, malaria infected over 300 million people. It killed nearly 2,000,000—most of them in Sub-Saharan Africa. Over half of the victims are children, who die at the rate of two per minute or 3,000 per day—the equivalent of 60 fully loaded school buses plunging over a cliff every day of the year. Since 1972, over 50 million people have died from this dreaded disease. Many are weakened by AIDS or dysentery, but actually die of malaria.

In addition to these needless deaths, malaria also saps economies and health care resources. It keeps millions home from work and school every day. Chronic anemia can sap people's strength for years and leave victims with severe liver and kidney damage, while cerebral malaria can cause lifelong learning and memory problems.[18]

Ruckelshaus once explained his ruling on DDT by observing that "in such decisions the ultimate judgement remains political."[19] His explanation may have been more honest than he intended. That his decision was not based on the existing scientific evidence, which was abundant even then, is obvious. Rather, it was a reaction to public pressure generated by environmental activists to "do the right thing." As such, it was the first major public health decision in the era of modern environmentalism that can truly be described as "eco-centric"—that is, it elevated environmental concerns—as defined by activists in and out of government—above all other considerations.

Even though the consequences of the eco-centric campaign against DDT have been well documented by the World Health Organization, the National Academy of Sciences, the Institute of Medicine, and the National Research Council, as well as by such writers as Tina Rosenberg, Indur Goklany, Malcolm Gladwell, Paul Driessen, and the late Aaron Wildavsky[20], the one American agency in a position to do something about it refused to do so. The United States Agency for International Development (USAID) appeared more interested in saving face than in saving lives. "For us to be buying and using in another country something we don't allow in our own country raises the specter of preferential treatment," E. Anne Peterson, assistant administrator for global health at USAID, told the *New York Times Magazine*'s Rosenberg. "We certainly have to think about 'What would the American people think and want?' and 'What would Africans think if we're going to do to them what we wouldn't do to our own people?'"

One African who has given considerable thought to such matters is James Shikwati of the Inter Region Economic Network, a think tank based in Nairobi, Kenya. "For rich countries to tell poor nations to...ban chemicals that help control disease-carrying insects—and then to claim to be responsible, humanitarian and compassionate—is to engage in hypocrisy of the most lethal kind," he points out.[21]

The campaign against DDT in the 1960s, and USAID's refusal to support its use in malaria-stricken areas, wouldn't be so harmful if there were effective malaria-fighting alternatives to DDT. There are alternatives to DDT, but none is as effective in controlling malaria as the chemical so roundly excoriated by environmental activists. Two alternatives, malathion and deltamethrin, have not shown themselves to be as effective at repelling mosquitoes, and both cost more than DDT. Cost is a crucial factor in developing countries where the average household spends more than 50 percent of its income on the most basic of necessities—food. What this means on a national level can be seen in Belize's use of deltamethrin to fight malaria. Deltamethrin, which costs three to four times more than DDT, consumed 89 percent of Belize's malaria-control budget by the early 2000s. This, Goklany notes, "starves funds from surveillance, elimination of mosquito breeding grounds, and even malaria treatment."[22]

Another alternative to DDT, widely used because it costs only pennies a day, is chloroquine. As resistant strains of malaria have evolved, however, chloroquine now fails 80 percent of the time. Bed nets treated with an insecticide have become a fashionable way of protecting people from mosquitoes, and they can be quite effective.

But, as Rosenberg points out, they have serious drawbacks. They are expensive, and the insecticide wears off after a while, requiring constant re-treatment.

The fact that the "alternatives" to DDT don't measure up either in terms of cost or effectiveness in fighting malaria, or both, has not moved officials in international agencies to reconsider their position on the chemical—despite the rising death toll. Indeed, USIAID was not the only offender. The 1980 and 1990s saw the rise of environmental sections within health organizations and international donor agencies. The World Bank, for example, flatly rejected a recommendation from the Pan American Health Organization in 1999 that Ecuador use DDT to combat malaria in the wake of a severe El Nino. Walter Vergara, who headed the World Bank's environmental section at the time, defended his decision to Tina Rosenberg with the following explanation: "DDT has an awful impact on the biosystem and is being eliminated by the world community. There are alternatives. We're not the only species on the planet."

Vergara is correct is saying that human beings are not the only species on the planet, but his remarks ignore the consequences of the World Bank's stance for humans living in poor countries—the very nations the World Bank is supposed to assist. "The U.S. and other rich countries are siding with the mosquitoes against the world's poor by opposing the use of DDT," Nicholas Kristof, a *New York Times* columnist, commented in January 2005. Kristof added that "most Western aid agencies will not pay for anti-malarial programs that use DDT, and that pretty much ensures that DDT won't be used." In an odd turn of events, two influential environmental NGOs, Greenpeace and the World Wildlife Fund, have—belatedly—changed their tune on the use of DDT. "If there's nothing else and it saves lives, we're all for it," said Rick Hind of Greenpeace. "Nobody's dogmatic about it."[23]

"All I can say is: It's about time," Paul Driessen comments. "Better late than never. But why did so many people have to die over the past three decades, because of the near global de facto DDT ban, which these groups promoted so incessantly?" Steve Milloy, adjunct scholar at the Cato Institute, was even more blunt: "It might be easy for some to dismiss the past 43 years of eco-hysteria over DDT with a simple 'never mind,' except for the blood of millions of people dripping from the hands of the WWF, Greenpeace, Rachel Carson, Environmental Defense Fund, and other junk science-fueled opponents of DDT."[24]

The Precautionary Principle

It would be comforting to think that the acknowledgement by Greenpeace and WWF that the chemical they once demonized can, in fact, be used to save lives signals a maturing of the movement, including a fundamental reassessment of environmentalism's attitude toward science and public policy. Sadly, there is little reason to believe this is the case. While attributing motives is always a risky undertaking, the—partial—revision of their stance on DDT by some environmental groups is probably a reflection of their recognition that it is no longer in their interest to defend the indefensible. The death toll from the spread of malaria is so high, and the publicity given to it by such traditional supporters of environmental causes as the *New York Times* so widespread, that the blanket condemnation of DDT has become untenable.

However, by the time some environmental groups had begun to distance themselves from their earlier positions on the use of DDT, a certain genie was already out of the bottle. The genie in question was the well-orchestrated environmental scare campaign designed to rid society of products or technologies said by activists to pose an unacceptable risk to human health and/or the environment. So successful was the campaign against DDT that, over the next couple of decades, it inspired activists to launch similar attacks against products as diverse as saccharin, Alar, medical devices made from plastics, virtually everything containing chlorine, genetically-modified crops, and fossil fuels—just to name a few.[25]

What was lacking in the early years of environmentalism, however, was some kind of guiding principle that activists—in and out of government—could use to win widespread acceptance of policies they advocated. Ideally, that principle would spare them the burden of looking to science or epidemiology (the study of the transmission and control of epidemic disease) to justify their claims, because data from these two sources couldn't always be relied on to produce the desired results. Over time that void would be filled by what has come to be known as the "precautionary principle." The origins of the precautionary principle are somewhat murky. At first glance, the idea of exercising caution in public policy would seem to be little more than an extension of the age-old warning, "Better safe than sorry." But there is far more to it than that. Some scholars trace its use in regulatory policy to the gradual adoption by activists and officials in the 1970s and 1980s of the German term *Vorsorgeprinzip*, which translates as "precaution" or "foresight" principle.

As the environmental movement grew in influence, the precautionary principle—long before it had a name, much less an agreed-upon definition—began to appear in various guises in certain international environmental agreements and proclamations. In 1982 the United Nations World Charter for Nature, for example, stated that when "potential adverse effects [of activities likely to pose significant risks to nature] are not fully understood, the activities should not proceed."[26] Similarly, the 1989 Nordic Council's International Conference on the Pollution of the Seas called for eliminating pollutants "even where there is inadequate or inconclusive scientific evidence to prove a causal link between emissions and effects."[27]

In 1992 delegates to the United Nations Conference on Environment and Development (UNCED) in Rio de Janeiro adopted different versions of the precautionary principle which they inserted into the Rio Declaration of Environment and Development (Rio Declaration), the United Nations Framework Convention on Climate Change (UNFCC), and the Convention on Biological Diversity (CBD). Principle 15 of the Rio Declaration, for instance, states that:

In order to protect the environment, the precautionary approach shall be widely applied by States according to their capabilities. When there are threats of serious or irreversible damage, lack of full scientific uncertainty shall not be used as a reason for postponing cost-effective measures to prevent environmental degradation.

The version of the precautionary principle included in the Convention on Biological Diversity reads as follows:

"That it is vital to anticipate, prevent and attack the causes of significant reduction or loss of biological diversity at source,...

When there is a threat of significant reduction or loss of biological diversity, lack of full scientific certainty should not be used as a reason for postponing measures to avoid or minimize such a threat.[28]

While both of these versions state that "lack of full scientific certainty" (rarely achievable in the best of circumstances) is no reason not to take action, neither mandates such action, and the Rio Declaration even allows for "cost-effective" measures. This degree of flexibility, however, proved frustrating to a growing number of environmental activists who saw in the emerging precautionary principle both a means to emphasize the risks of technologies not of their liking, and a way to downgrade the role of science in trumpeting those risks. In

1998 thirty-one activists from five countries gathered in rural Wisconsin at the behest of the North Dakota-based Science and Environment Health Network (SEHN). Citing an array of maladies, from cancer to climate change, the activists adopted their own definition of the precautionary principle, one that quickly won favor among their fellow environmentalists the world over. Known as the Wingspread Declaration (after the conference center where the meeting was held), it reads as follows:

> When an activity raises threats of harm to the environment or human health, precautionary measures should be taken even if some cause-and-effect relationships are not fully established scientifically.

As one of Wingspread's organizers, SEHN coordinator Carolyn Raffensperger, wrote with her colleague Joel Tickner, the "burden of scientific proof has posed a monumental barrier in the campaign to protect health and the environment."[29] Indeed, by separating the alleged "threats of harm" from "cause-and-effect relationships," this new version of the precautionary principle opens the door to a world in which mere conjecture becomes the driving force behind health and safety regulations.

Though the Wingspread activists could not have known it at the time, environmental officials from over 180 countries would soon adopt their own version of a stricter precautionary principle—one not that far removed from the spirit of Wingspread. Even better, from the activists' standpoint, the precautionary principle would be applied to a technology that had incurred the wrath of global environmentalists: agricultural biotechnology. In January 2000 negotiators crafting the text of the Cartagena Protocol on Biosafety, a subsidiary agreement to the Convention on Biological Diversity adopted at Rio in 1992, made repeated references to the precautionary principle. In Articles 1 and 4, respectively, it served as a basis for decision-making and risk assessments with respect to the transboundary transfer (and associated handling and use) of genetically modified organisms (GMOs) "that may have adverse affects on the conservation and sustainable use of biological diversity, taking also into account risks to human health."

Although it is not as strict as the Wingspread language, the Cartagena Protocol, as Frances Smith and Indur Goklany note, is nonetheless seen as a "major victory for the more absolutist version of the precautionary principle and for its advocates."[54] The precautionary principle had now truly arrived, both as a regulatory instrument and as a tool for activists. Largely tucked away from public view, the precautionary principle can be used by NGOs and kindred spirits in regulatory bureaucracies to justify "erring on the side of caution" in crafting policies on public health and the environment.

"The so-called 'precautionary principle,'" Washington State University toxicologist Alan S. Felsot says, "essentially holds that when any concerns or allegations, no matter how spurious, are raised about the safety of a product, precautionary measures should be put in place and all burden of proof to the contrary should fall on the proponent of the allegedly unsafe product or activity."

Roger Bate, director of the health advocacy group Africans Fighting Malaria, has called it "the categorical imperative of environmentalists," which translates into "thou shall not tolerate even a risk of risk." Risks, of course, are a constant companion to all living things, ranging from the purely hypothetical or merely trivial to the severe. Putting risk into perspective, which the precautionary principle fails to do, columnist Holman Jenkins of the *Wall Street Journal* points out that, "The average human being comes into daily contact with a million species of bacteria and about 5,000 viruses." That people regularly exposed to such "risks" somehow manage to get on with their lives demonstrates the folly of letting speculation, rather than evidence, guide public policy decisions.[32]

"What this really says," University of Houston economist Thomas R. DeGregori points out, "is that the proponents of the precautionary principle have lost the debate on the evidence (otherwise they would argue the evidence), so they argue we should follow their policy prescriptions anyway."[33]

The growing controversy over the precautionary principle prompted the administration of George W. Bush to clarify its position on the doctrine. It did so in an unequivocal statement by John Graham, director of the Office of Information and Regulatory Affairs at the White House Office of Management and Budget. In an address at the Heritage Foundation in Washington in January 2004, Graham told his audience: "The United States government believes it is important to understand that, notwithstanding the rhetoric of our European colleagues, there is no such thing as the precautionary principle." Graham added that, while precaution in the public and private sphere is a "sensible idea," "there are multiple approaches to implementing precaution in risk management." "In both business and politics," he continued, "decision makers seek the right balance between taking risks and behaving in a precautionary manner."

According to Graham, who left the Administration in 2006, there are two major perils associated with an extreme approach to precaution. "One is that technological innovation will be stifled, and we all recognize that technological innovation has played a major role in economic progress throughout the world," he said. "A second peril, more subtle, is that public health and the environment would be harmed as the energies of regulators and the regulated community would be diverted from known or plausible hazards to speculative and ill-founded ones."[34]

Agricultural Biotechnology

What Graham meant by his reference to the threat to technological innovation, public health, and the environment posed by exaggerated sense of precaution can clearly be seen in the campaign by environmental activists against the "new biotechnology." Also known as genetic modification, genetic engineering, recombinant DNA engineering or gene-splicing, the new biotechnology here is understood to mean biotechnology that is applied to agriculture and food production.

Agricultural biotechnology is almost as old as agriculture itself. According to Henry Miller and Greg Conko, a primitive form of food biotechnology dates back at least 6000 years when the ancient Babylonians used microorganisms in fermentation to brew alcoholic beverages.[35] In modern times, ever-more sophisticated plant-breeding techniques have dramatically altered the composition of our food supply. Virtually all of the 200 major crops grown in the United States have been genetically engineered, or genetically improved, in some way. "Plant breeders—not Mother Nature—gave us seedless grapes and watermelons, the tangelo (a tangerine-grapefruit hybrid), and fungus-resistant strawberries," Henry Miller points out. "In North American and European diets, only fish and wild game and berries may be said not to have been genetically engineered in some fashion."[36]

"Conventional" biotechnology was a key component of the "Green Revolution," which, under the guidance of Iowa farmer and agricultural researcher Norman Borlaug, produced new varieties of high-yield crops, particularly rice, corn, and wheat. These high-yield crops germinate earlier in the year, grow faster and are more resistant to disease and drought. By far the biggest impact of Borlaug's use of conventional biotechnology was felt in poorer countries where the Green Revolution he spearheaded is credited with reducing the rate of malnutrition from 50 percent to 20 percent. For his work Borlaug was awarded the Nobel Prize for Peace in 1970.

The new agricultural biotechnology is a further refinement of techniques pioneered by Borlaug and others, albeit one which allows for much greater precision. It entails identifying single genes from one organism, isolating and removing them from the surrounding DNA, and then inserting them into the DNA strands of other organisms. "Because DNA in every organism is made up of the same basic chemicals— and because DNA works in essentially the same way, whether it's in a bacterium, a plant, or an animal—a gene can be moved from one organism to another and still produce the same trait," Miller and Conko write. "And the products of modern technology can be used for a variety of purposes—including modified bacteria for cleaning up oil spills; a weakened virus used as a vaccine; a protein, such as insulin, used to treat diabetics; or a crop plant modified to use less pesticides or to be more nutritious."[37]

Gene-spliced crops first made their appearance in the early 1980s and have since undergone extensive study to ensure their safety. Dozens of scientific bodies, including the U.K.'s Royal Society, the U.S. National Academy of Sciences, the World Health Organization, and the American Medical Association have studied modern biotechnology and gene-spliced organisms and reached similar conclusions about their safety:

- Modern genetic modification techniques are an extension, or refinement of earlier, far less precise ones.
- Simply adding genes to plants of microorganisms does not make them less safe to the environment or to humans.
- The risks associated with gene-spliced organisms are the same in kind as those associated with conventionally-modified organisms (and in both cases are extremely low).
- Regulation of the products of genetic modification should be based upon the risk-based characteristics of individual products, regardless of whether newer techniques are used in their development.[38]

In the roughly two-and-one-half decades since GM crops were introduced, their spread has been remarkable. By 2003, over 7 million farmers (most of them small farmers) in 18 countries were cultivating GM crops on 68 million hectares, or 206 million acres. It is estimated that 80 percent of the soya bean crop, 70 percent of cotton, and 38 percent of corn in the United States are now genetically modified. Over 4 million small farmers in China and many thousands in South Africa grow GM cotton. "GM cotton saved the cotton crop of Australia when it was on the verge of collapse from the build-up of pesticide resistance," Lord Taverne points out. "GM cotton is now being grown in India and Brazil and constituted one-third of the total cotton crop in Mexico."[39]

The clean bill of health the world's most prestigious scientific bodies have given agricultural biotechnology, and the positive results farmers have had in planting GM crops, have not, however, kept environmental groups from attacking the technology. On the contrary, environmental NGOs have launched a global campaign aimed at creating a groundswell of anxiety toward biotechnology by scaring consumers and intimidating regulators. Greenpeace, Friends of the Earth, Organic Consumers Organization, and the Sierra Club have been particularly shrill in their opposition to biotech. Other groups use less hysterical language in pointing to the alleged risks of biotechnology, but they clearly belong in the camp of the technology's antagonists. They include Environmental Defense, Union of Concerned Scientists, Pew Initiative on Food and Biotechnology, Resources for the Future, and the Center for Science in the Public Interest.[40]

Opposition to GM crops has been most widespread in Europe, where green activists eager to disparage biotechnology have skillfully exploited public concern over Bovine Spongiform Encephalopathy, or "Mad Cow Disease." Though Mad Cow Disease has nothing to do with GM crops, the outbreak of the disease in Great Britain in 2001 created enough public anxiety and confusion to raise doubts among European consumers about the safety of their food supply. Yet even before the outbreak of Mad Cow Disease, Greenpeace had set its sights on biotechnology by launching a scare campaign aimed at parents with infants. In early 1998 Greenpeace sent a letter to executives of the Swiss baby-food line Galactina, asking if their products contained biotech ingredients. Within days, Galactina's parent company, pharmaceutical giant Novartis, capitulated and promised to remove the offending products from store shelves and to forego biotechnology in baby food in the future.

Understandably pleased with its success, Greenpeace next went after Gerber Foods, the popular U.S. baby food brand also owned by Novartis. In May 1999 Greenpeace sent a fax to Gerber's headquarters in Freemont, Michigan demanding to know if Gerber used gene-spliced plants in its baby food. After initially defending the safety of its products, Gerber, fearful of a Greenpeace-led scare campaign aimed at its customers, eventually gave in and renounced the use of GM plants in its baby food and, for good measure, pledged to use only organic ingredients in the future. Ironically, Novartis, the parent company of Gerber and Galactina, was one of the world's leading producers of gene-spliced plant seeds. Its willingness to have its baby-food subsidiaries abandon a technology Novartis pioneered attests to the power of the mere threat of intimidation by a publicity-savvy environmental NGO.

Throughout Europe GM foodstuffs have been relegated to virtual leper status. Branded by activists as "Frankenfoods" whose cultivation will produce "Terminator Weeds" in the environment, GM crops face a bleak future in Europe. Public opinion, fed by hysterical claims in the tabloid press, has been reluctant to accept GM crops in its food supply. Even though the technology has been declared safe by the European Commission, EU member states, with the exception of Spain, have been generally reluctant to license them. Typical of the prevailing attitude among government officials in the EU are comments by Mo Mowlam, who served as minister for the Cabinet Office in the U.K. Writing in the London newspaper the *Express* in 1999, she boasted that the British government "had created one of the toughest regulatory systems in the world for GM foods." In remarks far more revealing than she could possibly have intended, Mowlam added, "If Elizabethan England had the kind of regulatory system we have now, there is no way the potato would ever have been introduced into this country."[41]

At this writing, few GM crops have been licensed to be grown commercially in the EU, and virtually no European supermarkets or shops carry them. European companies, once at the forefront of biotechnology R&D, have shifted their operations to the U.S. where the political climate is much more favorable. Not only is Europe rapidly losing its once-promising agricultural biotechnology industry, but, observes Dick Taverne, the Old World's "hostility to GM food in turn inhibits the production of GM crops in developing countries that might hope to export their produce to European markets."[42]

The lack of scientific evidence supporting their case against GM crops has made the precautionary principle a welcome refuge for green NGOs and regulators. One of the anti-biotechnology activists' favorite mantras is that "The absence of evidence of harm is not evidence of the absence of harm." Indeed, the Sierra Club justifies its opposition to genetically modified crops by specifically citing the precautionary principle. "According to the Precautionary Principle, we call for a moratorium on the planting of all genetically engineered crops and the release of all GEOs (genetically engineered organisms) into the environment, including those now approved. Releases should be delayed until extensive, rigorous research is done which determines the long-term environmental and health impacts of each GEO and there is public debate to ascertain the need for the use of each GEO intended for release into the environment."[43]

Greenpeace also focuses on what it says are the "unacceptable risks" of agricultural biotechnology. Its website states: "The introduction of genetically engineered (GE) organisms into the complex ecosystems of our environment is a dangerous global experiment with nature and evolution...GE organisms must not be released into the environment. They pose unacceptable risks to ecosystems, and have the potential to threaten biodiversity, wildlife and sustainable forms of agriculture."

"Note that Greenpeace is worried primarily about the hypothetical 'risks' of genetically engineered crops," says environmental writer Robert Bidinotto of the Washington-based Objectivist Center. "And the risks they are worried about are not to humans, but to 'biodiversity, wildlife and sustainable [organic] forms of agriculture. 'These risks—and not the risks of mass starvation—are 'unacceptable.'"[44]

Patrick Moore, who helped found Greenpeace in 1970, now accuses the organization of "abandoning science and following agendas that have little to do with saving the earth." He adds that "I believe we are entering an era now where pagan beliefs and junk science are influencing public policy. GM foods and forestry are both good examples where policy is being influenced by arguments that have no basis in fact or logic."[45]

In forsaking science for the precautionary principle, and in demanding preventive action by governments even in the absence of supporting data, Greenpeace, the Sierra Club, and kindred spirits throughout the environmental movement have opened a Pandora's Box from which much trouble will emerge—and in the case of DDT— already has emerged. Aaron Wildavsky recognized the implications of this development several years before the term "precautionary principle" had entered public consciousness. Shortly before his death in 1993, he wrote:

> If all is not known, that is, if a product or practice is not proved safe, then it must be banned or restricted. There is no need for opponents to demonstrate harm. It is up to the substance's supporters to prove a negative...—a task that requires comprehensive knowledge of all consequences.[46]

As Wildavsky well understood, comprehensive knowledge of all consequences is beyond human capacity. By demanding what they, too, know is impossible, green activists are playing a cynical game. They're also playing a dangerous game.

"Of all the activities that shape the environment, agriculture is the single most important, well ahead of whatever comes second," writes

Jonathan Rauch in the *Atlantic Monthly*. "Today, about 38 percent of the earth's land area is cropland or pasture—a total that has crept upward over the past few decades as global population has grown. The increase has been gradual, only about 0.3 percent a year; but that still translates into an additional Greece or Nicaragua each year." Rauch notes that the UN, in its mid-range projections, estimates that the earth's population will grow by more than 40 percent, from 6.3 billion people today to 8.9 billion in 2050. "Feeding all those people," he adds, "and feeding a billion or so of their hungry pets (a dog or a cat is one of the first things people want once they move beyond a subsistence lifestyle), and providing the increasingly protein-rich diets that an increasingly wealthy world will expect—doing all that will require food output to at least double, or possibly triple."[47]

While global population growth is expected to begin leveling off around 2050, providing some relief, the challenge of feeding people in the interim, particularly in poorer countries, remains a daunting one. According to Dennis Avery, director of global food issues at the Hudson Institute, "we have tripled the world's farm output since 1960. And we're feeding twice as many people from that same land." The dramatic rise in agricultural production Avery refers to was, of course, made possible by the Green Revolution. But the Green Revolution has reached the point of diminishing returns, because the world is running out of suitable land on which to grow crops, a trend that is likely to continue.

"By and large," Avery told the *Atlantic Monthly's* Rauch, "the world's civilizations have been built around the best farmland. And we have used most of the world's good farmland. Most of the good land is already heavily fertilized. Most of the good land is already being planted with high-yield seeds [Africa is the important exception.] Most of the good irrigation sites are used. We can't triple yields again with the technology we're already using."[48]

Making up for the fading effects of the Green Revolution in a world expected to experience a steady rise in population over the next four decades will require new sources of agricultural productivity. One of those sources could well be GM crops, but only if agricultural biotechnology is allowed to reach its full potential. A combination of fear-mongering by activists and empire-building by regulators, however, has retarded the growth of this promising technology. Despite favorable risk assessments of GM crops by the EU's Scientific Committee, several European countries in the late 1990s prevailed on the EU to block all new approvals of GM crops. The ban was finally lifted in May 2004, but only after the U.S. and several other countries had filed a lawsuit with the

World Trade Organization (WTO). By then, the EU had created an additional barrier to agricultural biotechnology by implementing rules mandating that all gene-spliced products undergo strict testing, labeling and tracing requirements.[49]

Although the regulatory climate for GM crops in the United States is far more favorable than it is in Europe, gene-spliced products still have to run a bureaucratic gauntlet before they are approved. Both EPA and the Department of Agriculture (USDA) require, among other things, case-by-case reviews and extensive field testing before gene-spliced products can enter the market, a process that costs applicants millions of dollars. This is a regulatory game that only the most well-heeled companies can play, and it is tailor-made to keep smaller firms on the sidelines. In addition to the financial barriers such a regime creates, an overly stringent regulatory scheme can raise unwarranted fears about the safety of a product. Testifying before a panel convened by the National Institutes of Health, Frances Smith observed: "For obvious reasons, the consumers views the technologies that are *most* regulated to be the *least* safe ones. Heavy involvement by government, no matter how well intended, inevitably sends the wrong signals. Rather than ensuring confidence, it raises suspicion and doubt (emphasis in the original)."[50]

There are many ways to raise doubts in the public's mind, and environmental NGOs have developed a clever division of labor when it comes to undermining confidence in biotechnology. Ever the blunt instrument, Greenpeace demands its "complete elimination [from] the food supply and the environment." On the other hand, groups such as Resources for the Future, Environmental Defense, Center for Science in the Public Interest (CSPI), Pew Initiative on Food and Biotechnology, and Union of Concerned Scientists take what appears to be a more measured approach by actually acknowledging the potential benefits of GM crops. At the same time, however, they are quick to raise scientific-sounding "concerns" about the "uncertainties" surrounding the technology. This attitude is a reflection of what William Nierenberg called The Law of Constant Concern which states that "no matter how much reassuring evidence is produced, another concern always rises."[51]

The tactics of the "moderates" show how the game is played. In February 2005 CSPI released a report finding that, due to the uncoordinated nature of the U.S. regulatory process and its "patchwork of legal authorities," the time U.S. regulatory agencies take to review new gene-spliced crop varieties had doubled since the late 1990s. "One would expect that the regulatory pathway for biotech crops in the 21st century would be quicker than in the 1990s," the report notes. "One would indeed," Miller and Conko counter, "unless one knew that NGOs such as CSPI had lobbied for years to make the regulatory process more burdensome, not less so."[52] In fact, CSPI's Greg Jaffe is credited with drafting legislation introduced in the U.S. Senate by Sen. Richard Durbin (D-Ill.) that establishes a rigorous approval process for foods made from GM crops. CSPI then orchestrated an—unsuccessful—campaign to drum up support for the Durbin bill while claiming to be a disinterested party that favored the legislation on its merits. Ironically, the Durbin bill, like the schemes already adopted by EPA and USDA, creates a regulatory framework for gene-spliced crops that is far more stringent than the one that governs conventionally produced food, even though the latter uses technology that is much less precise and predictable.[53]

In 2003, Steven H. Strauss, an Oregon State University professor of forest science, proposed a modest streamlining of the regulation of negligible-risk genetic constructions of gene-spliced plants. His proposal appeared in the journal *Science*. In a remarkable letter to *Science*, Jerry Cayford of Resources for the Future opined that Strauss' pleas "ignore the politics of the genetically modified food debate...Strauss' proposal, reasonable as it may be, asks critics to surrender a major bargaining chip—strict regulation of field trials—but offers them nothing in return." Unimpressed by Cayford's bargaining-chip argument, Strauss in a letter to *Science* responded by noting that "the cost to people and environment of effectively losing genetic engineering from most agricultural sectors as a result of excess regulations are too great for so simple-minded a political approach."[103] Lest the message be lost on Resources for the Future, Strauss added: "[W]ith the high level of regulation and stigma successfully implanted in places such as Europe, policies and attitudes may take a generation or more to change. The opportunity costs in dollars, and costs to human health and environment, will be incalculable."[54]

How incalculable the cost will be can be seen in the environmentalists' reaction to one of biotech's most promising products: "golden rice." In 2000, a team of researchers in Germany and Switzerland announced that they had been able to genetically modify rice so as to contain a precursor of vitamin A. Rich in beta-carotene, the new product became known as golden rich, for its yellow color. The development of rice enriched with vitamin A is vitally important to people in remote, rural areas of underdeveloped countries, where diets are low on vitamins and minerals, and where vitamin A supplements are largely unknown. According to the World Health Organization, 230 million children, predominantly from poor countries, are "at risk" for clinical or subclinical Vitamin A Deficiency (VAD)—and 500,000 go blind from it every year. VAD also impairs children's intellectual development and lowers the body's resistance to disease. As many as 2 million children die each year from problems directly related to VAD.[55]

"It is difficult to imagine any other development taking place at this time that has greater potential to enhance the well-being of women and children," DeGregori notes. "Nothing in scientific advancement or in the rest of life is guaranteed, but if using genetic modification to enhance the iron and vitamin A in rice work out in practice, then it is truly exciting."[56]

For its part, Greenpeace lost little time in attacking golden rice, saying it had too little beta-carotene and that a child "would have to eat about seven kilograms a day of cooked golden rice (equivalent to 3 kilograms of uncooked rice) to obtain the required amount of vitamin A." Greenpeace's assertion was contradicted by the Indian Council on Medical Research, which found that the daily consumption of golden rice would be the equivalent of 200 grams of uncooked rice, or one-fifteenth of the amount claimed by Greenpeace. Among the other mistakes Greenpeace made was its assumption that golden rice would have to supply *all* the vitamin A child needs. The problem in poorer countries is a deficiency in vitamin A, Lord Taverne notes, not a complete lack of it.[57]

Unmoved by the product's potential to benefit the world's most needy people, Greenpeace even attempted to keep the International Rice Research Institute from making golden rice available to farmers in Asia. Greenpeace activists intercepted a package of rice seeds that had been genetically modified for improved resistance to insects. The seeds were en route from Switzerland, where they had been developed, to the Philippines, where they were to be tested for their ability to increase yields using less pesticide. Greenpeace surreptitiously swapped the GM seeds for regular rice. "This may sound like a harmless prank until you consider that in the Philippines, rice is a staple food," Dudley and Norcross point out. "Insects and pests are a problem. The insect-resistant rice would have reduced the hazards Filipino farmers face when hand-spraying pesticides with little or no protective gear."[58]

Neither golden rice nor agricultural biotechnology in general is going to solve all the world's nutritional or health problems. But GM crops, along with other advances in science and technology, can contribute to healthier lives and higher standards of living in the world's poorest regions. Scientists in Egypt, for example, have genetically engineered a drought-tolerant wheat plant—containing a gene from the barley plant—that needs to be irrigated only once, rather than eight times per season. The new wheat is expected to increase wheat production dramatically in semi-arid climates.

In explaining his government's decision in 2002 to grant licenses for the planting of GM cotton in the face of strong opposition from green NGOs, Indian President A. P. J. Kalam called for biotechnology to be part of a "second green revolution." He said: "All our agricultural scientists and technologists have to work for doubling the productivity of the available land...400 million Indians are struggling to come out of poverty...Technology is the only tool we have."[59]

All of this raises one intriguing question: What is it about agricultural biotechnology that makes it so unacceptable to green NGOs? The environmentalists' war against man-made chemicals, misguided though it may be, is at least consistent with the—flawed—vision of Rachel Carson. But biotechnology actually obviates the need for millions of pounds of chemical pesticides, thereby reducing runoff into waterways and occupational exposures to farm workers. There is a sound environmental case to be made for its use. "For reasons having to do more with politics than with logic," observes Jonathan Rauch, "the modern environmental movement was to a large extent founded on suspicion of markets and artificial substances. Markets exploit the earth; chemicals poison it. Biotech touches both hot buttons. It is being pushed forward by greedy corporations, and it seems to be the very epitome of the unnatural."[60]

But just because something is "natural" does not mean it is benign. Ever since the first cave dwellers rubbed the proverbial two sticks together creating fire (a high-risk substance if there ever was one), people have endeavored to improve their lot by applying human ingenuity to the life-and-death challenges confronting them. Many of the threats to humans, animals, and the environment come from nature in the form of diseases, of which malaria is just one example, and natural disasters such as the tsunami of December 2004. Coping with such threats and devising ways to overcome them have been for millennia a preoccupation of creative minds. These efforts have entailed risks and trade-offs. Electricity has made our lives more comfortable, and safer, than our ancestors could have imagined, but people do get electrocuted. Penicillin has cured millions, but some people are allergic to it.

"[W]hat keeps economies running," historian Paul Johnson points out, "is precisely nonconformity, the new, the unusual, the eccentric, the egregious, the innovative, springing from the inexhaustible inventiveness of human nature."[61] Denying the fruits of innovation to those who need it the most in the name of protecting them from hypothetical or negligible risks is an exercise in what Paul Driessen calls "eco-imperialism." "If today's rich nations decide to stop or turn back the clock, they will still be rich," notes Wellesley College political scientist Robert Paarlberg. "But if we stop the clock for developing countries, they will still be poor and hungry."[62] This is where the precautionary principle so beloved by green NGOs and their counterparts in international agencies can take us. As Guy della-Cioppa and May Callan have noted, the precautionary principle applied to food production "would require that we grant legitimacy to the belief that scientifically unwarranted concerns for environmental safety take absolute precedent over providing a population with the means to feed itself."[63]

In the fall and winter of 2002-2003, an estimated 2.5 million people in the southern African countries of Zambia and Zimbabwe faced a severe famine. Their plight just happened to coincide with the UN-sponsored World Summit on Sustainable Development held in late August and early September in neighboring Johannesburg, South Africa. Johannesburg was the official location of the event, which focused on ways to alleviate poverty and hunger in developing countries. But the summit actually took place in Sandton, a wealthy suburb, whose posh hotels, fine restaurants, and spacious conference center were more attuned to the tastes of the participants.

The touchy subject of famine taking place only a short plane ride from the comfortable surroundings at Sandton was addressed in a way that speaks volumes about such gatherings and the pronouncement made at them. In response to the famine, the United States offered to distribute corn it had recently delivered to Zambia and Zimbabwe. To the approval of the green NGOs in Sandton and delegates from the EU, the governments of the two southern African countries rejected to offer because the corn may have contained trace elements of kernels of gene-spliced plants. Zambian President Levy Mwanawasa declared: "We would rather starve than get something toxic." Ignoring such words of wisdom, starving people in both countries stormed the lock warehouses and "liberated" the corn.[64]

Climate of Controversy

Of the various causes taken up by the environmental movement over the past 35 years, none has so preoccupied the attention of green NGOs as has global warming. Ever since NASA scientist James Hansen first sounded the climate alarm on Capitol Hill in the sweltering

Washington summer of 1988, environmental pressure groups the world over have been spreading the gospel of impending climate calamity caused by what they insist is mankind's abuse of the planet.

The religious metaphor in the preceding paragraph is highly appropriate. In the world of the global-warming faithful, there is a gospel to be taken literally. There is a litany to be ritually repeated to deepen the faith of the believers and to convert the heathens. There are acolytes, many of them in the media, to serve the high priests and to spread the word. There are heretics and infidels for whom—figuratively speaking— no public stoning or burning at the stake is too light a punishment. And there is a Doomsday that will assuredly be upon us unless we change our ways and repent our environmental sins.

Such zealotry seems oddly out of place for a subject as complex and—until recently—as poorly understood as the myriad factors that influence the earth's climate. Yet, from the environmentalists' perspective, the issue contains all the elements that comprise and re-enforce their view of the world, including "solutions" that, not coincidentally, promise to put considerable power in their hands. That vision includes greed-driven industrialists despoiling the planet by extracting hydrocarbons from pristine surroundings and converting them to fossil fuels whose heat-trapping emissions, especially carbon dioxide (CO_2), will inevitably lead to a catastrophic warming of the earth. This demands "urgent" action in the form of a global agreement, laid out in the 1997 Kyoto Protocol, to reduce emissions of greenhouse gases, with the ultimate goal of replacing fossil fuels with other forms of energy—wind, solar, biomass, hydrogen, and whatever else comes along provided it's not nuclear. And overseeing all this will be a giant bureaucratic apparatus with global reach staffed by climate stewards selectively plucked from the ranks of NGOs, international agencies, universities, laboratories, and government regulators—all of whom are to be accountable only to themselves. Indeed, the climate change debate we have experienced in the last two decades would have been unthinkable without the global greens. Through press releases, op-eds, books, interviews, conferences, demonstrations, textbooks, advertisements in print and broadcast media, websites, shareholder resolutions, collaboration with allies in Congress and the bureaucracy, and support for legislation at all levels of government, environmentalists have kept up a constant drum beat on the necessity of combating global warming. And in the time-honored tradition of environmentalist fear-mongering, no scare tactics—no matter how overblown—are to be shunned.

"They're here on American soil," a voice intones ominously "pumping poisons in the air, putting toxins like mercury in our water." As he speaks, a TV camera reveals a computer-enhanced landscape, zooming in on high resolution satellite images of a sprawling industrial complex. "We know how to stop them," the voice continues, "but the government won't."

And what are these alleged threats to our well-being? "They are dirty power plants that pollute, cause diseases and global warming," the voice informs us. "These are not weapons, but they cause mass destruction." "We have the technology to stop this," the voice assures us, "but the polluting power companies won't. If that's not a peril, what is?"[65]

Television viewers by the millions were exposed to this ad in late June and early July 2003. At a cost of approximately $360,000, the ad ran in Atlanta, Cleveland, Knoxville, Tampa, Philadelphia, and Washington, D.C., where it was shown on such cable outlets as *CNN, CNN Headline News, CNBC, Fox News,* and *MSNBC.* With its inflammatory rhetoric, defamation of things of which it disapproves, and skilled use of scare tactics, the ad could have come from any of a number of environmental groups. This one was sponsored by the Natural Resources Defense Council (NRDC), a relentless purveyor of fear in all things environmental and a key player in the global warming controversy. Indeed, the headline on the NRDC press release announcing the launch of the television campaign proudly stated: "Mass Destruction on American Soil: Graphic TV Ads Confront White House, Big Power Companies Over Toxic Mercury and Other Dangerous Chemicals."

While alarmist claims have long been a staple of environmentalist rhetoric, in the case of global warming, the level of fear-mongering is commensurate with the scope of the climate-change agenda. In pinpointing the cause of global warming in the burning of fossil fuels, advocates identified a culprit that happened to be the world's largest source of energy. Because energy is the life-blood of every economy, from the most advanced to the most backward, any plan to alter or restrict its use by regulatory means is fraught with pitfalls. Reducing emissions in the manner prescribed in the Kyoto Protocol, in the absence of viable alternatives to fossil fuels, would put an enormous strain the world's energy supply in the best of circumstances. As fate would have it, however, the scheme was concocted just when China and India, with one-third of the world's population, were beginning to emerge from centuries of backwardness as major economic players—with soaring demand for energy from all possible sources. For those seeking to suppress global energy use in the name of combating climate change, the timing couldn't have been worse.

46

Furthermore, in recognition of their special economic needs, China, India and all other developing countries are exempt from the global-warming treaty's restrictions on greenhouse-gas emissions. Yet developing countries are expected to be responsible for as much as 75 percent of global greenhouse gases by 2050. Thus, under the treaty adopted by over 180 countries, and enthusiastically supported by environmental NGOs, the group of nations producing the greatest amount of greenhouse gases by mid-century are required to do—absolutely nothing.[66]

In addition to having chosen the most inopportune time in modern history to embark on a scheme of international energy rationing, the advocates of the theory of anthropogenic global warming made a far more grievous error. They misunderstood their subject. "Climate is always changing, and on every spatial and temporal scale," writes Philip Slott, professor of biogeography at the University of London and editor of the *Journal of Biogeography*. "Climate is governed by millions of factors, from the lightest waft of a monarch butterfly's wing, through erupting volcanoes, shifting land surfaces, ocean currents, ocean salinity and atmospheric gases, to shifts in the geometry of the Earth, solar cycles, meteors, and meteorites. Even our most advanced computers can tell us little about this incredible and unpredictable complexity. The only true model for understanding climate change is the climate itself, and the myriad patterns of climate change from the past."

"The idea of global warming," Slott continues, "is potentially dangerous precisely because it gives the false impression that we might be able to halt climate change by fiddling with just one or two of the millions of factors involved. It is a serious lie. Even if we achieved all the cuts in emissions proposed, the effect would be a temperature change of probably less than 0.07 degrees Celsius, and, because of the millions of other factors involved, it might not happen at all."[67]

There is little reason to believe that those who so eagerly jumped aboard the global-warming bandwagon nearly two decades ago had any inkling of the magnitude of what they had set out to accomplish. Indeed, as we shall see, they still don't today. But, as always, the matter was "urgent," and the powers that be in the global environmental movement lost little time in creating structures to help move things along.

In 1988, the same year NASA's Hansen predicted a substantial rise in global temperatures over the next decade, the United Nations Environmental Programme and another UN agency, the World Meteorological Organization, jointly created a new entity, the UN Intergovernmental Panel on Climate Change (IPCC). The IPCC described itself as an" intergovernmental mechanism aimed at providing the basis for the development of a realistic and effective internationally accepted strategy for addressing climate change."[68] Note that the IPCC, in its own words, is a "mechanism" to provide the basis for "a strategy to address climate change." Far from being an independent scientific panel created to investigate climatic trends, the IPCC instead was a vehicle to promote the idea of climate change (global warming) through the development of an "internationally accepted" strategy. Though the IPCC would avail itself of the services of many reputable scientists over the years and would carry out extensive research on the factors influencing the earth's climate, the organization, nonetheless, had been politically compromised from its inception. In effect, the IPCC had made up its mind and assigned itself an agenda. It was time to put the show on the road, and the IPCC, green NGOs, and their political allies would put on quite a performance in the years to come.

In developing their strategy on global warming, environmental activists, in and out of government, drew heavily on their successful campaign from a few years earlier to ban the use of chloroflourocarbons (CFCs), halons, and other chemicals. A brief digression to the almost forgotten CFC controversy is instructive for understanding what later unfolded in the global warming debate. Once widely used as refrigerants, foamants, and as cleaning agents, CFCs, in the 1970s, were said by environmentalists and some scientists to be causing a thinning of the ozone layer, which protects the earth from the sun's ultraviolet rays. In the U.S., NRDC, warning of a "hole in the ozone layer," spearheaded a successful campaign by activists to get EPA to ban the use of CFCs as aerosol propellants in spray cans in 1978.

Their appetite sufficiently whetted, environmentalists turned their attention to the global arena, with calls for an international treaty to ban the production of CFCs. To that end, NGOs joined forces with national and international environmental officials to create a Coordinating Committee on the Ozone Layer under the auspices of UNEP. The committee, ably assisted in its lobbying by UNEP publications, issued periodic reports that made the case for global action on CFCs. These efforts bore fruit in 1985 with the adoption of the Vienna Convention for the Protection of the Ozone Layer, which bound signatories to exchange data on CFCs and ozone depletion and to continue to monitor the situation.

The Vienna Convention, however, contained no binding commitments, a situation that was rectified two years later when negotiators from UN member nations adopted the Montreal Protocol.

Officially known as the Montreal Protocol on Substances That Deplete the Ozone Layer, the pact, among other things, mandated the reduction of CFC consumption and production to 50 percent of 1986 levels by June 30, 1998. It also froze production of halons and banned trade in CFCs— as well as products made with CFCs—with all countries that had not signed the treaty. In a subsequent UN-sponsored agreement reached in London in 1990, the complete phase-out of CFCs and halons by industrial countries was mandated by 2000. Further revisions were made in an agreement adopted in Copenhagen in 1992, with phase-out dates moved up for CFCs, halons, methyl chloroform, and carbontetrachloride. Also, most hydrofluorocarbons, a chemical substitute for CFCs, were slated for elimination by 2020.

From the beginning, environmental groups played a decisive role in moving governments down the path of complete elimination of CFCs and related chemicals. From NRDC's hounding of EPA to ban CFCs in spray cans in the 1970s, to the Environmental Defense Fund's collaboration with UNEP in trumpeting the CFC-ozone-depletion connection in the mid-1980s, green NGOs kept up the pressure. By now, they were getting good at this sort of thing. Images of people getting skin cancer from CFC-induced ozone depletion were easy to conjure up and proved quite effective in driving the debate. But did science support global action on CFCs? At the time the Montreal Protocol was written, no ozone depletion had been observed. Richard Benedick, who negotiated the treaty for the U.S., has written that the theory of ozone depletion lacked scientific support and credits UNEP with keeping the issue alive.[69]

"The evidence that CFCs stay in the atmosphere, go up in the stratosphere, release chlorine, and destroy ozone is strong," Wildavsky noted, "but there is no clear evidence of global ozone depletion. Mitigating circumstances, such as concurrent emissions of methane, carbon dioxide, and nitrous oxide, as well as large natural variations of ozone, make the detection and prediction of a long-term thinning of the ozone layer problematic."[70] With the science as unsettled as it was, why did industry, after initial resistance, ultimately relent and even go so far as to create a U.S.-based corporate alliance that supported global regulation of CFCs? Sheehan argues convincingly that American producers and users of CFCs calculated that a global treaty was in their interest. After all, European and Japanese companies would have an advantage if Washington, under environmentalist pressure, took unilateral action to suppress CFCs. A global treaty, by contrast, would force foreign firms to comply with the same regulatory regime as U.S.

companies. "In this instance," he writes, "the fate of an international treaty depended on the willingness of private industry to bargain for comparative advantage rather than resist coercive demands."[71]

What's more, there were—albeit more expensive—alternatives to CFCs, which were either readily available or would be in time to meet the phase-out deadlines, making the transition to the post-CFC world a costly, but not overly disruptive, undertaking. This would not, however, be the case in the campaign to suppress the use of fossil fuels in the name of combatting global warming. Other than vague references to "renewable sources of energy" and "new technologies," green NGOs and their supporters have conspicuously failed to explain how the world's growing energy needs are to be met while the hated fossil fuels are confined to the dustbin of history. The 1987 Montreal Protocol was a stunning victory for the environmental movement, and the steps taken to reach it would serve as a model for activists to follow in pursuit of a treaty to curb the use of fossil fuels. But that treaty, the Kyoto Protocol, would have an entirely different fate.

The strategy that served the NGOs so well in the case of CFCs and was applied, with some modifications, to the issue of global warming, contained four key elements:

- claims that human activities are causing irreparable harm to the planet and endangering the lives of its inhabitants;
- assurances, arising from the timely and highly publicized release of "studies," showing that the emerging science supports such claims;
- creation of official panels, preferably with a scientific veneer and operating under the auspices of the UN, that help move the process toward the ultimate goal of global "action;" and
- adoption of global agreements—initially voluntary, but later mandatory—aimed at the ultimate removal of the offending substance(s) from the marketplace

From the very beginning, environmental groups and high-profile green activists engaged in a lively competition to see who could make the most hysterical claims about the threat posed by global warming. Here's a small, but representative, sample of the rhetoric employed in the years leading up to 1997 Kyoto Protocol:

- [W]e are going to see massive extinction ...we could expect to lose all of Florida, Washington, D.C., and the Los Angeles basin...we'll be in rising water with no ark in sight. *(Paul Erlich, Zero Population Growth, May 3, 1988)*[72]

50

- The world is on a truck careening down a highway toward a future of unlimited and irreversible global warming. Unless the U.S., the world's largest greenhouse-gas polluter, steps on the breaks and makes significant cuts in emissions, the Earth risks a plunge over the precipice of climate catastrophic. *(Michael Oppenheimer, Environmental Defense Fund, Nov. 7, 1990)*
- The message is clear: humankind is headed for deep trouble unless we drastically cut our emissions of greenhouse gases into the atmosphere. *(Jerry Leggett, Greenpeace U.K., 1990)*
- "Global warming poses an unprecedented threat to our environment and our economy...Never before has the Earth's climate been altered so severely and rapidly."[73] *(Sierra Club 1994 Congressional Platform)*

The alarmism was not limited to green activists; politicians and scientists also got into the act. In one celebrated example, climatologist Stephen Schneider, once a proponent of the idea of global cooling. even justified the use of scare tactics to promote global warming;

On the one hand, as scientists we are ethically bound to the scientific method, in effect promising to tell the truth, the whole truth, and nothing but— which means we must include all the doubts, the caveats, the ifs, ands, and buts. On the other hand, we are not just scientists but human beings as well. And like most people we'd like to see the world a better place, which in this context translates into working to reduce the risk of potentially disastrous climate change. To do that we need to get some broad-based support, to capture the public's imagination. That, of course, means getting loads of media coverage. So we have to offer up scary scenarios, make simplified dramatic statements, and make little mention of any doubts we might have.[74]

Over time, the scary scenarios Schneider was so eager to see offered up would include claims of melting glaciers, rising sea levels, spreading tropical diseases, vanishing species, and surging incidences of destructive weather—from hurricanes and tornadoes to floods and droughts. As for the scientific basis for anthropogenic global warming, the argument of choice was the assertion that the issue was "settled" because a "consensus" of scientists had reached that conclusion. As early as 1986, Tennessee Senator Al Gore declared "there is no longer any significant disagreement in the science community that the greenhouse effect is real and already occurring." Even in the early years of the climate-change debate, Gore would go so far as to contend that 98 percent of the scientific community agreed that a greenhouse emergency had begun. His contention was without merit. The much-proclaimed scientific consensus on the issue did not exist then and does not exist now. In February 1992, several years into the debate, the Gallup Organization polled members of the American Geophysical Union and the American Meteorological Society found that only 17 percent of those responding believed that greenhouse-gas-induced global warming was taking place.[75]

Furthermore, there was then, and is now, ample confusion over who are the scientists speaking out on climate change. Until the global warming issue came to the fore, climatology had been a backwater in the larger discipline of atmospheric science. There were only a few dozen Ph.D. climatologists in the whole world when the IPCC was formed in 1988. According to Michaels and Balling, only 70 of the 214 people (33 percent) listed as "lead authors" or "contributors" to a 1990 IPCC report raising concerns over global warming had been specially trained in climatology.[76] The confusion over the qualification of scientists expressing themselves on global warming served the interests of those promoting the idea of a scientific "consensus" on climate change. In 1990, for example, the Union of Concerned Scientists (UCS) organized a petition—signed by what *Science* called "heavy hitters," including nearly half the members of the National Academy of Sciences and 49 Nobel Prize winners—urging President George H.W. Bush to take seriously the threat of global warming.[77] Of the 700 scientists who signed UCS's petition, no more than four had any background in climatology.[78]

As the campaign to promote the idea of global warming unfolded, advocates found that the phrase "scientific consensus" could be used as a rhetorical tool to shut off debate on the matter. After all, if there was a consensus that man-made greenhouse gases were heating up the climate to the point of crisis, then the only matter left to discuss was how best to deal with it. Richard S. Lindzen, professor of meteorology at the Massachusetts Institute of Technology, traces the notion of a consensus on global warming to the IPCC's September 1990 report on climate change, one of several the IPCC would release in the years to come. Though the voluminous document, which relied heavily on notoriously inaccurate climate models, was quite ambiguous in its conclusions, that was not the impression the public was given. The IPCC had the political acumen to preface the document with a much-shorter Policymakers Summary, which ignored the report's numerous caveats and, instead, conveyed the impression that the expectation of global warming was firmly based on science. Essentially a PR document, the summary's "findings" were cited by the media and trumpeted by environmental groups as providing conclusive evidence that global warming was a real threat. It would not be the last time the IPCC would try to sway public opinion with what Lindzen calls "sophistry."[79]

The claim of a scientific consensus on global warming has had a long shelf-life, and references to it have become second nature to many in the media. In a July 22, 2005 op-ed, for example, *Washington Post* columnist David Ignatius wrote of global warming that a "consensus is finally emerging," "a growing scientific consensus," and, in case anybody missed the point, "a consensus is emerging." His colleague at the *Post*, Justin Blum, reporting a few days later on the change of CEOs at ExxonMobil, noted that the firm "questions whether fossil-fuel emissions are the primary cause of climate change, defying a growing scientific consensus." He added that the company "has long questioned the increasing accepted science behind global warming."[80] The *Post* is hardly the only offender, and, to its credit, it has occasionally published opposing views on the subject.[81]

If anything, reporting on global warming in the foreign press has been far more unbalanced—sometimes to the point of hysteria—than in the U.S. In one glaring example from July 2001, Munich's influential *Süddeutsche Zeitung* devoted an eight-page special section to the alleged horrors of climate change and related environmental trends. Not one of the section's 27 articles and side bars questioned the theory of catastrophic global warming. Not surprisingly, the section was headlined: "Forecast: Catastrophic."[82]

The alleged consensus on global warming is misplaced for a reason that goes directly to nature of scientific inquiry. "[S]cience is not a matter of consensus, as the histories of Galileo, Copernicus, Pasteur, Einstein and others will attest," former Secretary of Energy James Schlesinger reminds us. "Science depends not on speculation but on conclusions verified through experiment. Verification is more than computer simulations—whose conclusions mirror the assumptions built in the model. Irrespective of the repeated assertions regarding a "scientific consensus," there is neither a consensus nor is consensus science."[83]

With a quasi-permanent international bureaucracy in place to support the notion of a scientific consensus on global warming, and assisted by media culture with a fondness for the sensational, green NGOs had reason to believe that things would ultimately go their way. Following a series of conferences, at which NGOs and UN functionaries drafted and re-drafted language for a climate treaty and other environmental agreements, the stage was set for the Rio Earth Summit of June 1992. Closely watched, and in some cases advised, by activists who had flocked to the exotic Brazilian city by the thousands, delegates at the Rio Summit adopted the Framework Convention on Climate Change (FCCC). A seemingly innocuous document, the FCCC calls on—but does not require—all countries to reduce their greenhouse-gas emissions to 1990 levels by 2000, and to report annually on their progress.

The non-binding agreement allowed signatories to say that they had "done something" about global warming while committing them to do nothing. Like its role model, the Vienna Convention on CFCs, the FCCC was voluntary. And like the earlier agreement, the FCCC was to be followed by a series of meetings. In the case of the FCCC, the follow-up meetings were called "Conferences of the Parties" and concerned themselves with what further action on climate change should be taken. The action most desired by NGOs was what they hadn't been able to achieve at Rio: an agreement with binding reduction in greenhouse-gas emissions, complete with targets and timetables.

Moving the world of climate change from a non-binding agreement to a binding treaty would require a Herculean lobbying effort aided by political good fortune. Both would be forthcoming. To coordinate and intensify their lobbying efforts, green NGOs formed the Climate Action Network (CAN), a coalition of over 160 global environmental groups dedicated to promoting the notion of global warming.

Their work bore fruit at the first Conference of the Parties held in Berlin in March 1995, at which CAN assigned itself the role of conscience of the conference. Through the publication of a daily newsletter, *Ecos*, which was widely distributed and read at the conference, CAN berated the delegates for being too timid on global warming, recommended steps to overcome deadlocks, and never let decision-makers forget that they were being monitored. After CAN expressed its displeasure at being excluded from taking part in the conference's formal proceedings, one CAN activists was finally allowed to address the delegates. The blurring of the lines between environmental activism and official decision-making became even more evident when it was learned that *Ecos* was being funded in part by the environmental ministries of Germany and the Netherlands.

Green NGOs accomplished more in Berlin than just deepening their infiltration of global decision-making bodies. At their urging, delegates finally agreed to the "Berlin Mandate," which committed governments to meet in Kyoto, Japan in December 1997 to negotiate targets and timetables for curbing carbon emissions. This success, however, came at a price that would come back to haunt global-warming advocates in and out of government. Developing countries—including such heavyweights as China, India, Brazil, and Mexico—took advantage of the somewhat chaotic nature of the proceedings to exempt themselves from future emissions targets.[84]

Events were now set in motion to move from non-binding pledges to binding commitments—the ultimate goal of the global warming lobby. These efforts had been buoyed by the political good fortune of having the world's most powerful country, and biggest greenhouse-gas emitter, firmly in the camp of those seeking to reduce carbon emissions. While the Bush administration had paid little more than lip service to the issue, the Clinton administration, which came to power in January 1993, had a much deeper commitment to the climate change agenda. The new vice president, Al Gore, had been an outspoken environmental advocate since his earliest days in Congress, and had made an impassioned—to put it mildly—plea to deal with global warming in his 1992 bestseller, *Earth in the Balance.*

Gore's long-standing ties to the environmental movement enabled him to place green activists in key positions throughout the administration, notably at EPA, the Departments of Energy and Interior, and the White House Council on Environmental Quality. Among the most prominent were former Gore Senate staffers Carol Browner and Kathleen McGinty, who became EPA administrator and chair of the Council on Environmental Quality, respectively. Seasoned activist Eileen Claussen, who would later head the Pew Center on Climate Change, became undersecretary of state for environmental affairs and a key negotiator for the Kyoto Protocol. Former Wilderness Society president George Frampton, took over as director of the Council of Environmental Quality. Jonathan Lash, former president of the World Resources Institute (founded by the ubiquitous Maurice Strong) became co-chair the President's Commission on Sustainable Development. And this is just a short list.[85]

From their positions within the administration, these activists-turned-policymakers set out to translate their environmental vision into reality, and climate change was one of their top priorities. In October 1993, the administration launched its "Climate Change Action Plan," a cacophony of federally supported initiatives and voluntary industry programs aimed at promoting energy efficiency and renewable fuels, and—most important of all—keeping the idea of global warming in the public's mind. The administration also substantially increased the funding for research on climate change, which surpassed the $4-billion level by 2000, Clinton's last year in office. Not everything went smoothly, however. The administration's plans to enact a BTU tax, a tax on the use of energy, failed in Congress in 1993. Likewise, the Republican takeover of Congress in the wake of the 1994 mid-term elections put a damper on whatever far-reaching legislative initiatives on climate change the administration might have contemplated.

On the other hand, from the environmentalists' standpoint, having a supportive administration in power came in handy when the ever-fickle weather didn't conform with the theory of global warming. In February 1996, with cities throughout the upper Midwest recording record low temperatures, and with the mid-Atlantic and New England regions buried under heavy snowfall, President Bill Clinton—ever the artful dodger—attributed the frigid outbreak to...global warming.

Despite these setbacks, events moved inexorably toward the conclusion of the binding agreement so eagerly sought by activists and their allies in national and international agencies. Once again, it was the permanent bureaucracy of the IPCC that helped speed things along. In 1996, the IPCC issued another of its reports, this one known as the "Second Assessment," which contained many of the caveats and ambiguities that characterized the IPCC's 1990 report. Like its predecessor, the Second Assessment indulged in crass political manipulation, this one more egregious than the 1990 report's slick "Policymakers Summary." Displeased with the document's less-than-sensational findings, a small group of IPCC scientists took it upon themselves to re-write parts of the report—after the peer-review process had been completed. They also inserted a sentence into the report that would be cited countless times in the years to come as confirming that global warming was truly upon us. It read: "The balance of evidence suggests a discernable human influence on the climate."[86]

Actually the sentence is remarkable for what it doesn't say. No one could seriously doubt that the nearly 6 billion people living in the world in 1996, not to mention the untold billions who came before them, have had an influence on the environment, including the climate. The question is how humans have altered the climate and to what extent. This question goes conspicuously unanswered in the inserted sentence. Furthermore, the re-writing of the document by global warming enthusiasts made a travesty of the peer review process and showed the IPCC at its politicized worst. Frederick Seitz, the former president of the National Academy of Sciences, called the incident the most "disturbing corruption of the peer review process" he had ever seen. He warned that the effect of the re-write was "to deceive policy makers and the public into believing that the scientific evidence shows human activities are causing global warming."

As if on cue, EDF's Michael Oppenheimer seized the opportunity afforded him by the IPCC's chicanery and declared: "The IPCC's report serves as a clear warning: Humans have begun to influence the earth's climate and the outcome could be disastrous for many people and natural places."[87] But preparing the American public for the sacrifices resulting from a treaty to limit carbon emissions would require more than the standard environmentalist sound bites. Under the aegis of the Climate Action Plan, the Clinton White House teamed up with the Sierra Club, NRDC, EDF, and other environmental groups for an elaborate road show, featuring carefully staged "town meetings" in Austin, Boston, Miami, San Diego, San Francisco, and Seattle. Administration officials and activists presented their audiences with boiler-plate horror stories, focusing on how global warming would wreak havoc with local economies by destroying tourism, fishing, skiing, real estate, and forestry.

Kyoto: End of the Beginning and Beginning of the End

Considering the years of lobbying and untold hours of negotiations that preceded the Kyoto conference of December 1997, the event itself turned out to be something of an anti-climax. Attended by over 3,500 people packed into Kyoto's tastefully designed conference center, the event featured tedious behind-the-scene negotiations over the minutia of climate change issues, equally tedious speeches by delegates holding forth on the state of the talks and the future of the planet, and environmental groups passing out flyers, holding press conferences, and engaging in all manner of street theater to promote their cause. There were the usual receptions and, a special Japanese touch, even a "Sake Tasting Bar" that dispensed cups of the rice wine free of charge to thirsty attendees every evening.[88]

Economist Thomas Gale Moore of the Hoover Institution, who attended the conference, captured the essence of the proceedings in this memorable description of the arcane issues under discussion:

We were informed that the modality of the evolution was stymied, but that it would be taken up by a contact group; that, for unknown reasons, the European Union wouldn't budge on the bubble; and that the United States supported limited differentiation. The QELROs group debated the number of gases to be covered, and the United States insisted on joint implementation.

Note: If you understand the previous two sentences, please go to the next conference in my place.[89]

Even more revealing was the performance of a Russian official who chaired the plenary session in the final hours before the conference was scheduled to adjourn. Worried that the delegates wouldn't finish the final wording of the treaty on time, he exhorted his colleagues to speed things up, otherwise, he would miss his plane to Moscow. On the last day in Kyoto, the fate of the planet took a back seat to getting to the airport on time.[90]

Under the Kyoto Protocol, industrialized countries—led by the U.S., the EU, and Japan—are required collectively to lower their greenhouse-gas emissions to five percent below 1990 levels by 2008-2012. Developing countries are exempt from the mandates, and a host of special, and very complicated, arrangements were made for peculiar economic problems faced by former communist countries and for the poorer members of the EU. The targets and timetables in the treaty were supposed to be "legally binding," but delegates couldn't agree on what the term meant, and it was left for a follow-up conference to resolve. (It never was, and "legally binding" was later dropped and replaced by the—meaningless—term "politically binding.")

Vice President Gore made an unscheduled flight to Kyoto to help break one of the many deadlocks in the negotiations and to help raise morale among the often exhausted delegates and activists. In a brief, five-minute address before about fifty carefully selected media representatives, Gore declared: "We are altering the relationship between the Earth and the Sun." Changing mankind's behavior, he said, would require "humility because the spiritual roots of our crisis is pridefulness." To the assembled green NGOs, anxious that the agreement may fall short of their expectations, Gore said: "This is the step-by-step approach we took in Montreal ten years ago to address the problem of ozone depletion. And it is working."[91]

Gore was right about Montreal, but he would be wrong about Kyoto. In fact, the unraveling had begun, even before the long-awaited conference got underway. On July 25, 1997, the U.S. Senate, by a vote of 95 to 0, approved the Byrd-Hagel Resolution, which effectively instructed U.S. negotiators not to consent to a treaty that 1.) excluded meaningful participation of developing countries and 2.) harmed the American economy. The Kyoto Protocol violated both stipulations by exempting developing countries from the climate pact's mandates and by targeting fossil fuels, which account for 85 percent of U.S. energy needs. By ignoring the Senate's unmistakable warning, U.S. negotiators had doomed ratification. Knowing that the treaty had no chance of receiving the two-thirds vote the Constitution requires for ratification, the Clinton administration never bothered to submit the climate pact to the Senate.

Shortly after taking office, President George W. Bush, in March 2001, formally rejected the Kyoto Protocol, citing the damage the treaty would do to the American economy. The announcement met with predictable cries of outrage from the treaty's supporters. European leaders termed Bush's action "arrogant" and "irresponsible," and another example of American "unilateralisn," while Margot Wallstrom, the EU's Environmental Commissioner, declared, "We cannot allow one country to kill the process."[92] Wallstrom need not have worried about the "process;" it is very much alive. Since Kyoto, the UN has sponsored a steady stream of global warming conferences in such places as Buenos Aires, The Hague, Bonn, Marrakech, New Delhi, and Montreal, with more certain to take place in the years ahead. And despite its rejection by the U.S. (and later, Australia), the treaty, several years behind schedule, was finally ratified by enough countries to allow it to go into force in February 2005.

But while the process of Kyoto moves inexorably toward the next round of perfunctory meetings, ritualistic declarations, and empty pledges, it is the content of the treaty that is the real concern. It is becoming increasingly clear that those nations that so enthusiastically embraced Kyoto have—economically speaking—made a pact with the devil. Even the treaty's most outspoken advocates like France, Italy, and Canada are nowhere near to meeting Kyoto's emissions targets. According to the International Energy Agency, from 1990 (Kyoto's base year for measuring changes) to 2002, greenhouse-gas emissions in France *rose* 6.9 percent; Italy 8.3 percent; Greece 29.2 percent; the Netherlands 13.2 percent; Portugal 59 percent; and Spain 46.9 percent. Germany and Britain have seen their emissions decline by 13.3 percent and 5.5 percent, respectively, but both of these "successes" were the result of one-time savings created by special circumstances. After reunification in 1990, Germany closed many communist-era power plants in eastern Germany, which drastically cut its CO_2 emissions. Britain reaped the benefits of an earlier decision by its government to switch the country's utilities from coal (high CO_2) to natural gas (low CO_2).[93] But with the greatest reductions already having been achieved, Britain is now on track to fall short of its targets in the 2008-2012 period.[94]

In any event, these one-time savings by Britain and Germany will have been used up by 2012 at the latest, when the next phase of emissions reductions (the details of which are still to be negotiated) are scheduled to take effect. At that point, Germany and Britain will join their fellow EU members and other industrialized countries bound by Kyoto in trying to comply—or pretending to comply—with the climate treaty's mandates. "To reach Kyoto's drastic goal of cutting emissions by 2012 to levels 5 percent below those of 1990, developed nations have no choice but to slash energy use," notes James Glassman of the American Enterprise Institute. "That means slower growth, even widespread recession, with especially dire results not just for rich nations, but worse, for poor nations that rely on demand from the developed world for their goods and services."[95]

Glassman's remarks confirm a wry observation made by Aaron Wildavsky years before the Kyoto Protocol was written. Calling global warming the "mother of all environmental scares," Wildavsky wrote: "Warming (and warming alone) through its primary antidote of withdrawing carbon from production and consumption, is capable of realizing the environmentalist's dreams of an egalitarian society based on rejection of economic growth in favor of a smaller population eating lower on the food chain, consuming a lot less, and sharing a much lower level of resources much more equally."[96] Both Glassman and Wildavsky recognize that—aside from the problems faced by developed nations—those who can least afford restricted access to affordable energy are to be found at the bottom of the economic ladder. This includes both low-income people in developed nations and most inhabitants of developing countries. According to the World Health Organization, some 2.8 million people worldwide die annually because of indoor air pollution, mainly as a result of the burning of solid fuels (e.g. coal, wood, and dung) for heating and cooking in the home. Increasing fossil fuel prices—the inevitable result of Kyoto-style regulations—"would only make it harder for households using solid fuels to switch to cleaner, commercial fossil fuels."[97]

Attempts by countries bound by the treaty to square the Kyoto circle have already produced their first—quite predictable—casualty: the truth. In a July 7, 2005 letter to the *Washington Post*, Barbara Helfferich, speaking on behalf of the European Commission, made the absurd claim that "EU member states are on course to meet their Kyoto targets."[98] A far more honest assessment of the situation can be found in a question posed a few days earlier by Catherine Pearce, global climate change spokeswoman for Friends of the Earth. She was quoted in *The Guardian* as asking; "If Britain and the rest of Europe cannot get it right, then how can anyone expect the U.S. or developing countries to?"[99]

Unwilling to subject their economies to the energy diet that compliance with Kyoto demands, countries bound by the treaty are scrambling to find other ways to meet their obligations or, failing that, to keep up appearances. The climate pact offers such countries two options designed to lessen the pain of compliance. One option is the "Clean Development Mechanism," which allows an industrialized nation to receive emissions credits by investing in a "sustainable development" project, such as a modern power plant, in a developing country that reduces the latter's greenhouse-gas emissions.[100] The other option is an emissions trading scheme that allows countries that are exceeding their emissions targets to purchase credits from countries that are below their greenhouse-gas limits. Bureaucrats at the EU have developed an elaborate, three-tiered emissions trading scheme that enables countries like France, Italy, and Spain to purchase credits from Russia, Poland, Ukraine and other countries whose economies are still recovering from the communist era.[101]

The idea of emissions trading originated with the Clinton administration which saw it as a relatively painless way to cut emissions (at least on paper), and as a financial inducement to Russia and other former-communist countries to sign on to Kyoto. It was originally opposed by the EU and green NGOs which saw it—not without justification—as a cynical ploy by the U.S. to avoid making politically painful domestic cuts in energy use. With the U.S. having rejected Kyoto, emissions trading is now embraced by the EU and other treaty partners eager to spare voters the discomfort of reduced energy consumption. However, as most countries are far from meeting their current obligations, not to mention any new requirements that may be imposed after 2012, there is little reason to believe that either emissions trading or the Clean Development Mechanism will be enough to allow the treaty to function as its advocates expect.

"Post-Kyoto Era"

While some still persist in deluding themselves and the public that the Kyoto Protocol can be made to work, others have come to a different conclusion. Unveiled with precious little fanfare on July 27, 2005 in—of all places—Vientiane, Laos, the Asia Pacific Partnership for Clean Development and Climate Change may well emerge as the science and technology-based alternative to the Kyoto Protocol.

Initially composed of the United States, Australia, China, India, South Korea, and Japan, the partnership, according to the Bush White

House, will "allow our nations to develop and accelerate deployment of cleaner, more efficient energy technologies to meet national pollution reduction, energy security, and climate change concerns in ways that reduce poverty and promote economic development."[102] But behind what appears to be little more than the standard boilerplate of a White House press release is, in fact, an initiative that is as ambitious as it is subtle. Largely ignored by the media, the partnership not only breaks with Kyoto (without expressly saying so), but also parts company with many of the reigning tenets of modern environmentalism. Consider the following three passages from a White House fact sheet, the first of which is strongly reminiscent of Indira Gandhi's remarks introducing this chapter:

Overcoming extreme poverty will also improve the environment. Stagnant economies are one of the world's greatest environmental threats, because people who lack food, shelter, and sanitation cannot be expected to preserve the environment at the expense of their own survival—and poor societies cannot be expected to invest in cleaner, more efficient technologies.

Some have suggested the best solution to environmental challenges and climate change is to oppose development and put the world on an energy diet. But today, about two billion people have no access to any form of modern energy—and blocking that access would condemn them to permanent poverty, disease, high infant mortality, polluted water, and polluted air.

We oppose any policy that would achieve any reductions by putting Americans out of work or by simply shifting emissions from one country to another. Like us, developing countries are unlikely to join in any approaches that foreclose their own economic growth and development.[103]

In practical terms, the partnership will encourage investment in existing and emerging technologies and practices, including clean coal, liquified natural gas, bioenergy, next-generation nuclear power, the capture and use of methane, electrification of rural villages, and an assortment of advanced transportation technologies. The six founding partners of the pact account for 45 percent of the world's population, 48 percent of the world's greenhouse-gas emissions, and 48 percent of the world's energy consumption.[104]

A year in the making, and quietly initiated by the Bush administration (with assistance from Australia), the partnership is worlds apart from the Kyoto Protocol. It is a voluntary, non-regulatory pact, existing completely outside the structure of the UN, that sees technology—and not bureaucracy—as the key to address the world's growing energy needs, alleviate endemic poverty in developing countries, and cope with climate change, should global warming become a problem.[105]

"It's quite clear the Kyoto Protocol won't get the world where it wants to go...We have got to find something that works better— Australia is working on that with partners around the world," commented Australian environment minister Ian Campbell.[106] Of the pact's founding partners, two, the U.S. and Australia, have rejected the Kyoto Protocol; three, India, China, and South Korea, are exempt from Kyoto, have growing energy needs, and are major greenhouse-gas emitters; and one, Japan, has ratified Kyoto but has little chance of meeting its obligations.

Japan's participation in the pact is particularly intriguing because it sets a precedent for other industrialized countries to follow that are unable or unwilling to comply with the global warming treaty. For the time being, the Japanese will remain formally within the Kyoto framework—lest too many diplomatic feathers be ruffled. But Tokyo clearly views the partnership both as a far more appropriate way to address the country's future energy needs and as a mechanism through which Japan and the other partners can offer their emerging energy technologies to the rest of the world. Indeed, as Australia's Campbell suggests, the Asia-Pacific Partnership will become a global pact, offering countries, including those in the EU, an alternative to the burdens and inadequacies of Kyoto. Initially, the partnership will exist simultaneously with Kyoto but, over time, will ultimately supersede it. It is now clear what Bush meant at the G-8 summit in Gleneagles, Scotland on July 7, 2005, three weeks before the partnership was unveiled, when he spoke of the "post-Kyoto era."[107]

Because the partnership exists outside the formal structure of the United Nations, it also has no ties to the IPCC. This, too, is part of the "post-Kyoto era." We have seen that the IPCC was politically compromised from its very inception, that it was "designed to support a foregone conclusion."[108] Over the years, the IPCC used its quasi scientific status to function as a public-relations organ in support of the theory of anthropogenic global warming. The most egregious example of that support, however, has now come back to undermine the IPCC's credibility. In 2001, the IPCC issued one of its periodic reports on climate change. Known as the "Third Assessment Report" (TAR), the IPCC claimed that the increase in twentieth-century temperatures in the Northern Hemisphere is "likely to have been the largest of any century during the past 1,000 years" and that the "the 1990s was the warmest decade and 1998 the warmest year..."[109] Widely reported in the media, and trumpeted by green NGOs, the IPCC report appeared to provide further evidence of human-induced global warming.

The IPCC's findings were based on a 1998 study in *Nature* whose lead author was Michael Mann, at the time a geoscientist at the University of Virginia. Drawing on what are known as proxy data—tree rings, ice cores, corals, etc.—Mann and his two co-authors used computer models and mathematical calculations to conclude that, during the past 1,000 years, temperatures remained fairly constant until the twentieth century, when they began to rise, spiking dramatically in the 1990s. When placed on a graph, the results resembled a hockey stick lying on its back pointing upwards. Thus was born the "hockey stick" controversy within the larger global-warming debate.[110] The hockey stick contradicts the views shared by most paleoclimatologists, according to which the earth has experienced variations in climate throughout its history. As for the past 1,000 years, following the end of the Medieval Warm Period around 1450, the Northern Hemisphere went through the Little Ice Age, and began to warm again, in fits and starts, in the 17th century. The warming trend continued until about 1940, followed by a cooling trend for the next 35 years or so, with a slight rebound in temperatures, measured at ground level, since 1975.[111]

So startling were the findings of Mann and his colleagues that people with the requisite background began to try to replicate the study's results in order to test their validity. It was then that the hockey stick, and the IPCC, began to lose much of their luster. Two Canadian researchers, Stephen McIntyre and Ross McKitrick, were the first to discover significant problems in the methodology that produced the hockey stick. According to McIntyre, the mathematical techniques employed by Mann, when put to a graph, are prone to produce a hockey-stick image even when applied to random data. Statistician Francis Zwiers of Environment Canada told the *Wall Street Journal* that Mann's statistical method "preferentially produces hockey sticks when there are none in the data." Mann's reluctance to share the study's underlying data has only raised additional questions about the validity of his findings.

As the controversy unfolded, Mann's relationship with the IPCC and the environmental movement became the focus of growing attention. It seems that Mann was the lead author of the very chapter in the IPCC's 2001 TAR report that showcased his findings. What's more, someone in the IPCC saw to it that the hockey-stick graph was prominently displayed in the report's "Summary for Policymakers," where it was most likely to catch the attention of reporters. With his methodology coming under attack, Mann joined forces with the World Wildlife Fund to create a website, Realclimate.org, aimed at defending himself from his critics. But in teaming up with an outspoken advocate of global warming, Mann did little to allay the suspicion that he, like his partners at the WWF, was on a mission.

In late 2004, Joe Barton (R-Texas), chairman of the House Energy and Commerce Committee, launched an investigation into Mann and his two colleagues, Raymond S. Bradley of the University of Massachusetts at Amherst and Malcolm K. Hughes of the University of Arizona's Laboratory of Tree-Ring Research. Barton demanded that the three scientists turn over reams of documents containing data used to justify their conclusions. In a June 23, 2005 letter to Mann, Barton noted that in recent peer-reviewed studies in *Science, Geophysical Research Letters,* and *Energy & Environment*, researchers had questioned the validity of Mann's findings. He added:

> The concerns surrounding these studies reflect upon the quality and transparency of federally funded research and of the IPCC review process —two matters of particular interest to the Committee. For example, one concern relates to whether IPCC review has been sufficiently independent. We understand that you were a lead author of the IPCC chapter that assessed and reported your own studies, and that two study co-authors were also contributing authors to this very same chapter. Given the prominence these studies were accorded in the IPCC TAR and your position and role in that process, we seek to learn more about the facts and circumstances that led to acceptance and prominent use of this work in the IPCC TAR and to understand what this controversy indicates about the data quality of key IPCC studies.[112]

Skeptics could argue that because Barton is from Texas, a state that has long-standing ties to the fossil-fuel industry, he might not be kindly disposed to Mann's views. But it is also true that the IPCC's collaboration with Mann in the 2001 report was not the first time the UN panel engaged in activities that, putting it diplomatically, bore the appearance of being politically motivated. A public inquiry into the activities of the IPCC was long overdue. Whether the Energy and Commerce Committee's investigation of the hockey-stick dispute will resolve the issue remains to be seen. What is clear is that the IPCC, which finally distanced itself from Mann's work, is receiving a level of official scrutiny it has never before experienced.[113] The UN panel is expected to issue another climate report in 2007, and, if the past is any guide, it also will be supportive of the theory of anthropogenic global warming. What will be different, however, is that the IPCC, and the array of political interests tied to the Kyoto Protocol, will no longer be the only game in town. The partnership spearheaded by the U.S. has altered the political landscape on which the climate-change debate will play out.

Environmental NGOs lost little time in condemning the Asia-Pacific Partnership. "Skulking around, making secretive, selective deals will not accomplish this; signing up to the Kyoto Protocol will," said Greenpeace energy campaigner Catherine Fitzpatrick. "A deal on climate change that doesn't limit pollution is the same as peace plan that allows guns to be fired," commented Jenifer Morgan, head of the climate-change program of the World Wildlife Fund.[114] Reactions like these were hardly surprising. An energy and climate pact containing no mandatory emissions limits, having no ties to the IPCC, emphasizing economic growth instead of energy rationing, and having arisen without the advice and consent of green NGOs, was not going to warm the hearts of environmental activists. Yet for all the sound and fury of their protests, there is little indication that they grasped how much the pieces on the chessboard have been rearranged—to their detriment.

Having given up on Senate ratification of the Kyoto Protocol, environmentalists in the U.S. instead back efforts by individual lawmakers to enact legislation that would cap domestic greenhouse-gas emissions—a kind of Kyoto through the back door, or "Kyoto Lite." The most prominent of the efforts was a bill sponsored by Senators John McCain (R-Ariz.) and Joe Lieberman (D-Conn.). Defeated by a vote of 55 to 42 in 2004, the bill, slightly revised, went down to an even bigger 60-to-38 defeat in June 2005. The only point environmentalists were able to salvage was passage of a non-binding "Sense of the Senate" resolution on global warming—voted on after the McCain-Lieberman bill was rejected—which effectively committed the Senate to do nothing.[115]

True to form, the meaningless Senate resolution was quickly transformed into what NRDC President John Adams called "terrific news from Capitol Hill," a preposterous claim made in an appeal for more money. In a June 29, 2005 email message to members of the NRDC Action Fund, Adams described the Senate vote on the non-binding resolution as an "historic victory" and "the biggest leap forward in our global warming campaign in a decade." According to Adams, the resolution "calls on the Senate to enact mandatory limits on global warming pollution by the end of the decade." Adams conspicuously failed to tell his would-be donors that the resolution contains two provisos that stipulate emissions reduction "(1) must not harm the United States economy and (2) will encourage comparable action by other major trading partners and contributors to global emissions."

"Mandatory limits" on emissions would obviously harm the U.S. economy, the same reason why the Senate rejected the Kyoto Protocol and the McCain-Lieberman bill. And "comparable action" by other major contributors to global emissions is illusory because developing countries are exempt from the global warming treaty. These are two reasons why the Senate rejected the Kyoto Protocol and the McCain-Lieberman bill. The NRDC's Adams is hardly the first author of a political fundraising letter to play it fast and loose with the facts, but his declaration of victory after such a resounding setback for the proponents of mandatory emissions reductions borders on the comical.

Rebuffed at the national level, environmental groups and their political allies have tried to get states to take the lead in curbing greenhouse-gas emissions. In August 2005, officials representing nine northeastern states unveiled a plan to reduce greenhouse gas emissions from electric power plants by ten percent by 2020. The plan, expressly designed to "combat global warming," will effect over 600 power plants in New York, Massachusetts, Vermont, New Hampshire, Connecticut, New Jersey, Maine, Rhode Island, and Delaware. Essentially a regional version of the failed McCain-Lieberman bill, the plan establishes a mandatory cap-and-trade for carbon dioxide in which facilities will trade emissions credits. Emissions will be capped for the region at 150 tons of carbon dioxide beginning in 2009. After 2015 states will actually have to reduce their emissions in order to reach the goal of a ten percent regional cut by 2020.[116]

Two years in the making, and initiated by New York Governor George Pataki (R), the plan appeals to environmentalists, because it creates a model for other states to follow and is designed to build momentum for adoption of a nationwide mandatory program to curb greenhouse-gas emissions. "We're not going to solve the problem of global warming in the Northeastern states," commented Dale S. Bryk, a senior attorney with the NRDC, "but we're show that we have the American ingenuity to do this and we're setting a precedent in terms of the design of the program." Shortly after the northeastern plan was made public, officials in California, Oregon, and Washington announced that they would create a West Coast version of the emissions-reduction scheme. "We're making sure we have a uniform standard among the states in working toward greenhouse gas emissions," said Jon Myers, spokesman for California's Department of Environmental Protection. "California has a history of setting the bar a little higher." (For those who remember how "high" California set the bar when it developed its infamous energy deregulation scheme in the late 1990s, which led to rolling blackouts and brownouts across the state, Myers' remarks may sound ominous, indeed.)

With their embrace of mandatory targets and timetables, and the unquestioned faith of their supporters in the theory of anthropogenic global warming, the West Coast and Northeastern plans are in the tradition of Kyoto. In a glowing editorial, the *Boston Globe* affectionately—and accurately—dubbed the plan the "Northeast's little Kyoto." That most countries bound by Kyoto are unable to meet their targets under the treaty, appears to have escaped the attention of those intent on imposing Kyoto-like solutions on an unsuspecting public. And just as the guiding spirits of Kyoto devised a scheme to ration energy at a time of skyrocketing global demand for fuel and power, the architects of the regional efforts to curb emissions chose to increase regulatory burdens on power plants just as energy costs were feeling the effects of soaring oil prices. While the regional plans' effect on the climate is likely to be negligible, their impact on what consumers pay for electricity will be considerable.

Also at the state level, green NGOs and friendly lawmakers have joined forces to curb tailpipe emissions of greenhouse gases. Hoping to create what environmentalists have dubbed the "clean car corridor," officials in Oregon and Washington are moving their states toward adoption of so-called "California standards" for tailpipe emissions of greenhouse gases, particularly CO_2. In 2002, California lawmakers approved legislation directing the California Air Resources Board (CARB) to develop rules to achieve "maximum feasible and cost-effective reductions in greenhouse gas emissions from motor vehicles." Set to be phased-in beginning in 2009, the California plan is to be fully implemented by 2016. Once Washington and Oregon follow suit, the "clean car corridor" will stretch along the West Coast, from the Mexican to the Canadian border. By 2016, all new cars, SUVs, and light trucks sold on the West Coast will have to comply with the new standards for emissions of greenhouse gases.[117]

"People realize that having more advanced-technology cars on the road will enhance our oil security and begin to address global-warming issues," observed Rob Sargent of the National Association of Public Interest Research Groups (PIRG). PIRG has been pushing other states to join California and its two neighbors to the north to adopt the new standards for CO_2 and other greenhouse gases. Six Northeastern states—New York, Massachusetts, Vermont, New Jersey, Connecticut, and Maine—are expected to finalize California-style rules by the end of 2005. The federal Clean Air Act (CAA) allows California to set emissions standards for cars and trucks that are more stringent than federal standards. Other states have the option of adopting either

California or federal standards. This provision of the CAA, however, pertains to conventional air pollutants regulated by EPA. Carbon dioxide, which is not considered a pollutant by EPA, is another matter. The main greenhouse gas emitted by vehicles is CO_2, an inescapable byproduct of the combustion of gasoline and other carbonaceous fuels.

Attempts to regulate tailpipe emissions of CO_2, however, run afoul of substantial technical and legal barriers. According to EPA in a 2003 report:

> No technology currently exists or is under development that can capture and destroy or reduce emissions of CO_2, unlike other emissions from motor vehicle tailpipes. At present, the only practical way to reduce tailpipe emissions of CO_2 is to improve fuel economy."[118]

Hence, the only feasible way to carry out the California standard for tailpipe emissions of greenhouse gases is by regulations that reduce the amount of fuel consumed per vehicle miles traveled—i.e., fuel economy. Federal law, however, expressly forbids states to regulate fuel economy for motor vehicles. The Federal Energy Policy and Conservation Act of 1975 states:

> "When an average fuel economy standard prescribed under this chapter is in effect, a State or a political subdivision of a State may not adopt or enforce a law or regulation related to fuel economy standards or average fuel economy standards for automobiles covered by an average fuel economy standard under this chapter."[119]

It's no wonder that the auto industry, through the Alliance of Automobile Manufacturers, has sued CARB, arguing that it cannot achieve "Maximum feasible" greenhouse gas reductions without setting de facto fuel economy standards, which is prohibited under federal law. Lest anyone be confused about the legality of what California and like-minded states are trying to do, the Bush administration included language in new fuel economy standards it unveiled in August 2005 saying that "a state law that seeks to reduce motor vehicle carbon dioxide emissions is both expressly and implicitly preempted."[120]

With the legal deck stacked heavily against state efforts to curb vehicle emissions of greenhouse gases, PIRG and its allies appear headed for a defeat in the courtroom. For years, green NGOs have exhorted their followers to "think globally, and act locally." The attempt by state governments, backed by environmental groups, to reduce greenhouse-gas emissions, whether from power plants or from vehicles, is but one example among many of the "think-globally, act-locally" strategy. As we shall see in Chapter III, this approach has been quite successful in other areas of environmental policy, especially in affecting land-use decisions at the local, state, and regional levels. Its applicability to the climate change debate, however, is problematic, given the paramount role of federal statutes governing air quality and fuel economy. What is not open to question is the willingness and ability of green NGOs to pursue every conceivable avenue to forward their agenda, even those that may lead to a dead end.

The post-Kyoto era is a work in progress. With scientists around the world receiving grants to investigate every imaginable aspect of climate change, global warming has a well-funded constituency with a vested interest in keeping the subject alive. The U.S. federal government alone spent $2 billion on climate change research in fiscal year (FY) 2004. And more than 2,000 separate climate change-related grants were distributed by federal departments and agencies in FY 2002, the latest year for which comprehensive data are available.[121] In addition to public funds, private foundations donate a minimum of $35-50 million annually to non-profit organizations and universities to comment on or study various aspects of the climate change debate. This level of funding is more than sufficient to hold the interest of the scientific community and advocacy groups for years to come. Environmental organizations intent on ridding the world of fossil fuels will find ample opportunities to ply their trade, some of them in unsuspected places.

The Rise and Fall of Mercury

"Mercury is a real horror show," the League of Conservation Voters (LCV) proclaimed in the summer of 2005. "It comes out of power plants, into our air and causes brain damage in children. And now the Bush administration actually wants to increase the amount of mercury in our environment." Friends of the Earth also sounded the alarm on mercury, claiming an advertisement in *USA Today* that "...kids are being poisoned by deadly mercury from power plants." NRDC and MOVEON.ORG joined the fray, alleging in an advertisement in the *New York Times* that the Bush administration was planning to allow power plants to release "more mercury into the air."[122]

The claim that "kids are being poisoned by deadly mercury from power plants" is standard environmentalist fear-mongering. Also in the alarmist tradition is a variation on this theme, namely, that pregnant women eating fish containing trace elements of mercury are putting themselves and their yet-to-be-born offspring at risk. The Environmental Working Group (EWG), with its well-documented history of fomenting hysteria aimed at mothers and children, warns on its website that: "EWG has advocated that the FDA give strong, clear advice to pregnant women on fish consumption, and that the federal government cut mercury pollution from coal-burning power plants and other sources to eventually make tuna 'baby safe.'" The power plants that EWG, NRDC, LCV, the Sierra Club, and others condemn with righteous indignation are of the coal-burning variety. And, the argument goes, mercury emissions from these coal-fired power plants are "poisoning kids" and making seafood unsafe to eat, a situation made all the more intolerable by policies of the Bush administration. This is the charge; the reality is another matter altogether.[123]

Mercury is a naturally occurring element that is ubiquitous in the environment. Most of the mercury existing in the environment is released through natural processes. These include surface volcanic eruptions; deep sea vents and volcanic activity; hot springs such as the geyser basins in Yellowstone National Park; evaporation from ocean basins, other water bodies and soils; and erosion. The oceans alone contain millions of tons of naturally occurring mercury. Forest fires and the burning of other types of vegetation also contribute to the presence of mercury in the environment. To appreciate the role of natural geological forces in shaping the world around us, it is worth noting that, according to the Smithsonian Institution, there are more than 5,000 surface and submarine volcanoes in the world erupting 50 to 60 times a month. Volcanic activity may well be the largest source of oceanic and atmospheric mercury.

All told, these natural sources account for approximately 61 percent of the annual mercury deposition in the world. Another 37 percent comes from anthropogenic sources outside the U.S., with the biggest contributors being China, India, the EU, and Zaire. Anthropogenic sources in the U.S. account for the remaining two percent, with coal-burning power plants responsible for slightly less than half of that, or roughly one percent of annual global mercury deposition.[124]

The debate over mercury can be traced to a relatively obscure section of the voluminous 1990 Clean Air Act amendments which required EPA to determine whether there was a risk-based need to regulate emissions of what were called "hazardous air pollutants" from power plants, including mercury emissions. When EPA subsequently missed a reporting deadline it was promptly sued by NRDC. The ensuing litigation resulted in EPA being forced into a rulemaking process, in which the agency was to decide how mercury emissions from electric utilities were to be regulated. Carol Browner, who headed EPA during the Clinton administration, waited until December 14, 2000—five weeks before Clinton's term ended—to issue her decision.

Browner, who embodied the dual role of environmental activist and environmental official, chose the most inflexible, indeed, impractical regulatory course available to her.[125] She proposed in a "Notice of Regulatory Finding" to deal with mercury through a very strict regulatory regime known as Maximum Achievable Control Technology (MACT). MACT, however, is uniquely ill suited to deal with the tricky problem of curbing mercury emissions from power plants. The 1,032 coal-fired power plants in the U.S. vary in age, design, type of equipment, and kind of coal used (lignite, sub-bituminous, bituminous, and anthracite). There is simply no single "maximum achievable control technology" for mercury that can be successfully applied to the electric utility industry. This was made abundantly clear in an April 2003 report by the U.S. Department of Energy which concluded that "...there is no currently available technology that can consistently and cost-effectively capture mercury from coal-based power plants."[126]

Having inherited Browner's mercury proposal when it took office in January 2001, the Bush administration took it under advisement(for four years, no less), along with an alternative cap-and-trade approach. The latter would allow power plants to trade emissions allowances as mercury-control technologies developed. Interestingly, the cap-and-trade approach had also been viewed by the Clinton administration's Office of Management and Budget as the best way to regulate mercury from power plants, but Browner spurned OMB's recommendation. In addition to the technical difficulties associated with applying the inflexible MACT approach, there were important energy policy implications to be considered. Imposing a MACT regime on utilities would be so costly that many power plants would be forced to switch from inexpensive coal to more expensive natural gas to continue serving their customers. While America's supply of coal is abundant, most of the nation's—substantial—reserves of natural gas on the Outer Continental Shelf are off limits to drilling, due to federal moratoria. A switch from coal to natural gas would put enormous strains on the nation's already stretched energy supplies and place substantial financial burdens on ratepayers.

In light of these considerations, it should come as no surprise that the Bush EPA, in March 2005, announced that it would regulate mercury emissions from power plants through a cap-and-trade program, with the goal of cutting emissions by 70 percent by 2018. Predictably, the decision was greeted with howls of protest from environmental groups.[127]

The mercury controversy is instructive for several reasons. First of all, the "problem" identified by environmental activists had been taking care of itself for years. Anthropogenic emissions of mercury in the U.S. declined by 40 percent (97 tons) between 1990 and 1996 due to the closure of domestic mercury mines in 1991 and pollution controls for mercury emissions from medical, municipal, and hazardous waste incinerators. Though mercury emissions from power plants were not regulated at the time, they too declined, by 38 percent, from 1995 to 1999 as a result of pollution controls designed to reduce other kinds of air emissions. Yet, as we have seen, falling levels of anthropogenic mercury in the U.S. since the early 1990s coincided with environmentalist rhetoric aimed at scaring people into believing that consuming fish containing trace levels of mercury was hazardous to health. This is a claim, however, that not even Browner's EPA was prepared to endorse. In its December 2000 "Notice of Regulatory Finding," EPA discussed the health effects of methylmercury (the organic form of mercury found in trace levels of fish) and concluded:

> It is acknowledged that there are uncertainties regarding the extent of the risks due to electric utility mercury emissions. For example, there is no quantification of how much of the methylmercury in fish consumed by the U.S. population is due to electric utility emissions relative to other mercury sources (e.g., natural and other anthropogenic sources.[128])

Recent peer-reviewed studies cast further doubt on the alleged link between global mercury emissions and deposition and methylmercury concentrations in fish. A 2003 Princeton University study, funded by EPA, compared mercury analysis of recently caught Pacific tuna with similar tuna that had been caught in the 1970s. Princeton's researchers found that mercury levels in the tuna had not changed over time. The concluding statement in the study reads as follows:

> The bare fact that the concentrations of Hg (methylmercury) in tuna were identical in 1971 and 1998 either reflects a remarkable coincidence or indicate that, regardless of mechanisms, these concentrations are not responding to atmospheric pollution.[129]

Similarly, a twelve-year study conducted in the Seychelles Islands and published in *Lancet* in 2003 reported no negative effects from dietary exposure to methylmercury as a result of regular fish consumption. The Seychelles population consumes an average of 12 fish meals per week and has hair methylmercury concentrations approximately ten times higher than the U.S. population. Indeed, a far bigger threat to public health would result from people, spooked by incessant fear-mongering, reducing their consumption of fish. Peer-reviewed research has demonstrated that a diet rich in omega-3 polyunsaturated fatty acids from fish has beneficial health effects for people with heart disease and various types of cancer, including breast, prostate, and endometrial. Moreover, as Louis Sullivan, M.D., former secretary U.S. Department of Health and Human Services, points out, the United States has the most stringent safety margins for mercury in fish in the world. "That is because we build in a 10-fold safety factor," he explains, "meaning that if pregnant women and young children follow the government's advice (consuming up to six ounces a week of canned albacore tuna, for example) they will consume mercury levels that are at least 10 times lower than the lowest level for any known risk."[130]

In truth, the mercury controversy has little to do with safe levels of fish consumption but is merely an extension of the debate over global warming. Though methylmercury is not a greenhouse gas, like greenhouse gases, it is the inevitable byproduct of coal-burning power plants. As such, it has served environmentalists as a proxy for CO_2. Unable to get Congress to regulate CO_2 emissions, green groups turned to mercury as another way to attack fossil fuels. It was in this spirit that the Sierra Club's Nat Mund claimed in the *Wall Street Journal* in August 2005 that, "Coal-burning power plants are the single largest source of mercury pollution in the U.S." As we have seen, however, the single largest source of mercury pollution in the U.S.—and the rest of the world, for that matter—is none other than the planet itself through natural processes.[131]

A week before the Sierra Club's Mund made his erroneous claim, the U.S. Court of Appeals for the District of Columbia rejected a motion by environmental groups to block EPA from implementing its new mercury regulation. In turning back the suit by Environmental Defense, National Wildlife Federation, Chesapeake Bay Foundation, and other green groups, the court found that the environmentalists had not made a strong enough case. "Petitioner has not satisfied the stringent standards required for a stay pending court review," the one-page order said.[132]

By targeting mercury, rather than relying on the traditional greenhouse-gas bogeyman, environmentalists were inadvertently confirming that they too had entered the post-Kyoto world. That this world is upon us was underscored by no less than British Prime Minister Tony Blair, once one of the Kyoto Protocol's most enthusiastic supporters. Speaking of Kyoto at the Clinton Global Initiative in New York on September 15, 2005, Blair bid the global warming treaty a not-so-fond farewell. "We have got to start from brutal honesty about the politics of how we deal with it," he said. "The truth is, no country is going to cut its growth or consumption substantially in light of a long-term environmental problem. What countries are prepared to do to try to work together cooperatively to deal with this problem in a way that allows us to develop the science and technology in a beneficial way." Lest anybody miss the point, Blair added that he didn't think world leaders would "start negotiating another major treaty like Kyoto."[133]

In early December 2005, negotiators from nearly 200 countries gathered in Montreal for yet another UN-sponsored "Conference of the Parties" to ponder the fate of the Kyoto Protocol. As always there were claims of impending environmental doom unless "prompt action" was taken to cut greenhouse-gas emissions. Delegates also lost no time in telling reporters of their dismay over the Bush administration's rejection of the global warming treaty. In a remarkable performance, former President Bill Clinton urged the faithful to embark on a new round of talks aimed at producing additional binding commitments starting in 2012. Clinton's remarks were warmly received, and no one seemed to notice that this was the same Bill Clinton who, as president, had refused to submit the Kyoto Protocol to the Senate for ratification. In effect, Clinton and Bush were closer on Kyoto than most people realized.[134]

The conference ended inconclusively, with industrialized nations—minus the U.S. and Australia—agreeing to hold further talks on binding limits on emissions. Separately, a much broader coalition of countries agreed to an "open and nonbinding dialogue" that would not lead to any "new commitments" on reducing greenhouse gas emissions. The first agreement keeps Kyoto on a life-support system but with no prospect of recovery. The second agreement effectively abandons the Kyoto approach altogether in favor of a voluntary arrangement not unlike the Asian-Pacific Partnership on Clean Development and Climate Change.

Coming on the heels of Tony Blair's defection to the Bush camp on climate change, these meager results failed to lift the spirits of the green activists who had journeyed to Montreal. Jenifer Morgan of the World Wildlife Fund said of the renewed "commitment" by some countries to continue the dialogue on mandatory emissions cuts: "In the end it will only be as strong as what the governments have agreed to commit to. We've only set up a process here." If Morgan seemed resigned to whatever the "process" brought forth, Eileen Claussen, president of the Pew Center on Climate Change, remained defiant. Dismissing the idea of voluntary steps, Claussen told reporters: "If you really want results, you have to do something that's mandatory."[135]

During the Clinton administration Claussen had been instrumental in crafting the policies that led to the Kyoto Protocol, and in Montreal she was not inclined to entertain any radical departures from the path she and her colleagues had chosen a decade earlier. For Claussen and her environmental brethren, however, the problem was that most of the countries that loudly proclaimed they really wanted "results," were ultimately not willing to do what was "mandatory." This is why most EU countries had missed their first set of Kyoto targets, and why their "commitment" to pursue a new round of emission reductions cannot be taken seriously.

In Montreal to cover the conference, *New York Times* environmental reporter Andrew Revkin took stock of the proceedings: "[T]here is a sense that the whole idea of global agreements to cut greenhouse gases won't work....Some veterans of climate diplomacy and science now say that perhaps the entire architecture of the climate treaty might be flawed," Revkin noted. These thoughts were an acknowledgement that the conferences at Kyoto and Montreal were separated not just by eight years and several thousand miles, but also by the gradual awareness, even among some of the treaty's supporters, that the whole enterprise was far more perilous than originally thought. "The major reason the optimism over Kyoto has eroded so rapidly," he wrote, "is that its major requirement—that 28 participating industrialized countries cut their greenhouse emissions below 1990 levels by the year 2012—was seen as just a first step toward increasingly aggressive cuts."

Not only are such cuts unpalatable to relatively prosperous industrialized countries, they are completely at odds with the economic aspirations of developing countries. As Revkin explained: "Developing countries—China and India being the most dramatic examples—want to burn whatever energy they need, in whatever form available, to grow their economies and raise the standard of living of their people." None of these observations could have pleased the green activists assembled in Montreal. But Revkin saved the unkindest cut of all for the substance the environmental lobby had been pummeling for two decades. "Carbon dioxide," he pointed out, "is generated by activities as varied as surfing the net, driving a car, burning wood or flying to Montreal. Its production is woven into the fabric of industrial society, and, for now, economic growth is inconceivable without it."[136]

REACHing Beyond Their Grasp

While the debate over the Kyoto Protocol has consumed so much attention in recent years, climate change has not been the only major international effort undertaken by the global greens. Although it lacks the captivating imagery of melting ice caps, flooded coastal areas, and devastating cyclones, an environmental regulatory initiative by the European Union is no less ambitious and potentially every bit as harmful as the energy rationing foreseen in the Kyoto Protocol.

In the early 2000s, the EU began work on a new, comprehensive proposal to regulate chemicals in Europe. Known as REACH, an acronym for "Registration, Evaluation and Authorization of Chemicals," the scheme had taken form by mid-decade when its far-reaching implications were clear for all too see. The "Registration" provision of REACH requires manufacturers and importers to submit hazard, exposure, and risk information on over 30,000 chemicals, the vast majority of which are already on the market. The REACH regime also extends to any new substances that are produced or imported into Europe in annual quantities exceeding one metric ton. An additional 4,000 substances manufactured or imported into the EU in quantities exceeding 100 metric tons will be subject to "Evaluation" by the newly established European Chemical Agency to determine whether further testing is needed. Substances in lower quantities are also subject to "Evaluation" if they are deemed by regulators at the European Chemical Agency to be "of concern." Finally, there are approximately 1,500 substances of "very high concern" which fall under REACH's "Authorization" provision, and these chemicals require specific permission from EU regulators before they can be approved for certain uses.

REACH's regulatory reach goes far beyond the 30,000 or so chemicals targeted for review. It also extends to "downstream" products derived from or containing those chemicals. Downstream users are required to carry out additional testing "if the exposure or use of the product exceeds that foreseen by the manufacturer." "Because chemical products are ubiquitous in automobiles, aircraft, home construction and furnishings, and workplaces," analysts Angela Logomasini and Henry Miller point out, "REACH intrudes deeply into the life of every European. And given the massive amount of U.S.-European trade, it will also exert profound effects on American businesses and individuals." The same holds true for Japan, China, Australia and any other country doing business in Europe.[137]

The procedural labyrinth the EU has constructed to regulate chemicals is not, however, the most objectionable aspect of REACH. Of far greater concern is the scheme's underlying doctrine, which ties REACH directly to the global environmental movement. By requiring companies to prove that their products are safe before they can be put on the market, REACH bears the unmistakable imprint of the precautionary principle. "Precautionary regulation shifts the burden of proof from the regulator, who previously had to demonstrate that a new technology was likely to cause harm, to the innovator, who now must demonstrate that the technology will not cause harm under any circumstances," Miller and Gregory Conko remind us. "Since manufacturers can't prove anything is 100 percent safe," Angela Logomasini adds, "this policy [REACH] will likely produce arbitrary bans of many relatively safe substances and discourage innovation."[138]

Supported by the World Wildlife Fund, Greenpeace, and other environmental groups, and backed by Europe's green parties and environmental officials, REACH has undergone only modest changes on its way to its scheduled promulgation in 2007. In response to protests from the EU business community and from a growing chorus of critics from outside of Europe, the EU has staunchly defended its new chemical policy. Given what is known about the human cost of the ban on DDT, it is significant that an EU white paper extolling the virtues of REACH cites the DDT bans as an "accomplishment" whose only fault was that it didn't come soon enough.

Using the ban on DDT as an argument in support of REACH tells us much about how the proponents of the EU's new chemical policy view the future. Indeed, the future is already upon us in efforts by the Organization for Economic Cooperation and Development (OECD) and the United Nations Environmental Programme to apply REACH-style regulation at the global level. Logomasini is correct in saying that REACH will be the focus of the UN's Strategic Approach to International Chemicals Management (SAICM), a relatively new, "voluntary" initiative designed to coordinate global chemical and waste policies. While the details of SAICM are still being worked out, the UN initiative already shares commonalities with the word and spirit of REACH. For example, SAICM's Draft Global Plan of Action clearly advocates taking precautionary measures "even where there is a lack of full scientific certainty as to a chemical's environmental or health effects." National sovereignty also receives short shrift in the draft document which calls for "development of [global] liability and compensation schemes in relation to damage to human health and the environment caused by the production and use of chemicals."[139]

SAICM, like REACH, continues the global greens' war on manmade chemicals, a war which was launched with the attack on DDT. Among the 288 "concrete measures" proposed in SAICM's Draft Global Action Plan are plans to "restrict availability" of "highly toxic pesticides," "promote substitution of hazardous chemicals," "regulate the availability, distribution, and use of pesticides," "halt the sale of and recall products" that pose "unacceptable risks," and "eliminate the use" of certain "hazardous chemicals." "While SAICM negotiators don't want to acknowledge it," Logomasini notes, "many products are valuable because they are toxic and even 'highly toxic.' These properties provide important advantages, and their risks can be managed. Pesticides, for example, should be highly toxic to the vermin they are supposed to kill, while having little impact on human when used properly."[140] Indeed, chlorine's ability to remove life-threatening pathogens from drinking water would be unthinkable without the presence of toxic chemicals in the compound. And the standard SAICM and REACH regulators will use to determine what is "toxic," a "hazard," or a "risk" is none other than the precautionary principle.

Though still a work in progress, SAICM is being groomed by its promoters at the UN to become an international chemicals regulatory body, with the EU's REACH serving as a role model. Chemicals that are banned in Europe under REACH will be prime candidates to be *verboten* under SAICM at the EU's instigation. An international environmental bureaucracy based on the idea of REACH would also build momentum for global bans on chemicals as called for in various agreements, including the UN's Global Convention on Persistent Organic Pollutants (POPs). POPs already bans 12 substances, and the treaty contains provisions for additional bans to be imposed. Logomasini points out that European nations are already using the POPs treaty to propose worldwide bans on substances they have already eliminated domestically, even when such products have valuable uses in the United States and elsewhere. Indeed, Malaysia has already accused the EU of using REACH as a non-tarrif barrier to hinder access to its markets.[141]

In REACH, SAICM, and POPs, old-fashioned protectionism joins forces with modern environmentalism to rid the planet of both unwanted competition and unwanted chemicals. The same two forces were at work in the EU's failed efforts to get the U.S. to submit to the Kyoto Protocol, a step that would have taken the American economy down to the level of its less-competitive European counterparts. In an unguarded moment, EU Environmental

Commissioner Margot Wallstrom admitted as much in commenting on President Bush's rejection of the global warming treaty. "This is not a simple environmental issue, where you can say this is an issue where the scientists are not unanimous," she said. "This is about international relations, this is about economy, about trying to create a level playing field for big businesses throughout the world. You have to understand what is at stake and that is why it is serious."[142]

As the EU's environmental commissioner, Wallstrom played a leading role in the adoption of REACH, a scheme that has been called "the golden child of the environmental movememt." She and her colleagues in international bureaucracies and among green NGOs are what John O'Sullivan calls transnationals, or "Tranzis." "By manipulating UN conferences on issues from climate change to sustainable development," he explains, "they have imposed a sort of political agenda for 'global governance' on national governments." No less than French President Jacques Chirac said of the Kyoto Protocol in November 2000 that it was "the first component of authentic global governance."[143]

As we have seen, those striving for global governance invariably do so in the name of protecting us from the insidious effects of our technological pretensions. "In other words," says Thomas DeGregori, "they are condemning the forces that have benefited them, and they are restricting access to these same benefits by those who have not been so privileged."[144]

"'Global warming' is part of a misguided agenda that seeks stability when change is the norm on this ever-restless Earth," Philip Slott reminds us. "the same agenda is employed against the use of biotechnology, against the genetic modification of crops, against the very things that help humankind outpace change in population, pests, diseases and, above all, climate—whether hotter, wetter, colder, drier, or a mixture of all four." "Above all,' he explains, "it is about re-finding a lost Garden of Eden, a purer world, detoxified of industry, horrid iron and steel, chemicals and those teeming millions of unwanted folk."[145]

Postscript

In May 2006, USAID reversed over 30 years of policy and announced that it had authorized the use of DDT to help combat malaria in Africa. By late 2006, the agency will begin using DDT as part of its malaria-control efforts in Mozambique, Ethiopia and Zambia, with more African countries expected to join the indoor-spraying program in the coming years. "We think DDT is safe when used correctly," said Richard Green, director of the Office of Health, Infectious Diseases and Nutrition at USAID. "We think DDT is an excellent insecticide and that, in some circumstances, it has some advantages over some other insecticides that are available."

The decision, belated though it may be, marks a significant break with the postulates of *Silent Spring*. As such, it could not be welcome news to environmental advocates who have built their empire on chemo-phobia. "DDT is not a silver bullet for malaria control in Africa," commented Kristin Schafer, program coordinator for the San Francisco-based Pesticide Action Network. "We strongly support the 2001 Stockholm Convention on Persistent Organic Pollutants, which has been ratified by 122 nations, which calls for the [eventual] elimination of DDT."[146] Given the choice between fealty to an international agreement and saving lives in Africa, she chose the former with no hesitation.

Chapter 3

"THIS LAND IS MY LAND"

The moment that the idea is admitted into society that property is not as sacred as the laws of God, and that there is not a force of law and public justice to protect it, anarchy and tyranny commence. Property must be sacred or liberty cannot exist. [1]

JOHN ADAMS

One day in September 2002, Arizona rancher Jim Chilton was reading his local newspaper when his eye was drawn to a notice published by the Center for Biological Diversity (CBD). The notice described environmental destruction on U.S. Forest Service land leased to a rancher who used the acreage to graze his cattle. Readers interested in finding out more were directed to check out the CBD's website. That's exactly what Chilton did, because it was his cattle on his grazing allotment that had allegedly despoiled the environment.

CBD's website did, in fact, contain photos showing barren, unattractive patches on Chilton's grazing allotment, but they bore little resemblance to the terrain he knew so well. Chilton concluded that the environmental group had posted photos carefully selected so as to present a completely distorted picture of how the rancher used the land he leased.

What was to be done? As Chilton later told the *Wall Street Journal*: "I had to decide whether I was going to be a cowboy or a wimp. I decided to be a cowboy...and not ignore people saying bad things about my ranch." [2] But instead of reaching for his six-shooter, Chilton grabbed his telephone, called his lawyer, and soon thereafter sued the CBD for defamation. At the trial in January 2005, Chilton showed that two could play the camera game and produced photos showing that lush grasslands surrounded the barren patches the CBD had showcased on its website. It was also revealed in court that one of the uglier spots shown in a CBD photo resulted not from Chilton's grazing cattle, but from an annual May Day campout, whose numerous participants included an employee of the Center for Biological Diversity. Convinced that Chilton was the victim of an unseemly effort to distort the rancher's stewardship of the environment, the Arizona Superior Court in Tucson awarded him $600,000, including $500,000 in punitive damages from the CBD.

The clash between rancher Jim Chilton and the Tucson, Arizona-based Center for Biological Diversity is but one of thousands of such conflicts that have spread across the rural West like wildfire over the past three decades. These battles have pitted ranchers, farmers, loggers, miners, and other landowners against environmental groups that are often in league with government regulators. The only difference between the case of Jim Chilton and countless others that have inflamed passions in the rural West is that, in this instance, the rancher won. It didn't hurt that Chilton, a fifth-generation rancher who also is president of a Los Angeles municipal investment bank, had the financial wherewithal to tangle in the courtroom with the well-heeled environmental group. Other landowners, however, whose pockets are not so deep, have not fared nearly as well.

To those living outside the rural West, the posting of a few misleading snapshots on a website may seem like little more than a childish prank, carried out by over-zealous activists who let their exuberance get the better of them. But this would be a complete misreading of both the Center for Biological Diversity and the cause to which it and its fellow environmental groups are dedicated. It was, as the old Marxists were wont to say, "no coincidence" that a Western rancher ran afoul of the CBD, and that the conflict ultimately wound up in a courtroom.

Like so many other environmental groups, CBD's vision of the world is couched in the most apocalyptic of terms. "Ancient forests, free-flowing rivers, living oceans and deserts and the abundance of life they contain: all these, having evolved over millions of years, are in danger of vanishing from the world within decades," CBD's website asserts under the heading, "The Extinction Crisis." "In the grip of an explosion of extinctions that is unprecedented in history," the group explains, "we are now seeing the disappearance of biological and habitat diversity across the globe as wild lands and waters are desecrated and species are driven extinct." The culprit in all this is "the advance of a rapacious and homogenizing global economy driven by human population growth and resource consumption..." CBD's solution to the ills that have befallen the planet entail "[c]ombining conservation biology with litigation, policy advocacy, and an innovative strategic vision" and "working to secure a future for animals and plants hovering on the brink of extinction, for the wilderness they need to survive, and by extension for the spiritual welfare of generations to come."[3]

With revenues in 2003 of just over $2.9 million, and assets totaling $2.4 million, the CBD pales in comparison with such well-funded environmental organizations as the Nature Conservancy, Sierra Club, Conservation Fund, or Wilderness Society. But what it lacks in size it more than makes up for in its ability to make life miserable for those it targets. Its weapon of choice is the federal Endangered Species Act (ESA), a powerful, highly prescriptive statute, which CBD has wielded with devastating effectiveness in recent years.

In 1994, for example, CBD (then known as the Southwest Center for Biological Diversity) sued the U.S. Forest Service to halt its plans to permit logging in New Mexico, Arizona and Colorado forests, claiming the plan threatened over 40 endangered species, including the Mexican spotted owl. In June 1995, U.S. District Judge Carl Muecke ordered the U.S. Fish and Wildlife Service (FWS) to set aside habitat for the owls, whereupon FWS designated 4.6 million acres as "critical habitat" in eleven Southwestern national forests. Muecke also ordered all logging on the land suspended until the Forest Service had completed a study on the impact of logging on the owls, a suspension that lasted until November 1996. With logging banned for such an extended period of time, sawmill after sawmill shut down in the Southwest. The region's forest products industry and timber-dependent communities never recovered from the forces CBD's lawsuit set in motion.[4]

Between the late 1990s and the end of 2005, CBD filed nearly 60 ESA-related lawsuits. Assisted by funds generously donated by the relatively obscure but influential Foundation for Deep Ecology, CBD's litigation has also involved efforts to curtail cattle grazing on public land. The results have been nothing but impressive. Alexander J. Thal, director of the department of business economics and public administration at Western New Mexico University examined the damage wrought by CBD's lawsuits. He found:

- A loss of over 3000 jobs in 13 rural communities in Arizona and New Mexico.
- A loss of $60 million in cattle production in Arizona, which forced many small family ranches into insolvency.
- Devastated communities that faced such problems as destabilized families, increased mental health issues, reduced public services, and out-migration of youth looking for employment.[5]

Nowhere on the CBD's website is there any mention, much less expression of regret, about the human costs of the group's activities. Indeed, human costs are of little concern to an organization that specializes in "combining conservation biology with litigation." Conservation biology is a school of thought within the environmental movement that "puts emphasis on biodiversity and sustainability over time," according to Richard Everett, a scientist with the U.S. Forest Service. "It is concerned only with plant and animal habitat and does not consider human use of the land."[6] The field supports a journal called *Conservation Biology*, founded by Rutgers University ecologist David Ehrenfeld, and even a Society for Conservation Biologists, which holds annual meetings at which discussion focuses on ways to combat the extinction of species.

As it gradually took flight in the 1980s and 1990s, conservation biology became a potent force in the hands of activists who grasped its potential to transform traditional thinking on the relationship between humans and the rest of nature. And no wonder. A doctrine that sees plants and animals and their natural surroundings as forever threatened by humans, and that seeks to protect wildlife through the creation of vast wilderness areas that are as devoid as possible of human interference, is a doctrine aimed at the radical transformation of rural life as we know it.

CBD's commitment to conservation biology, and its willingness to litigate in the name of saving endangered species, has made it a favored grantee of the Foundation for Deep Ecology (FDE). Founded in 1989, and originally known as the Iri-Hiti Foundation, FDE is the creation of Douglas Tompkins, who, together with his first wife, made a fortune in the outdoor clothing company Esprit. After his first marriage ended in divorce, leaving him with $150 million from the sale of his share of Esprit, Tompkins remarried, this time to Kristine McDivett, CEO of Patagonia, another highly successful outdoor clothing company. Along the way, Tompkins, like fellow-multi-millionaire Ted Turner and such Hollywood luminaries as Barbara Streisand, Robert Redford, and Harrison Ford, became enthralled with the environmental movement.

In choosing to re-name his organization the Foundation for Deep Ecology, Tompkins was paying homage to an idea that has provided the philosophical underpinnings for conservation biology and related environmental causes. The brain-child of Norwegian-born philosopher and mountaineer Arne Naess, Deep Ecology rejects the idea that some living things have greater value than others. Rather, Naess claimed "the rights of all forms [of life] to live is a universal right which cannot be quantified. No single species of living being has more of this particular right to live and unfold than any other species." In 1984 Naess and environmental activist George Sessions put together a Deep Ecology Platform of eight Principles, three of which are of particular interest:

Humans have no right to reduce this richness and diversity [of life forms] except to satisfy vital needs.

Present human interference with the nonhuman world is excessive, and the situation is rapidly worsening.

The flourishing of human life and cultures is compatible with a substantial decrease in human population. The flourishing of nonhuman life requires such a decrease."[7]

Not content to leave such ideas to the realm of philosophical discourse, Tompkins has sought to move Deep Ecology from theory into practice. This requires money, and Tompkins FDE is flush with cash and eager to bestow it on worthy recipients. FDE had over $3.8 million in revenues in 2004 and assets totaling $48 million. Among the causes FDE has funded is one that embodies the spirit of both conservation biology and Deep Ecology: the Wildlands Project. Described by *Science* magazine as "the most ambitious proposal for land management since the Louisiana purchase of 1803," the Wildlands Project calls for "a network of wilderness reserves, buffer zones, and wildlife corridors stretching across huge tracts of land—hundreds of millions of acres, as much as half of the continent." According to *Science*, the long-term goal of the Wildlands Project "is nothing less than the transformation of America from a place where 4.7 percent of the land is wilderness to an archipelago of human-inhabited islands surrounded by natural areas."[8]

According to its website, the Wildlands Project has a "one-hundred-year vision." Eschewing even the hint of self-restraint, that vision is:

To create a continental-scale network of connected wildlands, linking together wildlands from Mexico to the Yukon, from Florida to the Yukon, from Baja California to the Brooks Range and the Bering Sea. Connections between the North Woods the Great Plains and great northern boreal forests must also be recreated.

The idea for the Wildlands Project originated at an FDE meeting in 1991. Dave Foreman, formerly with the Wilderness Society and founder of Earth First!, guided the project's fortunes in its early years, together with two prominent conservation biologists, Michael Soule and Reed Noss. Originally located in Tucson, Arizona, the Wildlands Project is now based in Richmond, Vermont. Its 2003 tax returns show that it had $1.3

million in revenues and assets of just over $238,000. Not surprisingly, its biggest donor in recent years has been Tompkins' FDE, which has provided $560,000 in funding since 1999.[9]

Audacious in scope, the Wildlands Project aims to return 50 percent of the continental United States to a "natural" state. It calls for establishing a system of core wilderness areas where human activity would be prohibited. Biological "corridors" would link the "core areas," serving as highways allowing nonhuman to pass from one to another. Buffer zones would be established around the core areas and their interlocking corridors. Only outside the core areas would human activities such as agriculture and industrial production be permitted. The goal is to overcome what conservation biologists Soule and Noss refer to as the "fragmentation of habitat."

In September 1999, the *Los Angeles Times* reported in a feature story on the group that the Wildlands Project's ambitions go far beyond merely setting aside land. "[T]he group also envisions 'rewilding' parts of the West by winning government approval to bring back major carnivores like mountain lions, wolves and grizzlies to maintain ecological checks and balances," the *Times* said. Needless to say, introducing large carnivores into rural area might so frighten local residents that many, fearing for the safety of their children, would leave—exactly what the supporters of the Wildlands Project want. In this ecocentric view of the world, the survival of flora and fauna takes precedence over all other considerations. "Our goal is to create new political realities based on the needs of other species," the Wildlands Project's Foreman told *Science News* in 1993.

It would be easy to dismiss such ideas as the ravings of delusional malcontents living on the edge of society. But a variation of the scheme has actually made its way into legislation introduced in the U.S. House of Representatives. The misnamed Rockies Prosperity Act, introduced by Representatives Christopher Shays (R-Conn.) and Carolyn Maloney (D-New York) garnered 177 co-sponsors in 2005—four-fifths of the number necessary for passage. In keeping with the goals of the Wildlands Project, the bill would designate over 23 million acres of federal lands in Idaho, Montana, Oregon, Washington, and Wyoming as wilderness area. Designation as wilderness area would ban not just mining and logging, but also motorcycling, bicycling, and snowmobiling. In a bow to the vocabulary of Deep Ecology, the bill further sets aside 8.5 million acres of land as "biological connecting corridors" in order to "protect the life flow" between the wilderness areas. Most resource-based economic activity—logging, mining, oil and gas exploration, and road construction—would also be banned in these areas as well. It is worth noting that Shays and Maloney represent districts that are located over 2,500 miles from the region that would bear the economic consequences of their environmental vision.

That a scheme that originated on the outermost fringes of the environmental movement could find its way into legislation supported by over forty percent of House members is testimony to the power of ideas—in this case, a very bad one. It also is a reflection of the reach of the intertwining networks that pervade the environmental movement. The Alliance for the Wild Rockies, a grantee of the FDE, calls the Rockies Prosperity Act "the legislative realization of [our] vision: bioregion-wide protection of the Northern Rockies." Another FDE grantee, the Sierra Club, lobbied Congress for the bill in 2001 and 2003. As Philip J. Maslar and David Hogberg have pointed out, the Shays-Maloney legislation stipulates that the law's implementation be monitored by a report that "shall be produced by a panel of independent scientists appointed by the National Academy of Sciences, in consultation with the Society for Conservation Biology." The Society for Conservation Biology, Maslar and Hogberg note, was founded by none other than Michael Soule of the Wildlands Project, and his colleague Reed Noss who sits on its board.

All this helps explain why the Center for Biological Diversity posted unflattering, carefully cropped snapshots of what it said was Jim Chilton's grazing allotment on its website. The purpose of the exercise was not just to defame Chilton but to discredit ranching, particularly when that ranching involved the use of public land. Keeping ranching, logging, and other related activities off public land moves that land one step closer to the "core areas" and "corridors" the CBD and its allies are so eager to create. Chilton, his cattle, and the environmental damage they were said to have caused were merely the pretext for the imposition of a far larger agenda. Dave Foreman, who directed the Wildlands Project for 12 years, said it best when he opined that humans "are the cancer of nature" and the "optimum human population of earth is zero."

No one can seriously expect the Wildlands Project to be realized in the grandiose fashion its most star-struck proponents envision. But its underlying vision of vast wilderness areas cleansed of human interference has guided the words and deeds of environmental activists for many years. And far from being strictly the domain of green activists, the idea has made its way into the letter of U.S. environmental law. Though still largely unappreciated—indeed, unnoticed—by America's predominantly urban and suburban population, the consequences of this development for residents of affected rural areas and, ironically, for the environment, have been devastating.

"A New Metaphor of Nature"

When conservation biologists Soule and Noss speak of overcoming the "fragmentation of habitat," they are expressing a view of the unity of nature that is rooted in the pantheistic preservationism of Henry David Thoreau, John Muir, Joseph Wood Krutch, Aldo Leopold, Ansel Adams, and Rachel Carson. Contemporary proponents of this school of thought are fond of referring to the natural world as composed of "ecosystems." The idea of ecosystems is not new; in fact, it predates the environmental movement by decades. It was coined by British botanist Arthur G. Tansley in 1935, who described ecosystems as physical systems encompassing living and nonliving things and their interactions.[10] The term languished in relative obscurity for decades until it was unearthed by elements of the nascent environmental movement in the late 1960s and early 1970s. Ecosystems would play a central role in what philosopher Alston Chase has called "a new metaphor of nature," one "which would energize and direct their [activists] actions, stir discord, and eventually inseminate the entire body politic."[11]

"Based on the notion that nature was organized into networks of interconnected parts called ecosystems," Chase explains, "the new science seemed to say that conditions were good so long as ecosystems kept all their parts and maintained in balance." This was particularly appealing to more radical activists who combined ecosystems with older ideas of nature worship to create a new ideology, eventually known as biocentrism. "If everything is dependent on everything else, they reasoned, then all living things are of equal worth, and the health of the whole—the ecosystem—takes precedence over the needs and interests of individuals. This was the idea a generation was looking for." Chase elaborates:

The metaphor of the ecosystem revived the notion of nature as purposive and as the foundation of value. Since an ecosystem's 'health'—that is, its stability—was the highest good, then any human activity that upset this balance was not merely mistaken but immoral. The ecosystem would thus serve as scaffolding for the construction of a new, misanthropic ethic of nature to replace the older, humanistic one.

For public policy—especially, environmental policy—the implications of this doctrine were profound. If nature really did consist of ecosystems, then managing those systems so as to protect them from human disturbance would be the duty of every conscientious environmental policymaker or regulator. Once preservation of ecosystems—maintaining their "stability," "balance," and thus their "health"—became enshrined in environmental statutes, most prominently in the Endangered Species Act, the stage was set for a drama that would play out as tragedy throughout the rural West. It would be a tragedy not least because the underlying "metaphor of the ecosystem" conflicted with the natural world.

"Ecosystems," notes Allan K. Fitzsimmons, "are only mental constructs, not real, discrete, or living things on the landscape. They do not breathe, emerge from wombs, or spring from seeds. They are not real, organized entities, consciously seeking to perpetuate themselves against internal or external threats to their existence." According to Simon Levin, "what we call an ecosystem...is really just an arbitrary subdivision of a continuous gradation of local species assemblages."[12] Writing in 1999, in the midst of the Clinton administration's efforts to make "ecosystem management" one of the cornerstones of U.S. environmental policy, Fitzsimmons pointed out that:

> Sixty years after the ecosystem idea surfaced in the scientific literature; after decades of dominance on university campuses; after thousands of books, articles, conferences, and monographs, scholars cannot agree on the most fundamental matters regarding ecosystems. They do not agree on what constitutes the core characteristics of ecosystems. They cannot say where ecosystems begin or end in space or time, or tell us where one ecosystem replaces another on a landscape. They cannot agree on how to locate ecosystems. They offer no generally accepted definitions of or measures of health, integrity, or sustainability. The state of science concerning the ecosystem notion and its attendant ideas provides little scientific justification for the radical change in public policy proposed by the Clinton administration.

In other words, the metaphor of nature that so enthralled the environmental movement and, as we shall shortly see, drove environmental policy was itself deeply flawed. Not only did the things that were supposed to be preserved—ecosystems—not exist in the real world, but the attendant notions of an inherent "balance of nature" fostering ecological "stability" and "health," were likewise invalid. Indeed, rather than being orderly and balanced, nature is constantly in flux and demonstrably unstable. Rivers change course, altering the adjacent landscape; volcanoes erupt, destroying habitat, which later regenerates; earthquakes shake the ground and roil the seas, leaving destruction in their path; climates change, alternating between warmer and cooler and dryer and wetter periods; and species come and go, providing for constant variations in the flora and fauna that inhabit the earth. Nothing is as it was before.

Chaos and random disturbance are the norm in nature, and naturalists have long known how "ecological succession" keeps things in flux. "Tornadoes, windstorms, blizzards, landslides—all turn forestland back into open country, or prevent open country from turning back into forestland," Charles C. Mann and Mark L. Plummer point out. "On the level of the landscape, the result is a rough overall balance, as some areas move up the successional ladder while others are knocked down. On the level of an individual piece of land, though, the rule is perpetual change." And no one should be fooled into believing that, in the end, calm will prevail:

A few years or decades of tranquility may see grasses replaced by a stand of shrubs or trees that in turn may be flattened by a violent thunderstorm, permitting the grass to thrive again. After a while, the shrubs and trees come back — only to be wiped out by a flood. And so on.[13]

To Chase, this disruptive aspect of nature is its hallmark:

As biological systems are inherently unstable and evolutionary change produces a constant stream of unique conditions, no single state of affairs can be 'healthy' or 'unhealthy.' The earth can be 'healthy' for humans or 'healthy' for dinosaurs, but it is never just plain healthy. Habitat can be good for deer or good for owls, but never merely good for wildlife. The earth was neither ill or robust 4 billion years ago, before life began. Since then distinctive conditions have favored different creatures, and the extinction of one species was often a boon to another. The same is true today. Protecting tropical wetland helps mosquitoes but spreads malaria.[14]

The history of the Endangered Species Act is, in many respects, the story of how a statute based on a flawed understanding of nature has been used by environmental activists to "create new political realities," as the Wildlands Project's Dave Foreman put it. It was the misleading concept of "stable" nature that allowed activists "to believe that their subjective goals were objective," Chase notes. "If they could say that ecosystems functioned only when they were in balance, then they could also claim that only stable ecosystems were healthy. And if sustaining this condition required maximizing biological diversity, then keeping all the parts was a matter of life and death for the planet."

This "bias in favor of stability," according to Chase, was the rationale for the Endangered Species Act:

> The task was not merely to rescue creatures that humans had put at risk. It was to stop all extinctions. Fighting change would become the guiding vision. And like all teleological theories, the ecosystem idea would have implications far beyond science. The federal government would seize upon the idea as a rationale for extending its control, even as, unwittingly, true believers, guided by the metaphor of nature as a harmonious organism, went in search of places where it might be found.[15]

Enacted in 1973 during the Nixon administration, the ESA contains what conservation biologist David Ehrenfeld calls the "Noah Principle," the preservation of biodiversity—all of it, regardless of cost. Whether species are deemed useful to man is immaterial. Ehrenfeld believes they should be cherished "because they exist and have existed for a long time." Or, as Stanford University biologist Paul Ehrlich and his wife, Anne, famously put it, "our fellow passengers on Spaceship Earth...*have a right to exist* (emphasis in the original)."[16] Ehrenfeld and the Ehrlichs are completely in tune with the ESA. The law directs the Department of Interior's Fish and Wildlife Service to maintain a list of species that are either endangered (in imminent peril of becoming extinct) or threatened (likely to become endangered in the near future). Once a species is listed, people are not allowed to "harass, harm, pursue, hunt, shoot, wound, kill, trap, capture, or collect" it. Violators of this provision against "taking" a species are subject to stiff fines, as are people who disturb the "critical habitat" of a species. The FWS is required "to list every species in trouble and save every species on the list," Mann and Plummer point out, "Mammal or plant, bird or bug, all shall be saved."[17]

Such was the scope of the statute, and the strength of its enforcement mechanisms, that a federal appeals court judge would later call the ESA "the strongest piece of land use legislation in history." Yet there is little reason to believe that the Republicans and Democrats in Congress who voted overwhelmingly for the bill in 1973 had any inkling of what they had wrought. The bill was shepherded through Congress by Rep. John Dingell (D-Mich.), an avid hunter from whom nothing radical could be expected. Caught up in the spirit of the time—it was only three years since the first Earth Day—lawmakers were eager to do their part to save such impressive and threatened creatures as the bald eagle,

California condor, and the whooping crane. What they did, or thought they were doing, enjoyed widespread support, and almost no one bothered to read the bill closely.[18]

In the years immediately following enactment, things stayed calm, because the ESA was applied almost exclusively to government projects. Some federal projects were delayed and a few halted, but it all took place with little controversy. The discovery of the three-inch long snail darter, *P. tanasi*, in shallow water upstream from the nearly completed Tellico Dam in Tennessee, however, created the first ESA crisis. Because the dam was thought to spell doom for the tiny fish, the FWS halted work on the project, whereupon the dam's supporters filed suit. In 1978 the case reached the Supreme Court where, in *Tennessee Valley Authority v. Hill*, the high court ruled in favor of the snail darter. The court found that it was "the plain intent of Congress to halt and reverse the trend toward species extinction;" that species must "be afforded the highest of priorities;" that they must be protected "whatever the cost;" that the ESA "admits of no exception;" and that the value of an endangered species is "incalculable."[19]

"That decision was ominous," R.J. Smith of the Competitive Enterprise Institute notes. "It demonstrated that the ESA was a new and totally different type of law. It appeared to supersede all other laws and all other public policy considerations. No aspect of government had ever so completely ignored costs." Tellico's supporters were outraged and launched a campaign to save the dam. Thanks in large part to the efforts of Senator Howard Baker of Tennessee, Congress approved legislation exempting Tellico from the act. The project, begun six years before the ESA was enacted, could now be completed. Tellico's exemption, however, left the ESA intact, with the potential to cause trouble elsewhere.[20]

"The Endangered Species Act sprang less from informed policymaking than from the simple aspiration to save everything—to banish extinction from the face of the planet, or at least from the United States," Mann and Plummer comment. "*TVA v. Hill* demonstrated that turning this appealing aspiration into a duty would be harder and more fractious than anyone initially realized."[21]

Indeed, the power of the ESA was there for all to see. That Congress, contrary to the court's ruling, never intended for the law to have such power, that, in fact, lawmakers were wary of "dismantling civilization" for the sake of saving species—all this was now irrelevant. The beast was free to roam the countryside, and it did not take long for environmental activists to put this legal Frankenstein to good use.

Range War

We have already seen how the Center for Biological Diversity seized the opportunity the ESA presented and filed nearly 60 ESA-related lawsuits in recent years. Scores of other environmental groups, large and small, also joined the fray. The trick has been to locate a species thought to be rare in a certain habitat, petition the FWS (or the National Marine Fisheries Service [NMFS], in the case of aquatic species) to declare it "threatened" or "endangered," based, according to the ESA, on the "best available data." Once the FWS or NMFS has determined that a species is threatened or endangered, the agency, under the ESA, must set aside "critical habitat" for the plant or animal in question. That habitat, whether on public or private land, is subject to severe restrictions on the kinds of human activities that are allowed to take place in it. It is the ESA's "critical habitat" provision that has opened the floodgates to rampant litigation and the resulting economic dislocations that mark the history of the act in the wake of *Tennessee Valley Authority v. Hill.* For those determined to keep human "disturbances" from upsetting the "delicate balance of ecosystems," the ESA was made to order.

Until legislation is adopted that protects these forests, we need at least one surrogate, if you will, that will provide protection for the forests...Well, the northern spotted owl is the wildlife species of choice to act as a surrogate for old growth protection, and I've often thought that thank goodness the spotted owl evolved in the Northwest, for if it hadn't, we'd have to genetically engineer it.[22]

Thus spoke Andy Stahl, an attorney with the Sierra Club Legal Defense Club, in an address before the Sixth Annual Western Public Law Conference at the University of Oregon School of Law on March 5, 1988. In impressing upon his listeners the decisive role the northern spotted owl would play in "protecting" the "old growth" forests of the Northwest, Stahl (thanks to the conference transcript) was leaving more to posterity than just a few random thoughts on political strategy.

Stahl's remarks came in the midst of the biggest controversy in the turbulent history of the ESA. Within a few short years, a brilliantly orchestrated, and thoroughly dishonest, campaign spearheaded by the National Audubon Society and the Sierra Club Legal Defense Fund, and involving numerous other environmental groups, riveted the nation's attention and ultimately spread economic ruin through vast rural areas of the Northwest. And when all was said and done, the supposed object of the environmentalists' affection, the spotted owl, was worse off than it had been before.

As Stahl candidly admitted, the spotted own had been carefully selected to "provide protection for the forests." In other words, the bird was a means to an end. And what was that end? Consistent with the notion that ecosystems need to be protected from human interference, Stahl and his compatriots set out to end logging, or as much of it as they could, in the vast forests of the Northwest. Much of the area in question is federal land that is under the jurisdiction of either the U.S. Forest Service or the Interior Department's Bureau of Land Management (BLM). During most of the twentieth century, the Forest Service and BLM sponsored periodic timber sales on these lands that provided local communities with jobs, and consumers in the U.S. and abroad with a seemingly inexhaustible quality of high-quality wood products.

Commercial logging, a well-established industry with tens of thousands of employees, had been a mainstay of the region's economy for over a century. It could only be attacked successfully if environmentalists could convince enough people that destroying the habitat of the northern spotted owl would cause irreversible damage to the environment. If green activists could persuade the public— particularly government officials, the courts, and the media—to accept their view of nature, they could then impose their will on the forests of the Northwest. This was no easy task, but the ESA would make it possible.

Following what has become standard operating procedure in such matters, a newly-formed consortium calling itself the Ancient Forest Alliance, which included the Wilderness Society, the Sierra Club, and like-minded groups, submitted a petition to the FWS in 1987 to have the northern spotted owl listed as an endangered species. The FWS rejected the petition, citing a lack of data showing the owl was in trouble. Undaunted, local chapters of the National Audubon Society then filed separate suits against the Forest Service and the BLM questioning whether the owl could survive planned timber harvests on lands under their jurisdiction.

The environmentalists' claims rested on the argument that the northern spotted owl, *strix caurina occidentalis*, one of several subspecies of spotted owl, was in danger of going extinct because its primary habitat, old-growth forests, was threatened by commercial logging. As the drama unfolded, the term "old-growth forest" became a staple of the debate over the owl. Foresters use the term "old growth" in referring to mature forests in the final, or "climax" phase of succession. In the forests of the Pacific Northwest, Douglas fir and Hemlock are the dominant trees, reaching 200 feet in height at maturity. Such old-growth forests make for good habitat for spotted owls and flying squirrels. But owls also thrive in younger forests, where their favorite prey, the northern flying squirrel and other rodents, are in abundant supply. That the owl's survival depended on millions of acres of land made off-limits to logging was an unfounded notion spread by environmentalists.

Factual or not, the emphasis on old growth served an important public relations function. In the hands of skilled PR people, old growth quickly became "ancient," inspiring even more reverence and awe in a public largely unfamiliar with the intricacies of forestry. Not for nothing did the consortium suing the Forest Service and the BLM call itself the Ancient Forest Alliance. Activists didn't hesitate to refer to "eight-hundred to one-thousand-year-old trees," numbers, Ron Arnold and Alan Gottlieb point out, "picked out of a hat to sound impressive, as fewer than one percent of the trees in question grow to *half* that age."[23]

The media played a key role in getting out the environmentalists' message. *Time* magazine devoted a cover story to the owl, and the Audubon Society's "World of Audubon," which aired on PBS and Ted Turner's TBS, produced a special documentary on the subject: *Ancient Forests: Rage Over Trees*. Actor Paul Newman hosted the program, telling his audience that the controversy over trees goes to "the heart of society's values." Newman concluded the program by urging his viewers "to let Congress know what you want done with them." The Wilderness Society kept the message going with the publication of a book, *Ancient Forests of the Pacific Northwest*, in 1990. Sinking into the depths of utter tastelessness, Pulitzer Prize-winning political cartoonist David Horsey portrayed loggers as stupid, brutish, uncaring thugs, eager to lay waste to nature. That blue-collar workers performing extremely dangerous jobs could be attacked in this fashion, speaks volumes about prevailing attitudes in the media.[24]

"Sudden concern about the owl derived not from ecological calamity but from a new interpretation of how nature ought to behave," Chase observes. "Once society embraced a teleology that demanded balance, then actions such as logging took on new meaning. What had previously been seen as ordinary and even beneficial was suddenly perceived as an ecological calamity."[25]

The environmentalists' success in the media was matched by triumphs in the courtroom and the bureaucracy. Responding to petitions submitted by the Audubon Society and its allies to protect the old-growth habitat of the owl, federal judges William Dwyer and Helen Frye issued orders halting hundreds of timber sales on Forest Service and BLM lands in 1989. In May 1990 the Interagency Scientific Committee to Address the Conservation of the Northern Spotted Owl, composed of scientists selected by BLM, FWS, the Forest Service, and the National Parks Service, issued a report concluding that the lack of a consistent planning strategy had resulted in a high risk of extinction for the northern spotted owl. One month later, FWS, reversing its 1987 decision, proposed listing the owl as threatened.

Few federal panels have been so inappropriately named as the Interagency Scientific Committee to Address the Conservation of the Northern Spotted Owl. It was the committee's report on the situation of the owl that gave the FWS cover to list the species. The panel showed how far U.S. environmental policy had strayed from the rigors of science. "It offered no evidence that old growth was essential for the owls or that their numbers were truly declining," Chase notes. "On the contrary, data revealing an abundance of birds in young stands and clear-cuts continued to mount. But this evidence was explained away." Actually, the methods of the committee weren't scientific at all. Instead of studying the issue, the panel took what is known as the "Delphi approach," which involves taking opinion polls among scientists and making predictions based on the results. "It did not require actual research, hypothesis formation, and testing, which is expensive and takes time," Chase points out. "It protected bureaucrats from criticism, allowing them to say that their decisions were supported by a consensus of experts."[26]

In the end the bureaucracy had done the activists' bidding, without environmentalists ever having to disclose what they were really after: This, according to Arnold and Gottlieb, was "to reclassify historically commercial forests into new, non-commercial preserves." Indeed, all the steps taken to "protect" the spotted owl severely restricted the amount of federal land on which timber could be cut. "From 1988 to 1993, the levels of timber harvests in the national forests of the Pacific Northwest fell by 80 percent," notes Robert H. Nelson of the University of Maryland's School of Public Affairs. "The total federal land acreage within the range of the spotted owl is 24 million acres; about 5 million of those acres are now available for timber harvesting." Such a drastic reduction in harvests in what Nelson refers to as "some of the highest quality timberlands in the world," would have devastating economic consequences.[27] According to the House Resources Committee, at least 130,000 jobs were lost in the region, after more than 900 saw mills, pulp mills, and paper mills closed in the wake of the spotted owl imbroglio. "Many of these were family businesses and the effect on small communities was severe," the *Wall Street Journal's* Kimberley Strassel observes. "Divorce rates shot up; men committed suicide."[28]

Timber-dependent communities and consumers of wood products weren't the only losers in all this; the northern spotted owl is worse off today than it was when the FWS set out to rescue it in 1990. Despite the "protection" it receives from the ESA, the bird's numbers continue to decline—falling by seven percent in one year in Washington alone. The culprit, it seems, is not the much-maligned lumberjack but another species of owl. Barred owls began moving west from forests in eastern Canada and Minnesota in the early 1900s and had made their way into Washington and Oregon by the 1970s. Larger and more aggressive than the spotted owl, the barred owl has successfully invaded the smaller bird's territory and appears to be winning the competition for prey and, perhaps, ultimately for survival. "Clearly the barred owl is having more of an impact on the spotted owl than any of us anticipated ten years ago," Jerry Franklin, a University of Washington forest ecology professor told the *Associated Press* in June 2004. "The question now has to do with how much that impact is going to be."[29]

In fact, the barred owl was known to be causing problems for its smaller cousin at the time the debate raged over what to do about the spotted owl, but this was swept under the rug in the rush to save "ancient forests." The Clinton administration brushed aside any thought that the barred owl was a problem, when, at the behest of Katie McGinty, head of the White House Council on Environmental Quality, it ordered further reductions in logging in the Northwest in the 1990s and even prohibited the removal of dead and diseased trees from the region's forests.[30]

The barred owl's invasion of the Pacific Northwest is instructive for another reason. It further undermines the biocentric notion of stable, balanced ecosystems. The migration of barred owls over two thousand miles westward in the course of a century is another example of nature in flux—in this case, a species of bird seeking its fortunes elsewhere. Attempting to preserve, to freeze in place, that which is inherently chaotic and unstable is an exercise in futility that, as the case of the spotted owl shows, will do more harm that good. The intellectual justification for saving the spotted owl and, by extension, for the ESA, was already being discredited at the time of the controversy. Writing in 1993, environmental historian Donald Worster observed that the idea of the ecosystem was receding and being replaced by the "lowly patch." "Nature," he says, "should be regarded as a landscape of patches, big and little...changing continually through time and space responding to an unceasing barrage of perturbations." Instability as the norm was already receiving a boost from the emerging school of thought known as "chaos theory," which Worster says teaches that nature is *fundamentally* erratic, discontinuous and unpredictable," (emphasis in the original).[31]

It had been a titanic struggle, one that brought to the fore completely divergent views on man's relationship to nature; indeed, what actually constitutes nature. The cast of characters included comfortably middle-class green activists in and out of government, well-paid environmental lawyers, blue-collar lumberjacks, wealthy donors to environmental causes, reporters eager to highlight an impending environmental disaster, and scientists whose words of wisdom masked their own agendas. Viewing the spectacle, Alston Chase observes:

> As with all great social transformations, the fight was multidimensional. It was at once a battle over the future of great trees, a social revolution propelled by demographic change, and a scientific controversy over the relative importance of stability and change in nature. To loggers, mature forests were simply stands of decaying trees that had to be cut before they rotted away. To environmentalists, they were 'ancient forests,' embodying the permanence and constancy of nature. To many foresters, old-growth forests were 'biological deserts' containing few animals, such as elk and grouse, which they felt desireable. To environmentalists, they represented the biocentric ideal that confers equal importance on all living things, from elk to boring beetles.[32]

The ultimate irony in the events that played out in the Pacific Northwest is that, for those truly interested in fostering "biodiversity," nothing could have been better for the region's forests and the wildlife living therein than the status quo ante. The periodic clear-cutting of trees that had been the norm before the spotted owl imbroglio had reduced the danger of catastrophic wildfires by creating open spaces in the thick forests. Those open spaces and the young trees that eventually fill them in also provided habitat for a variety of species, plants and animals alike, that have no place in the vaunted old-growth forests of environmentalist lore.

"Little Real Conservation Benefit"

Nothing succeeds like success, and the green victory in the forests of the Northwest only encouraged more ESA-related litigation by environmental groups. "We're crazy to sit in trees when there's this incredible law where we can make people do whatever we want," commented an enthusiastic activist to the *New Yorker*.[33] In the aftermath of the owl controversy, the ESA wreaked havoc in rural areas across the country, entangling landowners in its web of regulations and restrictions:

- In arid, wildfire-prone Riverside County, California, the ESA prevented landowners, under threat of fines or imprisonment, from constructing firebreaks on their land and clearing brush around their homes lest they disturb the habitat of the Stephens' Kangaroo rat. When the annual fire cycle struck the area in October and November 1993, several homes burned, as did the rat habitat the ESA was supposed to protect. The kangaroo rat was placed on the endangered species list courtesy of a petition filed by the CBD.[34]

- North Carolinian Ben Cone shared the fate of many rural landowners who made the "mistake" of providing habitat for endangered species on their property. Cone's father purchased 8,000 acres of cut-over, timberless land on the Black River near the Atlantic coast. Cone replanted the land with pines and planned to manage the property as a place where his family could hunt and fish. Over the years, the pines grew tall enough to attract the endangered red-cockcated woodpecker. And the woodpecker attracted the ESA. Fearing the worst, Cone hired a professional forester who determined that the birds were nesting in over 1,100 acres of Cone's land. None of that acreage could be harvested without the risk of violating the ESA and facing fines or imprisonment.

In testimony before Congress in 1994, Cone said that "by managing [the property] in an environmentally correct way, my father and I created habitat for the red-cockcated woodpecker. My reward has been the loss of $1,425,000 in value of timber I am not allowed to harvest under the provisions of the Endangered Species Act. I feel compelled to change my previous practices and massively clear-cut the balance of my property to prevent additional loss."[35]

- In April 2001 the Department of Interior's Bureau of Reclamation (BOR), citing the ESA, cut off water to irrigation farmers in the Klamath River Valley along the Oregon-California border. Instead of providing water to potato farmers in the drought-stricken, high-desert area, the BOR diverted the water to Upper Klamath Lake, home of the shortnose sucker fish which, together with its neighbor, the coho salmon, was on the endangered species list. The decision meant that 90 percent of the area's farms—some 200,000 acres of land—were without water for irrigation. BOR's action left 1,500 farms high and dry, costing local farmers $54 million in 2001.

It was the administration of President Theodore Roosevelt that, in 1909, lured homesteaders to settle in the Klamath Valley with contracts in which the government pledged to provide water for irrigation. That pledge, honored for over 90 years, was suddenly cast aside in favor of the ESA and the endangered fish. Local farmers organized a grassroots campaign that garnered national attention and eventually persuaded the Bush administration to reverse course and provide water for irrigation.[36]

The farmers' cause was helped immeasurably by a National Academy of Sciences study that concluded that diverting water to the Upper Klamath Lake wouldn't necessarily benefit the fish. NAS's findings were a slap in the face to Interior Department charged with enforcing the ESA, and they were further evidence that the science behind the law is wanting. It also was a rare defeat for the environmental groups which, throughout the conflict, demanded rigid enforcement of the ESA at the expense of the potato farmers. "You don't have logging in Yellowstone, and you shouldn't grow potatoes in this splendid place," opined Bob Hunter, staff attorney for Waterwatch, an Oregon-based environmental group.[37]

In these, as well as in countless other cases, landowners were punished for having endangered species in their midst; indeed, in the spirit of biocentrism, they were punished just for being there. North Carolina's Ben Cone may have lost the economic use of much of his land to protect the red-cockaded woodpecker, but neither he nor any other landowner will be compensated by the federal government for the economic burdens the ESA imposes on them. This is no small matter, given that between 80 and 90 percent of all listed endangered species are found on private land. The Fifth Amendment to the U.S. Constitution states that: "...nor shall private property be taken for public use without just compensation." Under the ESA, however, no such compensation is paid.

By contrast, the ESA, like many other environmental statutes, has a "cost recovery" provision that allows a "public interest" plaintiff that brings a suit under the Act and wins to recover its costs at taxpayers' expense. In the first three-and-one-half years following the listing of the northern spotted owl, "public interest" plaintiffs in the case took their winnings to the bank in the form of cost-recovery settlements. The Seattle Audubon Society, Portland Audubon Society, Lane County (Oregon) Audubon Society, and the Sierra Club Legal Defense Fund, together, collected over $2,140,000 in spotted owl-related court costs.[38]

These groups can sue to their heart's content. In 2003, for example, CBD reported to the IRS that it received $383,558 in "court-awarded attorney fees and legal costs in pursuing the

101

organization's tax-exempt purpose of protecting endangered species and their habitats" and another $608,976 in "settlement of environmental cases." Some of these funds came from federal agencies CBD had sued. Eager to keep the gravy train rolling, CBD, in mid-2005, petitioned the Bush administration to list an additional 225 species as endangered—78 percent of which had been on the "endangered" candidate list for over ten years.[39]

Such are the burdens of the ESA that the Act has even exhausted the funds of the agency tasked to administer it. In an April 2005 report ending five years of litigation regarding the riverside fairy shrimp, a tiny crustacean found in vernal pools in California, the FWS declared: "The service's present system for designing critical habitat has evolved into a process that provides little real conservation benefit, is driven by litigation and the courts, rather than biology, limits our ability to fully evaluate the science involved, consumes enormous agency resources, and imposes huge social and economic costs."[40]

Yet the most absurd aspect of the law is that it has made rural landowners and rare wildlife into mortal enemies through what the Competitive Enterprise Institute's R.J. Smith calls the "perverse incentives of the ESA." "By threatening landowners who make room for nature with the uncompensated loss of the use of their land or crops," he says, "it encourages landowners to get rid of wildlife habitat and sterilize their lands. It creates the 'shoot, shovel, and shut-up syndrome,' whereby wildlife is viewed as a liability—as a threat."[41]

In May 2005, the House Resources Committee issued a comprehensive report on the ESA, the first such report ever undertaken by a congressional committee. Using data compiled from the Fish and Wildlife Service, National Marine Fisheries Service, and other government sources, the report, *Implementation of the Endangered Species Act (ESA) of 1973,* showed that the ESA had failed to accomplish what the public had been told was the Act's primary mission: to recover threatened and endangered species. According to the report, of the nearly 1,300 domestic plants and animals on the endangered species list, only 10 have recovered—a success rate of less than 1 percent. The report further pointed out the FWS currently has 283 species that are candidates for listing, and that it would cost $150 million to add them to the list. The entire 2004 FWS budget to list species, the report noted, was $12.1 million.[42]

Four months after the release of the report, the House of Representatives, by a vote of 229 to 193, approved the first major overhaul of the troubled statute in the ESA's 32-year history. "The

"Threatened and Endangered Species Recovery Act of 2005" (TESRA), sponsored by Rep. Richard Pombo (R-CA), abolishes the litigation-ridden "critical habitat' provision of the current law and replaces it with a more integrated recovery planning process that includes the identification of specific areas that are of special value to the conservation of the species which are then given priority in recovery efforts. It also authorizes federal grants to property owners who voluntarily take steps to protect species, and would pay them for losses incurred on land the government sets aside for endangered and threatened species.[43]

Even before the Pombo bill passed the House, environmentalists, who have a lot to lose if the ESA is altered along the lines of TESRA, were vehemently defending the status quo. Commenting on a report by the Property and Environment Research Center and the Pacific Legal Foundation that pegged the annual cost of the ESA at $3 billion, Brent Blackwelder, president of Friends of the Earth, said the authors wanted to discredit and gut the ESA and displayed "an incredible ecological ignorance." "They try to contrast species concerns with human needs, and we see those as totally compatible. We as humans need a healthy environment."[44] John Kostyack, senior counsel for the National Wildlife Federation, was unrestrained in his praise of the ESA. "What [critics] fail to acknowledge is that the Endangered Species Act has had an amazing rate of success in preventing species from going extinct," he said. "We have hundreds of species that would not be around today if not for the Endangered Species Act."[45] As the Pombo bill neared passage in the House, Susan Holmes, senior legislative representative at Earthjustice, observed that: "Even school children know you can't protect plants and animals if you don't protect the places where they live."[46]

At this writing, the bill to reform ESA reform is still before Congress. Will lawmakers, the vast majority of whom represent urban or suburban constituents, invest their political capital in an issue primarily of concern to rural voters, particularly those in the West? Conditions unique to the West—large-scale federal ownership of land, abundant natural resources, and breathtaking scenery—have made the region the main battleground between environmentalists and those they seek to expel from the land. Of these special conditions, none is more important, and more misunderstood by outsiders, than widespread federal ownership and management—not to mention, mismanagement—of the region's land.

"Having its Livelihood Taken Away"

The federal government owns more than 670 million acres, almost one-third of the land in the United States. Most of this land is located in the rural West—between the Rockies and the Sierra Nevada/Cascade mountain chain, as well as in Alaska. The amount of federal land in the West is staggering. According to the U.S. Statistical Abstract, the federal government owns 62 percent of Alaska, 44 percent of California, and a whopping 83 percent of Nevada. In Colorado, the comparable figure is 37 percent, Arizona 45 percent, Idaho 63 percent, and Utah 66.5 percent. In September 2003, the General Services Administration identified more than 5.1 million acres of federal land as "vacant" with no federal purpose. BLM alone has more than 3 million acres that have been identified as surplus and suitable for disposal.[47]

In addition to the billions of dollars in potential tax revenues lost to local governments in these states, the vast federal estate creates enticing opportunities for environmental activists to use the agencies administering these lands for their own purposes. As we have seen, activists groups regularly sue the BLM and the Forest Service, both omnipresent throughout the rural West, to get these agencies to take action against ranchers, farmers, loggers, mining operations, construction companies, and practically anyone else trying to make a living in the rural economy. Small wonder, then, that the Washington-based Wilderness Society, for example, an enthusiastic backer of the Wildlands Project and the Endangered Species Act, has for years advocated government ownership and management of natural resources. Depopulating rural areas in the name of protecting the wilderness, ecosystems or forests is what much of the green sound and fury is about.

Writer Chilton Williamson, a native of New York City who moved to Laramie, Wyoming over three decades ago, describes the influence of environmentalism on his adopted region:

> What they [environmentalists] really want is to put Westerners out of their livelihood. They want to shut down ranching, take cattle off public land. Once the ranchers are shut down and effectively expelled from the land, they'll be succeeded by developers who will put in theme parks and suburbs, which is far more destructive and painful to see than anything the ranchers can do...The environmentalists essentially want to shut down mining and logging in the West.

Asked what America stands to lose if the West ultimately succumbs to these pressures, Williamson replies:

104

It stands to lose the oldest part of American culture that exists in this country, which is to say rural self-reliance. The West represents what remains of the old America. And as it's progressively urbanized and suburbanized, and prevented from being a real culture—which is to say a living culture, which is to say a working culture—by having its livelihood taken away, it will have its culture taken away from it and stop being American.[48]

Ron Arnold of the Center for the Defense of Free Enterprise calls the attacks by environmentalists on resource-based livelihoods "rural cleansing." Besides ESA-inspired lawsuits, activists and bureaucrats have devised other ways to drive people off the land and destroy their economic prospects. A case in point is the behind-the-scenes collusion between the Clinton administration and environmentalists in establishing the Grand Staircase Escalante National Monument in 1996. That effort entailed misusing the obscure Antiquities Act of 1906, a statute enacted to protect archeological sites such as cliff dwellings and other artifacts of scientific interest. But clever minds devised a new purpose for an old law.

Since its founding in 1984, the Southern Utah Wilderness Alliance (SUWA) has dedicated itself to using the Wilderness Act of 1964 to keep large areas of federal lands in southern Utah free of roads, motorized travel, and resource extraction. Generously supported by the Rockefeller Brothers Fund, the Florence and John Schumann Foundation, the Pew Charitable Trusts and other foundations, SUWA joined hands with the Clinton administration in the months leading up to the 1996 presidential election to score its biggest success: the creation of a giant national monument in southern Utah.

According to Ron Arnold, who meticulously researched the confusing events, it happened like this: Katie McGinty, head of the White House Council on Environmental Quality (CEQ), orchestrated the drafting of a letter from President Clinton declaring the creation of a national monument in southern Utah. Under the National Environmental Policy Act of 1969 (NEPA), a letter from the president, unlike one from the Secretary of Interior, does not require a lengthy NEPA approval process and is thus a good way to avoid unwanted public scrutiny. However, the plan for the monument originated with McGinty's allies in the Interior Department, which meant that it was necessary to create the *appearance* that the letter came from the executive branch. This McGinty was happy to do. She oversaw several drafts of the Clinton letter until one finally reached the point where administration attorneys were satisfied that it could withstand a court challenge.

Utah Governor Michael Leavitt and the state's congressional delegation were kept in the dark about what the administration and its environmental allies had in store for their state. But according to press reports, administration officials kept SUWA, the Sierra Club, and other environmental organizations abreast of the pending monument designation. Utah officials were understandably stunned when they learned of the plan, courtesy of an administration leak, in the *Washington Post* a few days before President Clinton's formal September 18 announcement of the designation during a campaign stop in—Arizona. By this time, of course, state officials were facing a fait accompli, prompting Utah Senator Orrin Hatch to call the whole affair "the mother of all land grabs."[49]

The 1.7 million-acre tract of land that comprises Grand Escalante is interesting for another reason. "[B]eneath the preserve's Kaiparowits Plateau lies what may be the nation's largest untapped energy reserve," Arnold notes. "It contains an estimated 62 billion tons of clean-burning, low-sulfur coal, between 3 and 5 billion barrels of oil, and 2 to 4 trillion cubic feet of natural gas." Yet the area's monument status means that these resources will likely never be tapped—just as the Southern Utah Wilderness Alliance and its fellow environmentalists in and out of government intended. The loss of these resources has raised America's dependence on foreign sources of energy and boosted the price American consumers pay to heat and cool their houses and provide for their transportation.

The people of Utah were shut out of the decision and will never benefit from the energy-extraction jobs the monument effective killed. The lost opportunity confirms Chilton Williamson's observation that environmentalists want to put "Westerners out of their livelihood." And for all its talk of meeting America's growing energy needs, it is worth noting that the Bush administration has undertaken no steps to undo the damage inflicted by McGinty and SUWA a decade ago.

A Burning Question

For decades, American television viewers have borne witness to the annual ritual of firefighters battling fierce blazes that regularly sweep across hot, arid Southern California in late summer and early fall. But in recent years even the most casual observer has had to notice that the

106

wildfires have grown in size and intensity and are causing widespread death and destruction in areas far removed from Southern California.

Ill-conceived decades-long attempts by the U.S. Forest Service to stop all forest fires—including naturally occurring wildfires that cleanse the forest floor of excess vegetation—have allowed a combustible understory to grow and spread. The problem has become most acute in the West, where most forests are owned and managed by the federal government, and where the catastrophic blaze that swept through Yellowstone National Park in 1988 proved a harbinger of bad things to come.

And come they did. The wildfire seasons of 2000 and 2002 were among the most destructive in the United States in the past half-century. In 2002 alone, forest fires burned nearly 7 million acres at a cost to federal land management agencies of more than $1.6 billion. Between 2002 and 2003, South Dakota, Oregon, Montana, and Colorado experienced the largest wildfires in their histories. Colorado's infamous Hayman fire of 2002 consumed 137,000 acres and 133 homes before it could be extinguished. All across the West, the blazes destroyed homes, killed firefighters, laid waste to wildlife habitat, eroded the soil, damaged watersheds, and polluted the air by smoke rising from what had been the forest floor.[50]

In the midst of the human and ecological tragedy engulfing the forests of the West in the early 2000s, Thomas Bonnicksen, professor of forest science at Texas A&M University, took stock of the devastation. He warned against "the idealized image of historic forests which some people are trying to recreate on public lands, which depicts old trees spread like a blanket over the landscape." He explained:

A real historic forest looked more like a quilt than a blanket. It was a mosaic of patches. Patches of younger trees, bare spots, and open meadows served as natural firebreaks, while the weak and diseased trees under larger trees burned off frequently without turning into infernos.

Today, the patchiness of our forests is gone. Fires now spread across vast areas because we allowed all patches to grow thick with trees. The problem is even more serious because monster fires create even bigger monsters. Seedlings planted in huge burn areas grow into uniformly thick forests that are more dangerous the next time fire comes around.[51]

"The root of the problem is that when we protect our forests from wildfires, over time they become susceptible to disease and to catastrophic wildfires as fuel loads build up," added Patrick Moore, co-founder and former president of Greenpeace, who has since parted company with the organization. Moore's solution is to return to traditional concepts of forestry. Rejecting Greenpeace's view, expressed in a 2003 report, that it's better to let forests burn to the ground than to adopt programs that will reduce catastrophic wildfire, Moore urged policy makers "to actively remove dead trees and to thin the forest. The active management of these forests is necessary to protect human life and property, along with air, water, and wildlife."[52]

In the years leading up to the outbreak of the Western infernos, forests under federal jurisdiction were "actively managed," but not in the way Bonnicksen and Moore recommended. We have already seen how efforts to "protect" the Mexican spotted owl and the northern spotted owl drastically reduced the amount of timber cut in the Southwest and Northwest. But the Clinton administration's approach to forests was further guided by its adoption of "ecosystem management." Even when endangered species were not a factor, the administration proposed to sharply reduce timber sales on federal land. This policy had a predictable consequence: It allowed forests to become increasingly overgrown, tinderboxes ready to ignite in due time. For the Clinton administration, that time came in late summer 2000 when a prescribed burn by Park Service employees at the Bandelier National Monument near Los Alamos, New Mexico got out of control, spread to the Sante Fe National Forest, and left tens of thousands of acres of scorched earth in its path.[53]

The administration's response was telling: It removed the employee who oversaw the ill-fated prescribed burn and, four months later, launched an initiative that was certain to make national forests even more vulnerable to conflagrations. In January 2001, just a few days before it left office, the Clinton administration proposed a rule barring road construction and logging, as well as most forms of forest management on 58.5 million acres of national forest land in 39 states.[54]

Commonly known as the "roadless rule," the initiative was completely compatible with the biocentric notion of limiting the human "disturbance" of wilderness. What better way to minimize such disturbance than to ban the construction of roads in the forests? By the same token, what better way to make the forests even more combustible than to prohibit logging, even of dead and diseased trees? Finally, what better way to ensure that blazes quickly spread and become uncontrollable wildfires than to impede access by firefighters and their equipment to the raging inferno?

In November 2000, two months before the plan was put forward, the Forest Service reported that about half of the 58.5 million acres of newly designated roadless area in the lower 48 states consisted of forests in a moderate to advanced state of ill health and ecological deterioration—making them prime candidates for catastrophic wildfires. These forests were a disaster waiting to happen, and the administration's scheme, once implemented, virtually ensured that the infernos would come sooner rather than later. But this prospect was of little concern to an administration so blinded by its vision of what nature ought to be that it refused to see the harm its own policies inflicted on it. The roadless rule fit neatly into the world the committed environmentalists in the Clinton administration were determined to create. It embodied the "ecosystem management" idea the administration had embraced, and it put a few more nails in the coffin of rural Western economies by further destroying timber jobs. But, most important of all, it revealed a breathtaking ignorance of the natural world on the part of the scheme's guiding lights.

Those guiding lights, people with impeccable green credentials operating quietly behind the scenes to shape the administration's land-use policies, included the ubiquitous Katie McGinty in the White House; Mike Dombeck, head of the Forest Service; and Jamie Rappaport Clarke, director of the Fish & Wildlife Service. McGinty had been a staffer with Sen. Al Gore before joining the administration, and she now serves as head of the Pennsylvania Department of Environmental Protection. Dombeck and Clark went to the National Wildlife Federation after Clinton and Gore left office, and Clark later moved on to work for Defenders of Wildlife.[55] These are the kind of folks Thomas Bonnicksen had in mind, when he warned against "the idealized image of historic forests which some people are trying to recreate on public lands..."

Minions at Work

While McGinty, Dombeck, and Clark were the movers and shakers behind the administration's natural resources policies, the real grunt work on the roadless rule was performed by officials of lesser rank. In crafting the far-reaching forestry initiative, these second-tier officials worked hand in glove with carefully selected environmentalists on the outside. According to a February 2000 report by the House Subcommittee on Forests and Forest Health, the roadless policy was developed "in an environmental vacuum with virtually all input coming from a select few in the environmentalist community, primarily: Ken Rait of the Heritage Forest Campaign; Mike Francis, Bill Meadows and Charles Wilkinson of the Wilderness Society; Niel Lawrence of the Natural Resources Defense Council; Gene Karpinski of USPIRG; Marty Hayden of the Earth Justice Legal Defense Fund; Don Beard of the Audubon Society; and Carl Pope of the Sierra Club."[56]

After reviewing thousands of pages of documents provided upon request by the administration, the subcommittee concluded that, "These individuals had continuous communication with, and access to, the federal employees that were directly involved in the creation of the rule-making, primarily: Chris Wood of the Forest Service, Jim Lyons and Anne Kennedy of the U.S. Department of Agriculture, Dinah Bear and George Frampton of the Council on Environmental Quality, and John Podesta, Chief of Staff to the President."

"This access was not limited to meetings, which were numerous," the report notes, "but included the providing of draft language, legal memoranda, and survey research data to the Administration which was then used to justify and frame the roadless area rule." For example, NRDC's Niel Lawrence submitted an extensive legal analysis on the "Executive Branch's Authority to Protect National Forest Roadless Areas," and the Wilderness Society's Charles Wilkinson provided CEQ's Frampton with a memo titled "Roadless Area Policy: What's Feasible."[57]

In addition to uncovering the highly structured relationship between the administration and environmental activists in putting together a major federal rule, the report pointed to "the lack of any evidence of even a token effort by the administration to involve other interested parties." "This disregard for any balance in the advice being solicited," it went on, "is evidence of both the pretextual nature of the decision, which had clearly already been made, and of a lack of concern for any adverse consequences on the affected users of the forest lands in question."[58]

The Federal Advisory Committee Act (FACA) was enacted in 1972, the report points out, to combat the secrecy, wastefulness, and unbalanced representation typical of many committees advising the federal government on national policies. Among other things, FACA requires advisory committees to keep meetings open to the public; post notices of meetings in the *Federal Register*; keep minutes of meetings; and have a designated federal officer on hand at every meeting. However, as the report states, "the Forest Service relied on the advice of a group of outside interests with a stake in the roadless area rule-making—in violation of FACA—meeting numerous times over the course of the development of the rule-making."[59]

All of this is strikingly reminiscent of the collusion between Clinton administration officials and environmental groups in creating the Grand Staircase Escalante National Monument a few years earlier. Indeed, the national monument designation appears to have served as a role model for the roadless rule—right down to the creation of a fake paper trail to make it look as if the initiative for the roadless rule originated in the executive branch. An internal White House e-mail dated October 12, 1999 contains the following message from Judy Jablow to Janelle Erickson: "This is what the Forest Service gave me to say: The President is directing the Forest Service to develop a proposal to protect roadless areas in national forests."[60]

Yet for all the collusion between environmentalists in and out of government, the grandiose scheme to transform national forests into giant laboratories for ecosystem management never came to fruition. The roadless rule was challenged by Western states and timber companies in six courts and was eventually invalidated by a federal judge in Wyoming in 2003 for violating the Wilderness Act and the National Environmental Policy Act. Too timid to challenge the rule head-on, for reasons that were never fully explained, the Bush administration let the matter be sorted out in the courts before finally setting the rule aside in July 2004. The administration replaced it with a policy that allows governors to petition the federal government if they wished to keep areas roadless.[61]

Reaction from the environmental movement was not long in coming. "The Bush administration's announcement today will immediately imperil wild forests across the country, leaving them vulnerable to commercial timber sales and road building," commented Carl Pope, executive director of the Sierra Club. "These wild forests are special places of national significance and need a national policy to ensure their proper management." Doug Hannold, an attorney with Earthjustice, was even less charitable. "It's another case of the Bush administration having happy talk about the environment, but it's basically rape and pillage."[62]

Environmentalists also vigorously opposed the Bush administration's efforts to undo some of the harm that decades of counterproductive fire-suppression policies by the Forest Service had inflicted on national forests. This also entailed liberating a redirected Forest Service from much of the litigation and paperwork burdens hindering its ability to deal with problems of disease and fuel buildup before they got out of hand. Lawsuits, however, and the delays they inevitably produce had become the modus operandi of activists intent on "protecting" the forests from human interference. The confrontation was joined.

By the early 2000s, the government reported that 180 million acres of federal land were at high risk of catastrophic wildfire, insect infestation, and disease due to unhealthy forest conditions. According to U.S. Forest Service chief Dale Bosworth, forest managers were spending up to 60 percent of their time and energy doing paperwork, time that could have been spent preventing or putting out fires. The Bush administration's response was the "Healthy Forest Initiative," a legislative proposal to reintroduce traditional forest-management practices to the Forest Service and reduce the litigation and paperwork burdens hampering forest-recovery efforts.[63]

What emerged from a long, contentious congressional debate was the "Healthy Forests Restoration Act of 2003," which was signed into law by President Bush in December of that year. With the death and destruction wrought by the wildfires fresh in lawmakers' minds, a fierce lobbying effort launched by the Sierra Club and other environmental groups failed to kill the legislation.[64] The new law traded protection for old-growth forests for the thinning of up to 20 million acres of federal lands and the streamlining of the environmental review and appeals process for such thinning projects.[65] To Texas A&M's Bonnicksen, who lamented the "terrible human, financial, and ecological losses" suffered as a result of the giant forest fires, the law's real strength is that it "requires weighing the risk of action against the risk of inaction in making management decisions."[66]

Having for years preached the gospel of separating man from nature, green activists were not about to acknowledge any responsibility for the deplorable state of forests on federal land. Instead, they sought refuge in the old time religion of biocentrism and ecosystem management. Chad Hanson, a national director of the Sierra Club, wrote that "habitat fragmentation caused by logging and road building on public land" were taking "a heavy toll on our nation's forests." "If forest ecosystems are to recover and imperiled species to survive," he opined, "we must protect all remaining forests on federal public lands—roadless and otherwise."[67] As for confronting the problem of overgrown, highly combustible forests, about all groups like NRDC, Sierra Club, Greenpeace, National Wildlife Federation, and the Wilderness Society were prepared to support was the trimming of trees and brush around communities in fire-prone areas. But as R.J. Smith pointed out, this approach was woefully inadequate for dealing with the conflagrations threatening national forests:

"The Greens fail to mention that fires commonly spot ahead of the flame front considerable distances, jumping roads, rivers, interstates and firebreaks. And large conflagrations fueled by kiln-dry fuels and forests, high temperature, low humidity and strong winds create literal firestorms, with flames and balls of fire, clouds of red-hot embers and burning branches carried ahead—sometimes for miles."[68]

Some might find it odd that those who feel called upon to "saving the planet" lack even a basic understanding of what fuels a gigantic wildfire, and of how a wildfire behaves once it has been ignited. Yet the ignorance of how the natural world really works is largely willful. Modern environmentalism has given green activists unprecedented power to lord over the fate of much of the countryside. And this power takes precedence over all other considerations, including the well-being of the environment.

Chapter 4

TAKING CARE OF BUSINESS

"That civilization which makes the fullest use of human ingenuity in search of truth in order to control nature and transform matter for the service of mankind, to liberate the human spirit from ignorance, superstition and slavery to the forces of nature, and to reform social and political institutions for the benefit of the greatest number—such a civilization is highly idealistic and spiritual."

HU SHIH[1]

The mountain yellow-legged frog, *Rana muscosa*, began disappearing from the Sierra Nevada Mountains in the first half of the twentieth century, and the amphibian's decline has become even more pronounced in recent decades. Today, the frog is absent from almost all the Sierra Nevada's high-altitude lakes where it once thrived. The frog's seemingly inexplicable demise has provoked much speculation in the media and among scientists, with parasites, ultra-violet radiation, fungal disease, and, especially, pesticides blamed for the frog's troubles.

Intrigued by the idea that pesticides could be at fault, a team of researchers from the U.S. Geological Survey (USGS) began looking into the possibility that pesticides from fruit, vegetable, and nut tree farms in the San Joaquin Valley to the west of the Sierra Nevada were being blown into the mountains on prevailing winds. Once the pesticides reached the High Sierras, the theory went, they could damage the frogs' nervous systems and cause the drop in numbers of the colorful amphibian. To test their theory, the USGS researchers measured traces of pesticides found in tissue of Pacific tree frogs that reside, and thrive, in the same area where the mountain yellow-legged frog had declined in population. They then compared the mountain tree frogs' pesticide levels with those found in tree frogs from coastal and northern mountain areas of California isolated from farmlands.

"It is ironic," notes Alex Avery of the Hudson Institute's Center for Global Food Issues, "that these ecologists would approach the yellow-legged frog declines by looking for traces of pesticides in tree frogs that were abundant in the same environment where pesticides were suspected of ravaging yellow-legged frogs." The findings of the USGS researchers hardly appeared to confirm the pesticide explanation for the decline of the mountain yellow-legged frog. They found traces of pesticides slightly more often and at slightly higher levels in Sierra tree frogs east of the Central Valley than frogs from California's coast and northern mountains. However, the pesticide residues found in both groups of frogs were so minuscule that most could not be measured. As the researchers noted in the journal *Environmental Toxicology and Chemistry*, "because of the frequency of samples found below analytical detection limits at all study sites, no significant differences were found in [pesticide] residues of either age [tadpoles or adults] or across sites..."[2]

The USGS researchers also found that the activity of a nervous system enzyme was "depressed" in tree frog tadpoles from the mountains when compared with tree frog tadpoles from coastal regions. These differences, however, did not appear in adult populations, which were thriving in both mountainous and coastal regions. In other words, whatever the reason for the "depressed" enzyme in mountain tree frogs, it was of no reproductive significance.

This paucity of data, however, was enough to lead the researchers to conclude that "pesticides are instrumental in declines of [red and yellow-legged frog] species." Donald Sparling, who headed the research team, took this claim one step further, telling the *Los Angeles Times* in 2000: "Unfortunately, there now appears to be a close correlation between declining populations of amphibians in the Sierra Nevada and exposure to agricultural pesticides."

These "findings" by the USGS research team were all it took to spawn the inevitable lawsuits by environmental activists. The Center for Biological Diversity, Californians for Alternatives to Toxics, and other environmental groups identified the source of the frog's difficulties in traces of pesticides that had made their way to the lakes in the High Sierra from the farmlands far below. They sued the California Department of Pesticide Regulation and the U.S. EPA for failing to review the impact of pesticides on California frogs and other amphibians. The media lost no time in echoing these claims, with the *San Francisco Chronicle* reporting that "pesticides and herbicides drifting into the mountains from Central Valley farmlands are a known cause of declining frog populations."

The case of the disappearing High Sierra frogs turns out to have had an entirely different explanation. As far back as the 1880s, anglers, miners, and other settlers began stocking lakes, rivers, and streams in the West with all manner of fish. Trout were introduced into the glacial lakes of the Sierra Nevada, and by 1924 wildlife biologists noted that mountain yellow-bellied tadpoles and trout were rarely seen in the same lakes. They strongly suspected that hungry trout were the cause, and in 1938 a separate group of biologists observed and reported trout preying on mountain yellow-legged frogs. The stocking of Sierra Nevada lakes with trout continued, with thousands of fingerlings being dropped by aircraft in the 1960s. Trout ended up in high-altitude lakes where previously there had been no fish at all, but plenty of frogs. That soon changed. Before long the hungry trout were feasting on frog tadpoles, with very predictable consequences for the overall frog population.

In carefully controlled experiments carried out over eight years, Vance Vredenburg of the University of California at Berkeley began removing trout from five separate lakes in the late 1990s. Vredenburg saw frog "population explosions" in each lake over the following years. As he told the *San Francisco Chronicle*, "There are at least 10,000 lakes in the High Sierra. Ninety to 95 percent of them hold introduced species of trout but no more frogs at all. And there may be plenty of lakes that have plenty of frogs, but few or no fish. So the answer is pretty straightforward, and it doesn't get much simpler: with no trout you get an immediate and dramatic response."

Minnesota also has a frog story. In 1995, a group of middle school pupils found some deformed northern leopard frogs, *Rana pipiens*, and posted pictures of the poor creatures on the Internet. Before long, other Minnesotans reported finding deformed frogs in ponds and lakes throughout the state. The Minnesota Pollution Control Agency (MPCA) swung into action, determined to find the cause of the deformities. The agency strongly suspected that the cause was a chemical pollutant in the water, such as pesticide runoff from farmland. Using the embryos of the African clawed frog, *Xenapus laevis*, MPCA carried out lab tests to determine what was interfering with the frogs' development. By September 1997, MPCA was ready to announce the results of its tests at a press conference attended by the national media, including *PBS* and *ABC*'s "Nightline."

"We're here because we've found something in the water," an MPCA official announced. Then an MPCA scientist added ominously. "We found that water from sites where malformed frogs have been reported was very potent in deforming frogs in this laboratory

116

experiment." Although they didn't say exactly what the "something" was that they found in the water, MPCA officials began shortly thereafter to offer bottled water to families concerned that local wells were contaminated.

Bottled water may have eased the fears of local residents, but MPCA"s tests soon came under withering criticism from scientists with the U.S. EPA. According to EPA, it was simply a natural lack of calcium and other salts in Minnesota water that was deforming the laboratory-raised African clawed frog embryos, not a chemical contaminant. As lead EPA researcher Joe Tietge put it: "You could probably take tap water from any county in Minnesota and get results like this. In science, spurious correlations happen all the time," and they are, "one of the weakest forms of evidence to support an hypothesis." Added another EPA researcher: "Results don't mean anything if they are interpreted improperly. Anybody with a tropical fish aquarium knows that if you fill it with tap water it will kill the fish. That doesn't mean your tap water isn't safe to drink."

Despite EPA's comments, MPCA still sticks to its story, even though Minnesota officials have never identified the chemical they assumed was responsible for the deformities. There is, however, another explanation for the problem, which has gained considerable currency in recent years. "Northern leopard frogs in the wild are afflicted at an early age by a tiny parasitic flatworm called trematodes," Avery explains. The parasites are shed by snails in ponds where they are picked up by frog tadpoles. Once in the tadpoles, they cause cellular dislocations that lead to deformities in adult frogs.

The parasite theory was first advanced by Stanley Sessions of Hartwick College in New York and initially met with skepticism from other researchers and environmentalists. Their reluctance to abandon the pesticide explanation, even as evidence mounted that the parasitic flatworms were at fault, was seen by Sessions as a sign of the times. As explained by *Washington Post* reporter William Souder: "[Sessions] thought the whole frog investigation was being manipulated—and important evidence ignored—so as to promote further research funding. In essence, he seemed to think other investigators were tilting their hypotheses toward a chemical contaminant in an effort to catch the endocrine disruption wave."

Scare Campaigns Come of Age:
Endocrine Disruptors, Global Warming and National Geographic

This short excursion into the world of frogs shows how public consciousness has been shaped by modern environmentalism. Whether frogs were disappearing in California or deformed in Minnesota, the popular assumption is that a chemical is the cause. "Actually, when I first heard about the Minnesota situation, I immediately suspected a chemical substance," Stanley Sessions admitted. "That's the first thing everybody thinks of. You see a screwed-up animal in the field and that's the conclusion you jump to." Not even Sessions, who ultimately debunked the chemical hypothesis in the case of the deformed frogs, could initially resist the temptation. Alex Avery has dubbed this the Rachel Carson Syndrome in recognition of *Silent Spring's* lasting impact on our collective psyche.

The Rachel Carson Syndrome was alive and well in the mid-1990s when the frog stories were garnering attention in the media. Indeed, Sessions' suspicion that grant-hungry researchers were eager to "catch the endocrine disruption wave" was reinforced by a well-orchestrated scare campaign involving the 1996 book, *Our Stolen Future: Are We Threatening Our Fertility, Intelligence, and Survival?—A Scientific Detective Story*. Written by Theo Colborn, Dianne Dumanoski, and John Peterson Myers, *Our Stolen Future* attempted to popularize the idea that exposure to trace amounts of certain environmental chemicals that mimic the action of hormones could disrupt normal physiological events and result in adverse health effects. These environmental estrogens or "endocrine disrupters," as the authors preferred to call them, were the focus of *Our Stolen Future*.[3]

With a foreword by Al Gore and funding from the W. Alton Jones Foundation (today known as the Blue Moon Fund), the book contained chapters with such titles as "Hand-Me-Down Poisons," "Hormone Havoc," "Fifty Ways to Lose Your Fertility," and "Beyond Cancer." Among other things, it cited reports that male sperm counts were falling and claimed that breast cancer rates among women were rising. Both trends were ominously tied to exposure to pesticides. While there had been reports of declining sperm counts, there also were reports of sperm counts remaining constant or rising. *Our Stolen Future* only mentioned surveys showing the former. Similarly, the book's claim of rising death rates from breast cancer was contradicted by data readily available at the time of publication that showed a nine percent decline in death rates since 1940. Stephen Safe of Texas A&M University has pointed out that the human diet will have forty million times more naturally occurring estrogen-mimicking chemicals than a person gets by exposure to synthetic hormone-like compounds such as those found in many leading pesticides. But data like this did not persuade the authors of *Our Stolen Future*, who saw pesticides as the source of endocrine disrupters' threat to human health.[4]

The endocrine-disrupter hypothesis appeared to receive further support in 1996 when researchers at the Xavier/Tulane Center for Bioenvironmental Research at Tulane University led by John McLachlan published a study in *Science* that reached a startling conclusion. Demonstrating what was called the "cocktail" or synergy effect, the Tulane team claimed to have demonstrated that a combination of two or more estrogens would amplify their effect by 150 to 1,500 times. This impressive display of chemical potency was just what *Our Stolen Future* warned against. The world of toxicology was suddenly turned on its head. By a strange coincidence, the Tulane study appeared the same year that *Our Stolen Future* was published.

Alas, the sensation was short-lived. In January 1997, *Science* published a letter from scientists at the U.S. National Institute for Environmental Health Sciences, Texas A&M University, and Duke University reporting that the Tulane results could not be replicated. A month later, *Nature* published results from British researchers who also were unable to replicate the Tulane claims. Under fierce attack from toxicologists around the world, McLachlan, in July, 1997, admitted in a letter to *Science* that neither his laboratory nor any other research institute was able to replicate the Tulane team's original findings. The once-widely-heralded study was subsequently withdrawn by a chastened McLachlan. Eyebrows were subsequently raised when it was learned that John McLachan received funding at Tulane from the same W. Alton Jones Foundation that provided financing for *Our Stolen Future* (one of whose authors, John Peterson Myers, was (and is) a director of the W. Alton Jones Foundation/Blue Moon Fund.[5]

Like the infamous "hockey stick" of a few years later that purported to show a sudden warming of the planet in the latter part of the 20th century, the cocktail effect could not be replicated. "One of the basic principles of science and the scientific method," Milloy and Gough remind us, "is that the results of scientific research must be replicable by other scientists in other laboratories." But Theo Colborn, the lead author of *Our Stolen Future*, was unperturbed by the unfortunate turn of events, saying, "This is a growing field...just because we don't have evidence does not mean there are no effects." Her comments were consistent with the precautionary principle's emphasis on speculation over evidence, and they show how invoking the doctrine, even indirectly, had become second nature to those promoting environmental scares.

Even though its message was under increasingly unflattering scientific scrutiny, *Our Stolen Future* stirred the waters enough to prompt Congress to act. The Food Quality Protection Act of 1996 included a directive to EPA to study the impact of endocrine disrupters. The study, carried out by the National Academy of Sciences and the National Research Council, could find no epidemiological evidence nor could it define any biological mechanism by which the reported disruption took place. Notwithstanding these scientific findings, the endocrine-disrupter cat was already out of the bag—as Sessions had concluded from public reaction to the deformed frogs case—and the implications for public policy were profound, especially when lawmakers and public officials began allocating finite resources to study purely hypothetical risks. As Thomas DeGregori has explained:

> The problem is that, once a causal connection between a phenomenon, such as endocrine disrupters, and a human disorder is posited, an academic industry is generated: grants and research institutes are created and newly minted experts become media pundits on the subject. This constitutes a powerful force that is resistant to any research findings that is contradictory to the previously established presumption of danger. Any study refuting an alleged environmental danger is deemed to be fatally flawed. The real fatality may not be the new study but some cherished assumptions."[6]

Our Stolen Future struck a sensitive nerve in a public conditioned by years of orchestrated environmental scares to fear the worst from chemicals. Congress decided to leap before it looked on endocrine disrupters, to "do something" even if it knew nothing. And that suited the book's promoters just fine. To ensure that the public was sufficiently frightened by this latest scare campaign, the W. Alton Jones Foundation hired a Washington, D.C.-based nonprofit called Environmental Media Services to stir the pot. Headed by Arlie Schardt, who served as press secretary for Al Gore's unsuccessful 1988 presidential bid, Environmental Media Services arranged for Theo Colborn to appear on the *Today* show and organized several high-profile news conferences at the National Press Club in Washington.

The work of experienced hands, Schardt's group also could avail itself of the expertise of a high-powered PR firm, Fenton

Communications, with which it shared office space. A service provider in the 1980s to the communist governments of Angola and Nicaragua, Fenton's green clients over the years have included the Natural Resources Defense Council (NRDC), Greenpeace, the Environmental Working Group, National Wildlife Federation, World Wildlife Fund, Sierra Club, Rainforest Action Network, Public Citizen, the Pew Charitable Trusts, and George Soros's Open Society Institute.[7]

Fenton's carefully cultivated media contacts and years of experience at conducting environmental scare campaigns made it a valuable asset to green activists. In 1989, Fenton had joined forces with NRDC and *CBS's* "60 Minutes" to launch the Alar scare. Alar is a chemical growth regulator that was used in growing apples. Fenton convinced "60 Minutes" to do a segment on an NRDC study linking Alar to cancer, particularly cancer in children. The study, *Pesticides in our Children's Food*, was good enough for "60 Minutes" even though it had not undergone independent peer review and was not based on human exposure to Alar. In the panic ensuing after the broadcast, apples were removed from supermarket shelves, apples and applesauce were pulled from school lunch menus, and apple growers suffered losses estimated at $250 million. FDA assurances that it was safe to eat apples sprayed with Alar fell on deaf ears. The product's manufacturer, Uniroyal, withdrew Alar from the market in June 1989, less than four months after the "60 Minutes" broadcast.[8]

With its years of experience, it is small wonder that green activist groups could panic Congress into inserting the message of *Our Stolen Future* into legislation during the very year the book went on sale and persuade the public that endocrine-modulating chemicals were "gender benders." Once again, the environmental movement showed that it could set the terms of public and policy debate and move its anti-chemical agenda forward. That the wildest claims of *Our Stolen Future* were never confirmed was no more relevant to the movement's success than that the FDA years earlier had exonerated Alar. In both cases, the public was given what seemed a compelling reason to fear man-made chemicals, and that's what the game was all about.

What worked well to damage DDT's reputation in the early 1970s and cripple the apple industry in the late 1980s was growing in effectiveness. A network of NGOs, foundations, government agencies and research institutions that was rudimentary at the first Earth Day in 1970 had become a multi-layered system capable of exerting enormous pressure. David Fenton, founder of the PR company that bears his name, is part of the network, as is Arlie Schardt. "60 Minutes" didn't just stumble onto the Alar story; Fenton Communications and NRDC made it happen. The greens were becoming adept at carrying their message to mainstream institutions, and there was more to come.

In 1997 visitors to the Smithsonian Institution's Museum of Natural History were treated to an exhibition, "Global Warming: Understanding the Forecast." Displayed at the museum on the Mall in Washington, the exhibition featured an on-line, interactive version for the Internet, complete with computer simulations and video displays showing how the burning of fossil fuels for energy was overheating the planet, with dire consequences for future generations. This bit of propaganda was the result of a collaborative effort between the Smithsonian and the Environmental Defense Fund (today called Environmental Defense), an advocate for the Kyoto climate treaty. Donors to the Smithsonian-EDF exhibition included the National Aeronautics and Space Administration, EPA, the National Science Foundation, the Teresa and H. John Heinz Foundation, the John D. and Catherine T. MacArthur Foundation, the Geraldine R. Dodge Foundation, and the W. Alton Jones Foundation. Corporate sponsors included Turner Broadcasting System, Lehman Brothers, and Enron.

Pooling funds from agencies, foundations, and corporations to sponsor a Smithsonian exhibition touting a favorite cause of modern environmentalism was quite an accomplishment for EDF. Consciously or not, environmental activists were following the teachings of Antonio Gramsci (1891-1937), a neo-Marxist socialist philosopher and founder of the Italian Communist Party who decades earlier urged the Left to embark on the "long march through the institutions." Infiltrating, transforming, and redirecting institutions to influence public consciousness is a subtle and largely non-confrontational way to alter the political landscape. A family from the Midwest strolling through the Museum of Natural History could hardly expect to fathom the political forces arrayed behind what was publicly presented as a purely educational exhibition on climate change.

National Geographic magazine provides another case in point. Known to an older generation of readers as a reliable source of spectacular photographs and lively descriptions of the natural world, *National Geographic* has undergone a radical makeover in recent years. Beautiful photos still grace its pages, but political overtones have made their way into the magazine's traditional narratives. *National Geographic's* September 2004 cover story is a 74-page spread on climate change. Under the headline, "The Heat Is On," the magazine's table of contents has this to say to its readers:

There's no question that the Earth is getting hotter -- and fast. The real questions are: How much of the warming is our fault, and are we willing to slow the meltdown by curbing our insatiable appetite for fossil fuels?

Typical of the magazine's near-hysterical tone is its two-page color photo of a Bangladeshi woman standing in a flooded rice field. "Swells rise in the Bay of Bengal," the caption reads, "and splash into Nurzahan Bibi's rice field, which—as global temperatures rise and sea level climbs—becomes an ever more precarious means of support for the widowed Bangladeshi...There's little doubt that greenhouse gases released by industry, agriculture, automobiles, and coal-fired electric generation are a key factor in changing Earth's climate." Data readily available to the editors of *National Geographic*, however, show that sea levels in Bangladesh actually *fell* in the 1990s and, over the last-half century, have risen by an infinitesimal seven-tenths of an inch. This is "far too little," Michaels points out, "for anyone to notice, in Bangladesh or anywhere else."[9]

"Everywhere on Earth, ice is changing," *National Geographic's* Daniel Glick writes. "The famed snows of Kilimanjaro have melted more than 80 percent since 1912." This is true, but Glick neglects to tell readers that human-induced global warming has nothing to do with it. As *Nature* reported ten months before *National Geographic* addressed the subject:

> Although it's tempting to blame the ice loss on global warming, researchers think that deforestation of the mountain's foothills is the more likely culprit. Without the forests' humidity, previously moisture-laden winds blew dry. No longer replenished with water, the ice is evaporating in the strong equatorial sunshine."[10]

The *International Journal of Climatology* noted on March 15, 2004: "A drastic drop in atmospheric moisture at the end of the 19th century and the ensuing drier climate conditions are likely forcing glacier retreat on Kilimanjaro." The editors of National Geographic also could have consulted the *Journal of Geophysical Research* on the snows of Kilimanjaro:

> It has been speculated that general global warming is directly driving the retreat of Kilimanjaro's glaciers. However, detailed analyses of glacier retreat in the global tropics uniformly reveal that changes in climate variables related to air humidity prevail in controlling the modern retreat."[11]

The inaccuracies and misleading statements that pervade *National Geographic's* treatment of climate change are what you would expect to find on the websites of Greenpeace or NRDC. That they appear on the pages of a publication that for decades has enjoyed a status befitting a cultural icon is but another demonstration of the environmentalists' "march through the institutions." Many more people will read *National Geographic's* global warming issue—or at least look at the pictures—than will delve into the literature compiled in the *International Journal of Climatology* or the *Journal of Geophysical Research.*

In justifying *National Geographic's de facto* endorsement of the theory of human-induced global warming, editor-in-chief Bill Allen said he could "live with some canceled memberships" of those who disagreed with the magazine's position. "I'd have a harder time," he wrote, "looking at myself in the mirror if I didn't bring you the biggest story in geography today." Of course the "biggest story" didn't last very long. Three months later, a giant tsunami struck the southern Indian Ocean region, flooding low-lying areas under an enormous sea wave and killing an estimated 240,000 people. Caused by an undersea earthquake, the tsunami left a massive path of death and destruction in its wake. It was arguably a bigger story in geography and geology than the one Allen tried to pass off on *National Geographic* readers.[12]

The Money Tree

Green activists have adeptly affected the clash of competing interests that typically shapes public policy debate by making their own message—at least substantial parts of it—an almost automatic point of reference. They are no longer on the outside looking in. Still, entering the political arena as a serious player requires more than a mastery of sound bites, skill at coalition-building, cultivating the media and developing ties to politicians and bureaucrats. It also requires money—lots of it. Here too the greens are not wanting.

While environmental NGOs, particularly those on the global stage, garner funds generously provided by the UN, the EU, and other national and international agencies, a far more abundant source of money is the capitalist system the Left goes to such great lengths to condemn. Tapping into this source of wealth, and using it for the Left's own purposes, Jarol Manheim points out, dominates the thinking of today's progressive movement. Manheim argues that modern progressives are attracted to the social theory of "power elites" rooted in the writings of such social scientists as C. Wright Mills, G. William Domhoff, and Thomas Dye:

In general, it suggests that institutions and actors, such as political parties, the mass media, traditional interest groups, and public opinion were important only at the margins of the political system. Rather...the political system is powered by large volumes of money expended by corporations and wealthy individuals, which they channel through a collaborative network of private foundations, universities, and policy-development think tanks to generate a menu of policy options that are subsequently addressed by policy makers on Capitol Hill, in the executive branch, and even in the courts. Control over the flow of money is exercised directly—by deciding which institutions do or do not receive it—but also and importantly indirectly, through interlocks among directors of various companies, foundations, and other institutions. The exercise of power in this world view is subtle and seldom transparent. By selecting the issues that move through the system and by shaping the ways they are studied and framed, the rich (and therefore powerful) are able to place boundaries on the range of policy choices available to those who operate the expressly political components of the system."[13]

Whether this theory adequately or accurately explains the complex American body politic is a debate for another day. But Manheim makes a persuasive case that by the early 1980s this view of the world was adopted by progressive thinkers and activists and guided their political strategy. They sought to emulate the existing power structure by creating what Manheim calls a "parallel universe." This alternative power structure would set the progressive agenda by choosing the terms of debate, selecting the issues and funding institutions to promote them. It also would deny funds to those who opposed the preferred policies and strategies. In other words, the Left, which imagined itself out-of-power, proposed to operate as it imagined the in-power Right did.

Not coincidentally, this strategy took form in the early 1980s when Ronald Reagan's election sent shock waves through the ranks of older liberals and younger self-described progressives, who emerged from the New Left of the late 1960s. This latter group arrived at the most far-reaching conclusions about the meaning of Reagan's election. The most important conclusion was that, like it or not, money makes the world go round, especially the political world. The Left would vanquish the Right only when it had enough money to do battle on something approaching even terms.

But pursuing wealth created a dilemma for progressives. "[T]he Right had an ideology that assigned a social value to monetary wealth, while the Left had an ideology that disparaged it," Manheim notes. "So the first challenge was clear—to obtain, or at the very least gain control over, large sums of money in ways that harmonized with a critical view of capitalism."

Luckily the problem was solved in a way that more than met the Left's financial needs without compromising its rejection of markets and money. The solution was philanthropy. If progressives could gain control of the assets of foundations and charities, then they could distribute funding to worthy Leftist causes, of which environmentalism was among the most prominent.

By the last third of the 20th century, some of America's oldest foundations had undergone a change in leadership that reordered their priorities. The Pew Charitable Trusts, the Ford Foundation, the Rockefeller foundations and other major philanthropies led the way in redirecting their donations to social causes far removed from what their founders had intended.

The fate of the Pew Charitable Trusts is instructive. Founded in 1948, the Pew Memorial Foundation, as it was originally called, was established by the four children of Joseph N. Pew, Sr., who started Sun Oil Company (Sunoco) in the Pennsylvania oil fields in the 1880s. With its oil and gas wells, tankers, pipelines, refineries, and deep-water shipping facilities, Sun Oil exhibited all the characteristics of a vertically integrated petroleum company. After the elder Pew's death in 1912, the company stayed under family management and continued to prosper.

For decades the trusts Pew's children established reflected the spirit of the industrious oil man whose vast fortune made it all possible. The foundation supported the work of the Hoover Institution, the American Enterprise Institute, the Center for Strategic and International Studies, and other symbols of the American establishment. All that began to change in 1979 after the death of the last of the founding generation of Pews. By 1987, the foundation's new president, neurosurgeon Thomas Langfitt, had purged most of the old guard and installed as Pew's new executive director Rebecca Rimel, a former nurse and self-described "high school cheerleader turned executive feminist." What resulted was a complete break with the foundation's original intent and a redefinition of Pew's mission. "[A] foundation that was established by prominent advocates of free trade and limited government is now a leading funder of policy initiatives that are generally opposed by advocates of those same positions today." Dorothy Ridings, head of the Council on Foundations, was not exaggerating when she called the makeover of Pew "the most radical transformation of any charitable institution." The environmental movement would become one of Pew's chief beneficiaries.[14]

Even as America's first generation of foundations was in transformation, a new type of foundation was in formation, one designed from the outset to fund progressive causes. Young heirs like Joshua Mailman were developing the institutions of social venture philanthropy and corporate social investing to funnel private-sector funds to Leftist causes. Born in 1957, Mailman is heir to a fortune amassed by the Utica, New York-based Mailman Corporation, one of the nation's first conglomerates. In 1981, shortly after Reagan took office, he convened a secret meeting of mostly well-heeled activists to the Colorado Rockies to discuss how the Left could regain power in what they deemed was a hostile environment. Calling themselves "The Doughnuts," after a doughnut-shaped cloud that formed one day in the sky over their meeting place, the activists hit upon the idea of pooling their resources to support social and political activist causes dear to their hearts. Unlike corporate social investing, the money would come from individual, family and foundation philathropy.

In 1982 Mailman created a vehicle to translate his idea into reality. The mission of the Threshold Foundation is the promotion of peace, understanding, and environmental awareness through grant-making and educational activities. Following the model laid out by the Doughnuts, Threshold provides "a mechanism for pooling the funds of smaller contributors in an effort to maximize their social impact." This model has been replicated by other organizations such as the Funding Exchange. Though their assets are minor compared to the major foundations, foundations like Threshold that pool donor resources created financial leverage to help smaller radical activist groups. By 2000, Mailman's foundation was distributing $1.3 million annually to organizations that included the Rainforest Action Network and the Ruckus Society, groups noted for "direct action" tactics that produce violent confrontations over environmental and trade policy.

More important than the money changing hands is the political impact of Mailman's innovation. "What Joshua Mailman and a few others of the same era saw as an opportunity, and what they have accomplished over the past two decades, is the redefinition of what it means to be philanthropic," Manheim explains. "By pooling their funds, not only within foundations, as in the case of Threshold, but across foundations, and there are many such partnerships,...they began to create a resource base on which a Progressive-Left counter-revolution could be constructed."[15]

The Tides Foundation and Tides Center

Mailman's was not the only innovative mind on the Left. In 1976, California activist Drummond Pike teamed up with Jane Bagley Lehman, a granddaughter of tobacco magnate R.J. Reynolds, to establish the Tides Foundation. It operates from offices in San Francisco's lush and historic Presidio, the grounds of a former U.S. Army base that the Clinton Administration transferred to the Interior Department, which then leased quarters to Pike. Tides has become a powerful behind-the-scenes force in American politics.

Tides' innocuous mission statement suggests that it does little more than support traditional liberal causes:

> Tides actively promotes change toward a healthy society, one which is founded on principles of social justice, broadly shared economic opportunity, a robust democratic process, and sustainable environmental practices."

In fact, Tides is unique in the world of philanthropy. It acts like a giant umbrella sheltering donors from the unwanted scrutiny of the outside world. As the *San Francisco Bay Guardian* reported in 1997:

> Wealthy patrons give big chunks of money to Tides—and their names are kept confidential. The Tides donation is completely tax deductible. But the donor can discreetly designate an organization that he or she wants to see receive the money—and Tides will pass the donation along, minus a small administrative fee. Often, the recipient group doesn't know where the money really came from. And there's no way the public can find out either. By the end of the 1980s, Tides had significantly expanded another of its tasks: providing a tax shelter to smaller non-profits unable or unwilling to win tax-exempt status from the federal government."[16]

Tides' mode of operation became more intricate in 1996 when it created a separate Tides Center to handle the finances and administration of radical activist groups lacking independent tax-exempt status. It was initially run by Edward Fouhy, a former producer of the *"CBS Evening News"* with Walter Cronkite. In the division of responsibilities, the Tides Foundation focused on grant-making, while the Tides Center concentrated on "fiscal sponsorship," i.e., providing administrative and technical assistance to grant recipients. Patrick Reilly of the Capital Research Center explains the division of labor:

> Besides giving grants to leftist organizations through the Foundation, the Tides apparatus is set up to assist groups' organization and development

128

from the very beginning. The Tides Center allows fledgling groups to operate as projects of the Center. Not only does it fund affiliated groups, but the groups are encouraged to contract with Tides for financial, management, and program assistance."[17]

The Tides Center spin-off has helped protect the donor-dependent Foundation from lawsuits that might be brought against the Center's radical affiliates. This wall of legal separation between the two organizations reassures wealthy donors eager to protect their money while using it to promote a radical anti-corporate political and social agenda. The Tides Center now manages Mailman's Threshold Foundation.

Both the Tides Foundation and Tides Center are classified as 501(c)(3) charitable organizations by the IRS, which makes contributions to them tax-deductible and not subject to public disclosure. As "public charities," Tides entities cannot engage in "substantial" lobbying and political activities, but its affiliates no doubt engage in a wide range of "research and education" activities. What makes the operation work so smoothly, analysts Gretchen and Tom Randall point out, is that "the original donor can't be linked to the ultimate recipient."[18]

In its first quarter-century Tides has raised and distributed more than $225 million. Much of its money comes from corporations, including American Express, Arco, AT&T, Bank of America, Gap, Hewlett-Packard, IBM, Mattel, Philip Morris, J.C. Penney, Sara Lee, Sony Music, and Ticketmaster. Foundations also use Tides to screen and channel their grants: Topping the list is the Pew Charitable Trusts, now also classified as a 501(c)(3) charity. Here is a list of other foundations that in 2002-2003 disclosed their contributions to the Tides Center and Tides Foundation:

- Pew Charitable Trusts, $8,208,000
- Ford Foundation, $4,355,000
- Charles Stewart Mott Foundation, $1,100,000
- W.J. Kellogg Foundation, $1,987,000
- David & Lucile Packard Foundation, $1,573,900
- Rockefeller Foundation/Rockefeller Brothers Fund, $450,000
- New York Community Trust, $175,000
- William and Flora Hewlett Foundation, $1,245,000
- William Randolph Hearst Foundation, $300,000
- Richard King Mellon Foundation, $2,900,000
- Open Society Institute, $254,700
- Turner Foundation, $75,000
- Ben & Jerry's Foundation, Inc., $25,000

Foundations that have disclosed their donations to the Tides Foundations in the years 2000-2003 include:

- Ford Foundation, $5,200,000
- Open Society Institute, $1,112,693
- William and Flora Hewlett Foundation, $1,000,000
- New York Community Trust, $235.000
- Foundation for Deep Ecology, $218,783
- David & Lucile Packard Foundation, $115,000
- Rockefeller Brothers Fund, $100,000
- Turner Foundation, $50,000
- Barbara Streisand Foundation, $20,000 [19]

Not all the money, of course, has gone to environmental causes. In the 30 years since its founding, Tides has funded such groups as People for the American Way, the ACLU, Children's Defense Fund, Planned Parenthood, National Abortion Rights League, Association of Community Organizations for Reform Now (ACORN), National Lawyers Guild, the Institute for Policy Studies, and George Soros's Open Society Institute. Environmental groups receiving Tides' support include the Earth Island Institute, Earth Justice Legal Defense Fund, Environmental Defense, Environmental Media Services, Environmental Working Group, Friends of the Earth, Greenpeace, League of Conservation Voters, Living Earth Foundation, Natural Resources Defense Council, NGO Coalition for the Environment, Pesticide Action Network, Rainforest Action Network, Rocky Mountain Institute, Ruckus Society, Sierra Club, and the Wilderness Society.

For the Left and for environmental groups in particular, the ties between Pew and Tides represent an alliance of old and new: the venerable Pew has changed with the times, while Tides is thoroughly modern, a creation in the innovative spirit of Drummond Pike and Joshua Mailman. Pew and Tides are now joined by many other funding entities with deep pockets and a commitment to the agendas of modern environmentalism. The interlocking relationships of foundation grantmakers, NGO activists, and government officials are flourishing, their empires expand, and their money flows.

"The money came rolling in," Arnold notes, "but the brash little volunteer-driven environmental David of the 1960s grew not into a great king after Earth Day, 1970, but turned into just another well-heeled special interest Goliath strutting around Capitol Hill."[20]

Indeed, the environmental movement—barely three decades old by the end of the 20th century –was becoming a financial powerhouse. In his landmark, five-part series for the *Sacramento Bee* (April 22-26, 2001), appropriately titled "Environment, Inc.," Tom Knudson reported that U.S. green groups had taken in $3.5 billion in 1999, up 94 percent since 1994. Knudson found that individuals, companies, and foundations gave an average of $9.6 million *a day* to environmental organizations in 1999. Knudson's exhaustive research also turned up the unequal distribution of money flowing into the coffers of environmental organizations. Citing data on file with the IRS, he found that 20 of the nation's 8,000 green groups took in 29 percent of all contributions to environmental organizations in 1999. Indeed, the top 10 environmental groups earned spots on the *Chronicle of Philanthropy's* list of America's wealthiest charities.[21]

Despite the sluggish performance of the stock market in the wake of the bursting of the dot-com bubble and the terrorist attacks of 9/11, funds have continued to flow to the environmental movement. Money comes from individuals, corporations, government agencies (particularly EPA), and foundations. But the most reliable source is philanthropy. There are many players in this game, but a few of the more outstanding ones deserve special attention:

Pew Charitable Trusts: Rebecca Rimel has transformed a reliable backer of traditional U.S. charities into an enthusiastic supporter of a cacophony of leftist causes. The Philadelphia-based organization has about $4 billion in assets, and Pew's environmental program, directed by Joshua S. Reichert, has donated an average of $30 million annually over the past two decades to an array of environmental causes. Once described by the *Boston Globe* as the "man in charge of doling out the single largest block of money earmarked for environmental causes," Reichert told the *Globe*: "We are very product oriented. We need to demonstrate a return on these investments...that is measurable." Reichert likes to tell grant recipients what he wants done and "encourages" them to form coalitions to get maximum use out of Pew's money. He once told environmental writer Mark Dowie: "I don't want someone who knows the facts, or can articulate them persuasively; I want someone who wants to win and knows how."[22]

Pew's environmental interests are wide-ranging. It has become a scourge of ranchers, growers, loggers, and other resource users and property owners by funding such groups as the Center for Biological Diversity, the Wilderness Society, and the Earth Justice Legal Defense Fund, which use the Endangered Species Act to cripple local economies in the rural West. Pew also is active on the global-warming issue. With the John D. and Catherine T. MacArthur Foundation and the Rockefeller Foundation, Pew created the Energy Institute in 1991 to argue against use of fossil fuels. In 1998, it created the Pew Center on Global Climate Change whose director is former Clinton administration official Eileen Claussen, a twenty-year career employee at EPA. Within fours years of the Center's founding, Pew had pumped over $24 million into the project and persuaded the Turner Foundation, David and Lucile Packard Foundation, W. Alton Jones Foundation, and others to donate funds to it. Claussen's Center advocates Kyoto-like restrictions on the use of fossil fuels, using conferences, reports, and support for legislation such as the ill-fated McCain-Lieberman bill to curb greenhouse-gas emissions.

Here are a few of the environmental groups receiving Pew grants in recent years:

- Ducks Unlimited, 2000-2004, $25,300,000
- National Environmental Trust, 2000-2004, $20,500,000
- Earth Justice Legal Defense Fund, 2000-2004, $20,476,000
- Wilderness Society, 1998-2004, $2,596,400
- Trout Unlimited, 2000-2004, $2,312,000
- National Parks & Conservation Association, 2000-2004, $2,300,000
- Save Our Wild Salmon, 2000-2004, $2,250,000
- Sierra Club, Sierra Club Foundation, 1998-2004, $1,689,000
- Union of Concerned Scientists, 2000-2004, $1,100,000
- Conservation Law Fund, 2000-2004, $906,000
- Friends of the Earth, 1998-2004, 852,335
- Natural Resources Defense Council, 1999-2004, 830,247
- World Resources Institute, 2000-2004, $500,000
- Center for Marine Conservation, 2000-2004, $390,000
- National Religious Partnership for the Environment, 2000-2004, $320,000.

Pew also contributed $23,119,000 to the Tides Foundation and Tides Center between 2000 and 2004. Tides method of operation makes it all but impossible to determine where this money goes, which is how Tides and its donors want it.[23]

Nathan Cummings Foundation: Located in New York City, the foundation is named after Nathan Cummings (1896-1986), who turned a small tea and canned foods business in Baltimore into the giant Sara Lee Corporation. The foundation is dedicated to building "a socially and economically just society that values nature and protects the ecological balance for future generations." Lance Lindblom, its president and CEO, previously worked for George Soros's Open Society Institute. With assets of approximately $400 million, the foundation makes annual grants totaling around $15 million. Environmental groups receiving grants from the foundation in 2000-2003 include:

- Environmental Defense, $529,000
- Earth Island Institute, $474,500
- Wilderness Society, $275,000
- Sierra Club Foundation, $315,000
- Earth Justice Legal Defense Fund, $150,000
- Waterkeepers Alliance, $125,000
- Alliance for Sustainable Jobs and the Environment, $105,000
- Friends of the Earth, $100,000 [24]

Charles Stewart Mott Foundation: The distinctly blue-collar town of Flint, Michigan would seem an odd place for one of America's best-endowed foundations to call home. Charles Stewart Mott was a founder of General Motors, which is the basis of the foundation's wealth. But like the Ford Foundation, it has taken a decidedly anti-market left turn to the benefit of the environmental movement. Some of the recipients of Mott's largesse—NRDC, Sierra Club, Friends of the Earth— make little secret of their disdain for the automobile industry. Their attacks on cars, trucks, and the dreaded SUV for allegedly contributing to global warming are smiled upon by the Mott Foundation. Among the green groups receiving Mott grants in 2000-2004:

- Conservation Fund, $8,336,000
- Nature Conservancy, $5,807,800
- Friends of the Earth, $1,660,000
- World Resources Institute, $1,650,000
- National Wildlife Federation, $1,803,141
- Sierra Club Foundation, $1,234,000
- Alabama Rivers Alliance, $1,125,000
- American Rivers, $1,065,000
- Environmental Defense, $707,000
- Trout Unlimited, $574,000
- Earth Justice Legal Defense Fund, $530,000
- Conservation International/Conservation International Foundation, $480,000
- World Wildlife Fund, $331,000
- Natural Resources Defense Council, $300,000
- Worldwatch Institute, $300,000
- H. John Heinz Center for Science, Economics and the Environment, $200,000
- World Wildlife Fund, $171,000

John D. & Catherine T. MacArthur Foundation: Founded in 1978, the MacArthur Foundation, with over $4 billion in assets, ranks among America's ten largest philanthropies. From its Chicago headquarters

MacArthur dispenses nearly $200 million a year to leftist advocacy groups. Global in outlook, MacArthur has offices in Florida, India, Mexico, Brazil, Nigeria, and Russia. John MacArthur (1897-1978) was a high school dropout who made a fortune in the insurance business. MacArthur established the foundation shortly before his death but left no instructions on how the money was to be spent. As he told his lawyer, William Kirby, who helped him set up the foundation: "I figured out how to make the money. You fellows will have to figure out how to spend it."[25]

It's doubtful that MacArther would be pleased by his foundation. His son Rod urged the foundation to support leftist groups, including the ACLU, Institute for Policy Studies, Urban Institute, and the Tides Center. The foundation supports Friends of the Earth, Union of Concerned Scientists, and Environmental Defense. A favorite grantee is the Conservation International Foundation, which promotes climate change and biodiversity projects on four continents. Conservation International's board includes Harrison Ford, Queen Noor and movie mogul Barry Diller.

In 1974, John D. MacArthur referred to environmentalists as "bearded jerks" and "obstructionists" who "just throw rocks in your path." For the past two decades, his foundation has funded plenty of rocks. Environmental group grant recipients in 2000-2003 include:

- Conservation International/Conservation International Foundation, $60,370,000
- World Resources Institute, $735,000
- Environmental Law Institute, $680,000
- Nature Conservancy, $485,000
- National Wildlife Federation, $350,000
- Environmental Defense, $325,000
- Conservation Fund, $100,000

Rockefeller Foundation, Rockefeller Brothers Fund, Rockefeller Family Fund: The fortune amassed by John D. Rockefeller (1839-1937), founder of Standard Oil Company, is the stuff of legend. While the names of most of the 19th century Robber Barons are lost to public consciousness—Harriman and Gould come to mind—Rockefeller is still very much with us. The Rockefeller family over successive generations has been a powerful force in the world of philanthropy. Never opting for simplicity, the Rockefellers have devised many ways to support causes they favor. Together with his son, John D. Rockefeller, Jr., John D. Sr. established the Rockefeller Foundation in 1913. In 1940, John D. Rockefeller, Jr. and his six children set up the Rockefeller Brothers Fund. Yet another entity, the Rockefeller Family Fund, was incorporated in 1967 by the fourth generation of Rockefellers, the grandchildren of John D. Rockefeller, Jr.

Active for decades in medicine, education, and civil rights, the Rockefeller Foundation didn't get serious about funding environmental advocacy until the mid-1980s. One grantee, the Conservation Foundation, merged with the World Wildlife Fund (WWF) in 1990, enabling Rockefeller money to influence WWF's international agenda, including projects dealing with wildlife, wildlands, tropical forests, and climate change. By then, William Reilly, the former president of the Conservation Foundation, was head of the EPA (under President George H.W. Bush) and the chairman of the board of WWF was Russell Train, the EPA head during the Carter administration. Reilly and Train exemplify the well-oiled revolving door between government, foundations and activist groups. The Rockefeller foundations are old hands at networking in the world of the rich and powerful. Like Pew, Mott, and MacArthur, they know how to leverage their resources to maximum effect. The Rockefeller Foundation also has been a generous supporter of the Tides Center, donating over $3,300,000 to Drummond Pike's organization between 1998 and 2003.[26]

For decades, the Rockefeller Brothers Fund was a vehicle for the business and political interests of Laurance S. Rockefeller, a grandson of John D., Sr. and the brother of Nelson Rockefeller. "The Rockefeller Brothers Fund has been one of the two Mother Ships of the environmental movement for decades," Arnold and Gottlieb note, "the other being Laurance Rockefeller's American Conservation Association." The Rockefeller Brothers Fund has generously supported Greenpeace, Friends of the Earth, NRDC, the Sierra Club, Rainforest Action Network, and Environmental Media Service. The American Conservation Association, Laurance Rockefeller's other "Mother Ship," contributes to environmental groups and accepts funding from the Rockefeller Brothers Fund and the Jackson Hole Preserve, another Rockefeller philanthropy.

In one field of environmental advocacy, the Rockefellers were ahead of their time: They were pioneer proponents of depopulating and setting aside rural areas for the well-to-do. After World War II, Laurance Rockefeller spearheaded the family's investments in resort locations. As Ron Arnold explains it: "His clever deals—secretly buying up private land, donating it for national parks, and then getting the visitor concession—had built RockResorts, the family's for-profit hospitality industry empire, into a thriving venture." In buying private land and flipping it to the government, Laurance Rockefeller presaged some of the lucrative land deals later pulled off by the Nature Conservancy, another Rockefeller grant recipient.[27]

Interestingly, on the issue of genetically-modified (GM) crops the Rockefeller foundation empire parts company with substantial elements of the environmental movement. Greenpeace continue to rail against the use of GM crops, but the Rockefeller Foundation has teamed up with the U.S. Agency for International Development to promote agricultural biotechnology in famine-prone Sub-Saharan Africa. As part of the initiative, Monsanto, DuPont, Syngenta, and Dow Agribusiness will donate biotech seeds, patent rights, research tools and training in proper laboratory techniques to African scientists, relying on the new African Agriculture Technology Foundation in Kenya. It has received start-up funding from the Rockefeller Foundation.[28]

The Rockefeller Family Fund has its own unique finger in the environmental advocacy pie. It is the Environmental Grantmakers Association (EGA), an informal, unincorporated group of some two hundred foundations and several corporations that meet annually to set the agenda for, and dole out money to, environmental groups willing to follow its orders. The EGA was created in 1987 as little more than an extended bull session for foundation leaders comparing notes on each other's environmental programs. But one participant was Donald K. Ross, who in 1985 had become director of the Rockefeller Family Foundation. Under his auspices, the EGA grew steadily, adding new members. By the late 1990s, EGA members were collectively contributing half a billion dollars annually to environmental groups.

From the Fund's New York City offices, Ross coordinated EGA activities until he left the foundation in 1999. EGA annual meetings have become important strategy sessions for the environmental movement. Besides the Fund, other foundation kingpins are Pew, Cummings, and Blue Moon (formerly the W. Alton Jones Foundation) as well as the Bullitt Foundation (Seattle), Surdna Foundation (New York), Beldon Fund (Washington, D.C.), and the Joyce Foundation (Chicago). Companies belonging to the EGA include IBM and the leisure and sports clothiers L.L. Bean and Patagonia, Inc.[29]

The Rockefeller philanthropies are varied and not always altruistic. Early supporters of land conservation, they were late in coming to support environmental advocacy. But while they may stray on support for GM crops (and, earlier, on DDT use), they are pillars of support for modern environmentalism.

Environmental groups receiving grants from the Rockefeller Foundation in 2000-2003 include:

- Environmental Law Institute, $778,933
- Conservation Law Foundation, $770,000
- World Resources Institute, $717,138
- Resources for the Future, $459,884
- Nature Conservancy (Little Rock, Arkansas), $80,000

Environmental groups receiving support from the Rockefeller Brothers Fund:

- National Environmental Trust, 1997-2002, $1,950,000
- Friends of the Earth, 1994-2001, $1, 427,500
- Natural Resources Defense Council, 1991-2001, $1,377,510
- Environmental Defense, 1997-2001, $994,363
- Environmental Media Services, 1995-2001, $672,000
- Rainforest Action Network, 2000-2003, $600,000
- Greenpeace, 1997-2003, $780,000
- Sierra Club, 1995-2001, $710,000
- Earth Island Institute, 1995-2001, $562,400
- Environmental Working Group, 1990-2000, $560,000
- Wilderness Society, 1997-2000, $520,000

Blue Moon Fund: Founded in 1944 and known for over a half a century as the W. Alton Jones Foundation, the Charlottesville, Virginia-based Blue Moon Fund has combined an enthusiasm for all things environmental with a commitment to save the world from nuclear war. Its website explains:

The goals of the foundations are to—build a sustainable world by developing new ways for humanity to interact responsibly with the planet's ecological systems, and—build a secure world by eliminating the possibility of nuclear war and by providing alternative methods of resolving conflicts and promoting security.

W. Alton "Pete" Jones was a hard-driving oil man who in 1940 became president of Cities Service, the predecessor company to the CITGO Petroleum Corporation. But his lack of interest in environmentalism didn't keep his widow and children from pouring the wealth he created into an array of environmental causes. Deb Callahan, who later headed the League of Conservation Voters, was once the foundation's grassroots coordinator and helped make it synonymous with environmental grantmaking. As mentioned, John Peterson Myers, an author of *Our Stolen Future*, chairs Blue Moon's board, which explains why W. Alton Jones/Blue Moon doesn't shy away from contro-versy. Its very prescriptive environmental grants go to radical groups such as Greenpeace, NRDC, and the Rainforest Action Network.

Groups receiving Blue Moon Foundation grants in 2000-2003 included:

- Natural Resources Defense Council, $2,210,000
- National Environmental Trust, $900,000
- Friends of the Earth, $700,000
- Conservation International/Conservation International Foundation, $700,000
- Environmental Working Group, $495,000
- Union of Concerned Scientists, $481,500
- Environmental Defense, $400,000
- Greenpeace/Greenpeace USA, $390,000
- League of Conservation Voters Education Fund, $380,000
- Earth Justice Legal Defense Fund, $300,000
- National Religious Partnership for the Environment, $272,000
- American Lung Association, $260,000
- Nature Conservancy (Honolulu, Hawaii), $254,000
- American Lands Alliance, $245,000
- World Wildlife Fund, $285,000
- National Wildlife Federation, $200,000
- Clean Water Fund, $107,000
- Environmental Law Institute, $180,000
- Snake River Alliance, $135,000
- Rainforest Action Network, $90,000
- Ecology Center, Ecology Center, Inc., $80,000
- Earth Island Institute, $84,200
- Alaska Center for the Environment, $60,000

Richard King Mellon Foundation: The storied Mellon family of Pittsburgh owes its wealth to the business acumen of Andrew Mellon (1855-1937) whose creations included the Aluminum Company of America (Alcoa), Gulf Oil, and numerous mining, steel, and banking interests. Andrew Mellon was generous in philanthropy. An avid art collector, he gave his collection of Van Eyck, Rembrandt, Raphael, and Vermeer masterpieces to the U.S. government in 1937 and donated $15 million to build the National Gallery of Art, which opened in 1941, to house his paintings.

His nephew, Richard King Mellon oversaw many Mellon business interests but also continued the family's tradition of philanthropy. Established in 1947, the Pittsburgh-based foundation initially donated to hospitals, schools and other community-improvement projects in western Pennsylvania. Over time it developed an interest in cleaning up the grit and grime and pollution plaguing the "Steel City." Using his financial and political muscle, Mellon pushed to clean up Pittsburgh years before *Silent Spring* and the first Earth Day. As he put it: "We cannot get away from the fact that the very basis of our industrial society rests upon the environment in which we live."

We can only speculate about where Mellon's vision of the relation of industry to the environment might have led the foundation because he died in 1970. Within a few years, his widow Constance led the foundation down the path trod by Pew, MacArthur and Alton Jones. By 1977, 42 percent of the foundation's resources was going to purchase private land off-limits to development, and most of it went to the Nature Conservancy, which flourished under Mellon's patronage. In 1980, the foundation gave $15 million in initial funding for the Nature Conservancy's "Rivers of the Deep South" program, and in 1983 $25 million to launch its "National Wetlands Conservation Project," which aimed to identify "critical areas from the Atlantic coastal wetlands to the forests of Hawaii."

Mellon's focus was on what are known as land trusts. The Nature Conservancy and a host of groups of this type specialize in purchasing rural land, removing it from development or restricting its use, or selling (flipping) it to agencies of government—federal, state or local. Besides land trusts, Mellon has been a generous supporter of the Tides Center, which received $4,324,500 in 2000-2003.

Other environmental group recipients of Mellon grants in 2000-2003 include:

- Conservation Fund, $3,000,000
- Appalachian Mountain Club, $1,100,000
- American Farmland Trust, $1,000,000
- National Audubon Society, $610,000
- American Rivers, $200,000
- Izaak Walton League of America, $100,000
- Trout Unlimited, $100,000

The Heinz Foundations: The company founded by Henry John Heinz (1844-1919) made its name and money in pickles, not ketchup. Heinz was known as the "Pickle King" and he was a gifted marketer of processed foods, including pickles, vinegar, canned soups, and ketchup. The Pittsburgh-based H.J. Heinz Company became a global food giant, and the company stayed in the Heinz family for well over half a century before going public in 1969.

Like the Rockefellers, the Heinz family has not restricted its philanthropy to a single foundation. But the Howard Heinz Endowment,

Vira I. Heinz Endowment and Heinz Family Foundation have two things in common: they support environmental advocacy groups and Teresa Heinz Kerry, wife of Massachusetts Senator John Kerry, is a chairman or member of their board of trustees.

Born in Mozambique and educated in South Africa, Teresa Heinz, who changed her name to Teresa Heinz Kerry to help boost her husband's presidential ambitions, came to public attention during her husband's 2004 run for the White House. But for years the widow of Pennsylvania Republican Senator H. John Heinz III, who was killed in a freak helicopter-airplane collision in 1991, has been a force to be reckoned with. She is chairman of the board of the Heinz Family Foundation and the Howard Heinz Endowment and a member of the board of directors of the Vira. I. Heinz Endowment. Together they have over a billion dollars in assets and disburse tens of millions of dollars annually. Underscoring her unique role in deciding who gets what, Heinz Kerry once said, "I don't make money in my office. I give it away."[30]

Heinz Kerry donated $20 million in 1993 to create the H. John Heinz Center for Science, Economics and the Environment, a Washington, DC-based think tank that continues to receive Heinz grants. The environmental projects of the Tides Foundation also have benefited from grants from the Howard Heinz Endowment and the Vira I. Heinz Endowment. In 2001, Tides joined forces with the Heinz endowments to create the Pittsburgh-based Tides Center of Western Pennsylvania, which supports the 50,000-member Student Environmental Action Coalition (2200 chapters nationwide) and the Pennsylvania Energy Project II, which promotes "green" business. The Heinz foundations have given $3,009,500 to the Tides Center in 2000-2003. Interestingly, they also received money from the Tides Center for a "Pennsylvania Chemicals Partnership Project," which instructs chemical suppliers and customers in how to reduce their use of chemicals.[31]

Teresa Heinz Kerry's attempt to move to the White House with her husband relied on support from environmental advocacy groups that received support from the Heinz foundations. The Heinz Family Foundation contributed to the League of Conservation Voters (LCV), which endorsed John Kerry for president in January 2004, a time before the Iowa caucuses and the New Hampshire primary when Kerry's campaign appeared to be floundering. Kerry's campaign also received a boost from the LCV Action Fund, a so-called 527 group, which (under Section 527(h) of the U.S. Tax Code) can make independent expenditures on behalf of candidates. Kerry received $18,528 from the LCV Action Fund by late January. By mid-February, when the Kerry campaign had found its footing, LCV political director Mark Longabaugh acknowledged that his group had spent "six figures" on TV ads on Kerry's behalf.

Between 2000 and 2004, the Heinz foundations gave nearly $1 million to LCV, members of its board, and environmental groups those members represent, including Natural Resources Defense Council, Sierra Club, Environmental Defense, Earth Justice Legal Defense Fund, Wilderness Society, Trust for Public Land, National Wildlife Federation, Defenders of Wildlife, U.S. Public Research Group, and Environmental Working Group. All these groups are IRS tax exempt 501(c)(3) organizations often associated with 501(c)(4) lobbying groups, 527 political organizations, and other affiliated groups. Because money is fungible, it is not difficult to pass funds from 501(c)(3)s to 501(c)(4)s and to 527s with little regard for the legal niceties of campaign finance disclosure requirements. As a former Federal Election Commission official explained to the *Washington Post:*

"In the wake of the ban on party-raised soft money [McCain-Feingold law], evidence is mounting that money is slithering through on other routes as organizations maintain various accounts, tripping over each other, shifting money between 501(c)(3)'s, (c)(4)'s, and 527's...It's big money, and the pendulum has swung too far in their direction."[32]

A recognized mover and shaker in the world of environmental advocacy, Heinz Kerry was vice chair of Environmental Defense for 12 years. Environmental Defense is an advocacy group that has received nearly $2 million in grants from the Heinz Family Foundation and the Heinz Endowments since 1993. Green groups, including the Heinz Center, receiving donations from the Heinz Family Foundation, Howard Heinz Endowment, and the Vira I. Heinz Endowment in the years 2000-2003 include:

- H. John Heinz Center for Science, Economics and the Environment, $12,793,606
- Environmental Defense, $776,000
- Clean Water Action/Clean Water Fund, $497,000
- National Audubon Society (various offices), $290,000
- Chesapeake Bay Foundation, $135,000
- Wildlands Conservancy, $125,000
- Rocky Mountain Institute, $105,000
- Nature Conservancy, $100,000
- National Park & Conservation Association, $65,000
- Earth Force, $50,000

- American Farmland Trust, $40,000
- Allegheny Defense Project, $40,000
- Resources for the Future, $25,000

John Merck Fund: Boston-based Merck & Company is one of the world's largest pharmaceutical firms. While the company does battle with Pfizer and GlaxcoSmithKline, not to mention the Food and Drug Administration and the trial lawyers, its offspring, the John Merck Fund, channels money to liberal activist groups. From its headquarters on Beacon Street, the John Merck Fund, under leadership of former Conservation Law Foundation chairman Francis W. Hatch, has shown a special interest in environmental advocacy. The Merck Fund prefers to pre-select the groups it supports and discourages unsolicited applications. Often working closely with the Boston-based Jessie B. Cox Foundation, Merck has become a New England financial pillar of the environmental movement.

Environmental groups receiving 2000-2003 grants from the Merck Fund include:
- Clean Water Action, $903,000
- Tides Center, $829,500
- Natural Resources Defense Council, $665,000
- National Environmental Trust, $650,000
- Toxics Action Center, $249,000
- Izaak Walton League of America, $225,000
- Greenpeace/Greenpeace USA, $120,000
- Union of Concerned Scientists, $115,000
- Conservation Law Foundation, $85,000
- Sierra Club/Sierra Club Foundation, $60,000
- Appalachian Mountain Club, $60,000
- Friends of the Earth, $50,000
- Coalition for Environmentally Responsible Economies (CERES), $50,000
- National Wildlife Federation, $35,000
- National Audubon Society, $35,000
- Green Corps, $25,000
- Institute for Social Ecology, $25,000

Brainerd Foundation: Unlike Pew, Rockefeller, Mellon, and Heinz, which owe their existence to industrial-age money, the Brainerd Foundation is a child of the Age of Software. Computer wizard Paul Brainerd gave the world PageMaker, which launched desk-top publishing from the personal computer. His company, Aldus Corporation, was bought by Adobe Systems in 1994 for $525 million and

142

Brainerd pocketed about $120 million. He set up the Seattle-based Brainerd Foundation with $50 million.

A true believer in the nostrums of modern environmentalism, Brainerd has lavished funds on green groups, from the rich and powerful—Sierra Club, NRDC, Wilderness Society—to the lean and mean—Green Corps, Northwest Environmental Watch, and Earth Day Network. Paul Brainerd's activism owes much to the idea of the "alternative power structure" that Jarol Manheim has identified as the strategy guiding of the out-of-power elite. In 1997, for example, he founded a non-profit organization called Social Venture Partners. It is supposed to inspire fellow Microsoft Millionaires (to use Ron Arnold's term) to donate money to social causes to leverage their effectiveness in a way similar to a venture capitalist. Teaming up with the Bullitt Foundation, another Seattle grantmaker, Brainerd has used its software expertise to upgrade the computer capabilities of scores of environmental groups.

The Pacific Northwest has been the scene of many environmental battles that frequently pit largely urban elites against rural income earners whose jobs are in resource-based ranching, mining and logging. Brainerd and the Bullitt Foundation (endowed with old timber money later augmented by the King Broadcasting Company fortune), generously support activist groups on the urban side of the Northwest divide. Environmental groups, including the Tides Foundation and Tides Center, receiving donations from the Brainerd Foundation in recent years include:

- Sierra Club, $988,500, 1999-2003
- Northern Plains Resource Council, $667,500, 1996-2003
- Wilderness Society, $450,500, 1999-2005
- Oregon Natural Resources Council, $435,000, 1998-2002
- National Wildlife Federation, $236,050, 1998-2003
- Tides Foundation & Tides Center, $229,000, 2000-2005
- Western Organization of Resource Councils, $219,000, 1997-2003
- Environmental Media Services, $194,000, 1998-2003
- National Audubon Society, $129,000, 2000-2003
- League of Conservation Voters, $110,00, 2000-2004
- Greenpeace, $100,000, 2000-2001
- Green Corps, $73,000, 1999-2001
- Environmental Support Center, $70,000, 1998-2002
- Ecology Center, Inc., $60,000,2000-2003
- National Environmental Trust, $35,000, 2003
- Northwest Environmental Watch, $35,000, 1998-2000

- Consultative Group on Biological Diversity, $30,000, 1998-2000
- David Suzuki Center (Canada), $25,000, 2002
- Earth Day Network, $25,000, 1999
- Natural Resources Defense Council, $20,000, 1998
- World Wildlife Fund, $18,500, 2000-2003

Turner Foundation: No discussion of philanthropy to environmental advocacy groups can fail to mention the Turner Foundation. The creation of Ted Turner, the founder of CNN and Turner Broadcasting and former owner of the Atlanta Braves, the foundation was established in 1990 to distribute some of the flamboyant Georgian's vast wealth to his favorite causes. None is so dear to the outspoken "Mouth of the South" than environmentalism.[33]

The Turner Foundation is "committed to preventing damage to the natural systems—water, air, and land—on which all life depends." Ted Turner hired Peter Bahouth from Greenpeace USA to be its executive director, and the foundation began to fund an array of green groups including Greenpeace, the Ruckus Society and the Rainforest Action Network. What started off as a mere trickle of $582,700 in grants in 1991 became a flood: $69.7 million in grants in 2001, and over seventy percent went to environmental groups. Small wonder that Ted Turner was called "Daddy Greenbucks" by environmentalists. Turner, his five children, and his wife (now ex-wife) Jane Fonda served as foundation trustees.

In the late 1990s Turner established two more foundations. The Washington-based Better World Fund (now known as the Better World Campaign) has tried to drum up U.S. support for the United Nations, even to the point of taking credit for the Bush administration's 2003 decision to rejoin UNESCO (the UN Science, Education and Cultural Organization). The Reagan administration had pulled the U.S. out of UNESCO in 1984, citing mismanagement and concern about the organization's anti-democratic policies.. Even more intriguing is the Campaign's "Energy Future Coalition," which supports the use of "alternative fuels," which means anything other than coal, oil or natural gas. The Coalition vigorously promotes policies that support the Kyoto Protocol, including regulation of greenhouse-gas emissions. Representatives of Shell Oil, Goldman Sachs and the World Bank sit on the Coalition's advisory council. Among those who serve on the Coalition steering committee are Frances Beinecke of the Natural Resources Defense Council, Maggie Fox of the Sierra Club, Frank Lovejoy of the H. John Heinz Center for Science, Economics and the Environment, and former Colorado Senator Timothy Wirth.

Wirth also figures prominently in the other Turner creation, the

United Nations Foundation (UNF). In September 1997, Turner announced the establishment of the UNF, saying he would use the organization to contribute $1 billion to the UN over the next ten years. Wirth, who had been an international environmental official in the Clinton State Department after leaving the Senate, became UNF president. At the zenith of his personal wealth, Turner became the patron saint of the environmental movement and its indispensable global partner, the UN.

Turner thought he was now in a position to make things happen as his foundations proceeded to bankroll dozens of environmental groups. The League of Conservation Voters topped the list, taking in over $15 million in the Turner Foundation's first decade. NRDC, the Trust for Public Land, Defenders of Wildlife, National Wildlife Federation, Greenpeace, and the Conservation Fund all pocketed over $1 million in Turner Foundation donations during that period.

However, the good times didn't last. When Turner sold his media empire to Time Warner in 1996, he was paid in stock, which he held onto, even after Time Warner's disastrous merger with AOL in 2001. The value of AOL/Time Warner stock plummeted, as did Turner's fortune, which fell from $10 billion in 2000 to under $2 billion two years later. Turner's many beneficiaries soon felt the pinch. In 2003, the Turner Foundation, which has no endowment and whose wealth is tied to Turner's fortune, announced it would not accept new grant proposals until further notice. The $1 billion pledge to the UN also fell behind schedule, although Turner remains determined to fulfill it.

Turner is plotting his comeback. One vehicle, "Ted's Montana Grill," is a chain restaurant whose specialty is bison meat, much of it from the bevy of ranches Turner owns around the country. Turner is now in competition with California timber baron A.A. "Red" Emmerson to be America's biggest private landowner. He owns around 2 million acres of land on at least 14 ranches in seven states. His ranches raise bison, charge fees to hunters and fishermen to try their luck, and, no small irony, log trees. The same Ted Turner who, when the going was good, lavishly funded environmental groups with a long history of anti-ranching, anti-logging, anti-property rights activism, is himself a rancher, logger, and landowner.

Turner-funded environmental groups in the years 2000-2003, include:
- League of Conservation Voters/LCV Voter Education Fund, $16,657,126
- Natural Resources Defense Council, $2,645,000

- National Wildlife Federation, $1,275,000
- Greenpeace/Greenpeace USA, $1,050,000
- Tides Foundation/Center, $810,000
- U.S. Public Interest Research Group, $810,000
- Defenders of Wildlife, $807,000
- Conservation Fund, $800,000
- Trust for Public Land, $790,000
- Sierra Club/Sierra Club Foundation, $715,000
- Izaak Walton League of America, $635,000
- Green Cross International/USA, $620,000
- Nature Conservancy, $600,000
- National Parks & Conservation Association, $510,000
- Earth Island Institute, $505,000
- Global Green USA, $425,000
- Bluewater Network, $390,000
- Ducks Unlimited, $365,000
- WorldWatch Institute, $330,000
- Earth Justice Legal Defense Fund, $315,873
- Alliance for the Wild Rockies, $305,000
- National Environmental Trust, $300,000
- Wilderness Society $280,000
- Rocky Mountain Institute, $260,000
- Environmental Defense, $253,875
- Environmental Working Group, $225,000
- American Lands/American Lands Alliance, $220,000
- Center for Biological Diversity, $200,000
- Heinz Center for Science, Economics and the Environment, $200,000
- Keystone Center, $200,000
- Friends of the Earth, $198,000
- National Audubon Society, including local chapters, $190,000
- American Rivers, $120,000
- American Farmland Trust, $115,000
- National Forests Protection Alliance, $105,000
- Western Organization of Resource Councils, $105,000
- World Wildlife Fund, $100,000
- Conservation International/Foundation, $100,000
- Colorado Environmental Council, $90,000
- Rainforest Action Network, $80,000
- Alabama Rivers Alliance, $80,000
- World Resources Institute, $75,000
- Trout Unlimited, $75,000

- Waterkeeper Alliance, $70,000
- Montana Environmental Information Center, $65,000
- Union of Concerned Scientists, $50,000
- American Wildlands, $50,000
- Rainforest Alliance, $45,000
- Alternative Energy Resources Organization, $40,000
- Wildlife Forever, $30,000
- Save Our Wild Salmon, $20,000
- Clean Water Alliance, $15,000
- American Lung Association, $11,000

Energy Foundation: Founded in 1991 with $20 million in grants from the Pew Charitable Trusts, the Rockfeller Foundation, and the John D. and Catherine T. MacArthur Foundation, the San Francisco-based Energy Foundation is the creation of Hal Harvey, an activist for alternative energy. Earlier, Harvey spent three years at the Rocky Mountain Institute. There he was under the tutelage of the flamboyant Amory Lovins, an enthusiastic advocate of renewable fuels. Lovins sees "soft energy" as the wave of the future and believes in increased use of renewable energy—solar, wind, and biomass. To those who doubt the potential of renewable energy, Lovins has this to say: "The role of government is to steer the boat, not to row it—that is the job of business and others."[34]

Harvey's enthusiasm for alternative energy and government dictation inspires the Energy Foundation, a grant recipient (it also has received grants from the McKnight Foundation, the Joyce-Mertz-Gilmore Foundation, and David and Lucile Packard Foundation) that is a grant-maker to environmental groups that promote tighter government fuel efficiency standards for everything from home appliances to Corporate Average Fuel Economy (CAFE) regulations for automobiles.

Not surprisingly, the foundation's focus on energy has embroiled it in the subject of global warming. In 2002, the Energy Foundation, now under the leadership of Eric Heitz, helped create the official-sounding National Commission on Energy Policy (NCEP). NCEP is actually an advocacy organization funded by the Energy Foundation, Pew Charitable Trusts, David and Lucile Packard Foundation, John D. and Catherine T. MacArthur Foundation, and the William and Flora Hewlett Foundation (where Harvey is currently environmental program director). NCEP claims to promote "market-based" approaches to energy efficiency—as long as they are confined by a rigid regulatory structure. On climate change, for example, NCEP calls for the creation of a "greenhouse gas emissions trading program" under which the federal government will issue permits to companies before they are allowed to emit carbon dioxide or other greenhouse gases.

The Natural Resources Defense Council and Environmental Defense, both ardent supporters of Kyoto-style restrictions on energy use, have been primary recipients of Energy Foundation grants. Other grantees in the years 2000-2004 include:

- Natural Resources Defense Council, $3,678,348
- Environmental Defense, $2,312,923
- National Environmental Trust, $1,200,000
- Izaak Walton League of America, $550,000
- Conservation Law Foundation, $435,000
- American Lung Association, $387,000
- Tides Center, $375,000
- Union of Concerned Scientists, $350,000
- Rocky Mountain Institute, $302,000

There are many other major grantmaking foundations that support environmental advocacy groups, including the Ford Foundation, Surdna Foundation, Joyce Foundation, and the Winslow Foundation. They provide the life-blood of environmental activism and give green groups the visibility to be taken seriously in politics. The key foundation heads— Drummond Pike, Teresa Heinz Kerry, Ted Turner, Paul Brainerd, Francis W. Hatch, John Peterson Myers—are themselves ardent environmental activists, albeit ones with big checkbooks. Tapping this source of abundant wealth may be the greatest achievement of the American environmental movement.

Some environmental activists complain that the strings attached to the foundation grants have reduced their independence. They resent the carefully prescribed grants of the Environmental Grantmakers Association and the Pew Trusts. But they take the money, which shows that they regard these arrangements as the price of doing business.

Taxpayer Funding

While foundation grants, individual and corporate contributions and membership dues account for most of the money going to environmental groups, green activists have found another generous funding source: the American taxpayer. EPA grant programs and, to a lesser extent, those at the Departments of Interior and Energy have been a happy hunting ground for environmental advocacy groups who have figured out how to play the game. For EPA grants, this boils down to submitting a proposal with all the right buzz words, getting the grant approved, carrying out the conditions of the grant to the EPA grant officer's satisfaction and, as a now familiar face, submitting another grant proposal.

Each year, EPA awards about half of its annual budget—about $4 billion—in grants. This supports annually between seven and eight thousand grants or grant-related actions. EPA grants can be non-discretionary or discretionary. Non-discretionary grants typically go to state, local, and tribal governments for projects to improve environmental infrastructure. EPA awards discretionary grants to non-profits, universities, and government entities, and many of these discretionary grants find their way into the eager hands of environmental groups.[35]

In recent years, EPA grants management of discretionary grants has come under investigation by the Government Accountability Office (GAO), EPA's Office of Inspector General (OIG), and congressional oversight committees. They have focused their attention on EPA's practice of awarding non-competitive, non-solicited grants time and again to the same non-profits. The sometimes cozy relationship between EPA grant officers and certain recurring recipients of EPA grants was highlighted in an August 2003 GAO report:

> According to a 2001 EPA Inspector General report, program officials indicated that widespread solicitation was not necessary because 'word gets out' to eligible applicants. Applicants often send their proposals to these program directly to these program officials, who funded them using 'uniquely qualified' as the justification of a non-competitive award. This procedure created the appearance of preferential treatment by not offering the same opportunity to all potential applicants"

Testifying before the Senate Environment and Public Works Committee in March 2004, EPA assistant inspector general Melissa Heist described her investigation of the agency's procedures: "We found Agency managers continued to use the same grantees year after year and there has not been a lot of competition."

Heist's testimony identified five areas of concern:
- No link between funded projects and EPA mission,
- no assessment of probability of success,
- no demonstration of the reasonableness of the cost of the grant,
- no measurable environmental outcomes, and
- no deliverables in grant work plans.[36]

Heist gave the committee the OIG audit of five selected EPA grants totaling $4,714,638 to the Consumers Federation of America in 1996-2004. It concluded:

> Therefore, although EPA funds were awarded to a 501(c)(3) organization, in actuality, a 501(c)(4) lobbying organization performed the work and ultimately received the funds. This arrangement clearly violates the Lobbying Disclosure Act prohibition on a 501(c)(4) organization which engages in lobbying from receiving federal funds.
>
> In summary, the [Consumer Federation of America], a 501(c)(4) organization: (1) performed direct lobbying of Congress, and (2) received Federal funds contrary to the Lobbying Disclosure Act. Consequently, all the costs claimed and paid under the agreements are statutorily unallowable.[37]

EPA grants to non-profits vary in size—from well over $1 million to less than $3,000—and they are awarded to a kaleidoscope of groups—from the Girl Scouts of the Black Hills Council and the Michigan Small Business Association to Jesus People Against Pollution and the Natural Resources Defense Council. Unlike EPA non-discretionary grants, which generally fund infrastructure projects such as a water-purification facility, the discretionary grants to non-profits can easily be abused by funding programs with a political purpose. The Consumer Federation of America, for instance, had legally separate affiliates, each with a different tax status, but existing under one roof. Similarly structured green groups, and there are many, augment their income with government grants, enhancing their political clout

Moreover, the express purpose of these grants is often couched in language so vague that even an appropriately targeted recipient can do much as it pleases. In August 2002, EPA's Office of Prevention, Pesticides, and Toxic Substances awarded a three-year, $332,304 grant to the Children's Environmental Health Network (CEHN). Its stated purpose: "to increase the scientific information on children's health to CEHN and other non-governmental organizations." Like other EPA grants to CEHN (there were three others at the time), the grant was awarded without competition from other applicants. The GAO suspected EPA "preferential treatment" to grantees could well apply to CEHN. After all, Lynn Goldman, the chairman of CEHN's board of directors, headed EPA's Office of Prevention, Pesticides, and Toxic Substances in the Clinton administration from 1993 to 1999. She was a familiar face around the office. And what sort of "scientific information" on children's health would CEHN disseminate? The group's website provided a clue.

There one might read the "Children's Environmental Health Bush Administration Report Card," which gave the administration a grade of "F" for failing to protect children.

EPA also rewarded programs suggested by the litigious Natural Resources Defense Council. It received over $6.5 million in EPA grants from 1993 to 2004. A grant of $1,198,193 from EPA's Office of Air and Radiation for the period January 2002-December 2004 went for "Development of Long-Term Adoption of Energy-Efficient Products and Services, To work within the energy-efficiency and manufacturing community toward long-term market transformation of energy-efficient technologies and practices." It also was awarded without competition from other applicants and approved as a proposal submitted by NRDC.[39]

NRDC's appetite for federal grants does not keep it from biting the hand that feeds it. The self-described litigation arm of the environmental movement sues the government on everything from endangered species to climate change. In 2001-2002, NRDC sued the federal government ten times. But during the same period, it received no less than $1,591,570 in grants from EPA alone.[40]

Prodded by House and Senate oversight committees, EPA pledged to tighten its monitoring of grantees and introduce more competition for grants of $75,000 or more. The agency even has initiated a five-year plan to improve its grants management. However, observers of the EPA consider it a cumbersome, insular bureaucracy where accountability to outside authorities has never had high priority. Absent radical change to EPA's culture, its most familiar grantees are likely to retain their preferential treatment in future grant applications. And American taxpayers will continue to subsidize the already well-funded environmental movement.[41]

Selected environmental groups receiving EPA grants (2000-2004) include:
- American Lung Association, 72 grants, $8,732,146
- Nature Conservancy, 37 grants, $4,746,042
- American Farmland Trust, 7 grants, $3,768,090
- Natural Resources Defense Council, 13 grants, $3,931,117
- Environmental Law Institute, 14 grants, $3,255,220
- World Resources Institute, 11 grants, $2,8832,134
- National Audubon Society, including state and local chapters, 10 grants, $2,131,124
- Environmental Defense, 12 grants, $1,870,695
- Hudson River Foundation, 7 grants, $1,705,574
- Tides Foundation/Center, 11 grants, $947,822
- Izaak Walton League, 4 grants, $425,298

- National Wildlife Federation, 9 grants, $292,620
- Oregon Environmental Council, 4 grants, $218,000
- Conservation Fund, 4 grants, $231,805
- Conservation Law Foundation, 1 grant, $137,791
- Sierra Club/Sierra Club Foundation, 3 grants, $87,129
- Trust for Public Land, 2 grants, $80,000
- Friends of the Earth, 2 grants, $70,000
- World Wildlife Fund, 2 grants, $51,074
- Conservation Biology Institute, 1 grant, $40,000
- Rocky Mountain Institute, 2 grants, $40,000 [42]

"Nature's Real Estate Agent"

"I really believe that in the next century the most influential institutions on the planet will be nongovernmental organizations," declared Steven J. McCormick, president of the Nature Conservancy, at his organization's 50th anniversary meeting in October 2001. "I believe the Nature Conservancy will set that pattern."[43]

McCormick had good reason to be upbeat. The Arlington, Virginia-based Nature Conservancy is the world's richest environmental organization, with over $3.3 billion in assets, 3,200 employees, and operations in over 500 offices in every state and in thirty countries. It manages seven million acres of land of which it owns two million outright. Much of the land is held in 1,400 nature preserves, "the world's largest private sanctuary system."[44]

The Conservancy cultivates an image of civility and moderation. It shuns the antics of Greenpeace and the Ruckus Society and the overblown rhetoric of NRDC and the Environmental Working Group. It hovers above the fray, dedicated to only the noblest of goals. That air of gentility buttresses a once-sterling reputation. Its mission statement: "To preserve the plants, animals and natural communities that represent the diversity of life on Earth by protecting the lands and waters they need to survive."

Called "nature's real estate agent," the Nature Conservancy has been a magnet for donations from individuals, foundations, and corporations. Many of its 1,900 corporate sponsors are drawn from the Fortune 500 list, and many of these do not have cordial relations with other environmental organizations. ExxonMobil, Georgia-Pacific, General Electric, Southern Company, Philip Morris, General Motors, and American Electric Power are some of the corporate giants that have supported the Conservancy. Corporate CEOs serve on the

Conservancy's Board of Governors, and some pay $25,000 annually to take a seat on the group's International Leadership Council.

The ties between the Nature Conservancy and companies regularly branded as "polluters" by other environmental groups have sowed suspicion among some green activists. They suspect that the well-heeled group is selling out. "The Conservancy brings in board members who don't know much about conservation—or even care much about it," says Huey Johnson, former head of the Conservancy's western U.S. operations and founder of the Trust for Public Lands.

"Some of our brethren say we're dealing with the devil," counters Conservancy official Michael Horak. "Some of the deals we're making are quite extraordinary." Horak is not exaggerating; the Nature Conservancy's deals are in a class by themselves. And that's the problem.

In a series of articles in the *Washington Post* beginning in May 2003, reporters David Ottaway and Joe Stephens uncovered longstanding patterns of Conservancy mismanagement and abuse. Entitled "Big Green," the series triggered a Senate Finance Committee probe and an IRS "in-house" audit of the group. The revelations contained in the *Post* articles were stunning:

• The Conservancy repeatedly bought scenic properties, added development restrictions known as "conservation easements," and then resold the land at reduced prices to Conservancy trustees and donors. Buyers, some of whom were permitted under the easements to build homes on the property, then gave the Conservancy cash donations at roughly the amount of the discount. The donations were eligible for substantial federal income tax deductions. To the Conservancy, these transactions were known as "conservation buyer" deals.

• An audit report of the Conservancy-run Virginia Coast Reserve (VCR) found the project was debt-ridden and there were accounting problems and violations of IRS regulations. The Conservancy had hired a Virginia farmer to oversee leases on the property but paid his wife. The report explained: "VCR negotiated [the employment contract] in the farmer's wife's name and issued an IRS Form 1099 [which reports miscellaneous income to the IRS] in her name and social [security] number even though her husband performed all of the work under the contract. VCR wrote the contract in the wife's name so that the farmer could hide personal income."[45]

• On its nature preserve near Texas City, Texas, the Conservancy drilled for oil and natural gas under the nesting place of the Attwater's prairie chicken, one of the most endangered species. Drilling for oil and gas on nature preserves need not be incompatible with wildlife conservation, as the Audubon Society's decades-long experience on its Rainey Wildlife Sanctuary in Louisiana shows. However, the prairie chicken did not fare well under Conservancy stewardship. For instance, captive-bred birds scheduled for release in mid-summer were not set free on the preserve until November because a natural gas pipeline was uncompleted. The delay in their release made them prey for falcons returning to the area in the winter. Another group set to be introduced to the flock drowned because their holding pen was located in flooded area.[46]

The Conservancy's oil and gas drilling caused other problems on the preserve. While the Conservancy owned drilling rights in the preserve's south tract it shared the north tract rights with the Russell Sage Foundation and 39 other private investors. In summer 1999 the Conservancy drilled a well on the south tract that slanted northward. It tapped into a giant deposit of natural gas that lay under both tracts. The Conservancy removed the gas but failed to notify its co-owners that it was selling gas that also belonged to them. It did, however, have Texas oilman J.L. "Jack" Schneider write to the Russell Sage Foundation and offer to purchase its mineral rights, worth millions, for $26,176. The Sage Foundation had a consultant evaluate the offer. The consultant concluded, according to the *Post*, "that Schneider was fronting for the Conservancy; that the preserve's mineral rights were worth millions; and that the Conservancy had already begun draining the foundation's natural gas." In subsequent litigation, the Conservancy reached a $10 million settlement with the aggrieved parties.

An internal Conservancy audit obtained by the Senate Finance Committee described the attempted purchase of the Sage Foundation mineral rights as a "patently deceptive offer." "Were the events that transpired at the Preserve to become public knowledge, the Conservancy's good reputation could be badly damaged."[47]

• In 2001, the Conservancy acquired 215 acres of rare open sandplain on Martha's Vineyard for $64 million. The deal was part of its much-heralded campaign to save earth's "Last Great Places." However, the Conservancy only put development restrictions on half the land. It resold the other half to those who could afford Martha's Vineyard's sky-high prices. The *Post* reporters observed that this paved "the way for Gatsbyesque vacation houses on pristine beach and grasslands. Those buyers included a pair of Oracle software tycoons, a retired Goldman Sachs executive and comedian David Letterman."[48]

• In February 2001, the Conservancy hired Steven J. McCormick as its new president and reported to the Better Business Bureau that his compensation was $275,000 plus health and retirement benefits. Under the *Post* reporters prodding, it admitted that the compensation was

$420,000 and it gave McCormick a $1.55 million loan to help him buy a $1.7 million home in the McLean, Virginia, an upscale Washington, D.C. suburb. The loan's interest rate was 4.59 percent, well below the market rate and well below the 7-percent rate it originally reported to the *Post*. The loan was repaid after details of the transaction were published. Besides McCormick, twelve other Conservancy employees received home loans and five were charged no interest. The Conservancy's California director, Graham Chisholm, received a no-interest $500,000 mortgage.[49]

As the *Post* investigation intensified, the Nature Conservancy hunkered down. An internal Conservancy memo obtained by the newspaper attests the seriousness of the revelations and the remarkable self-awareness of Conservancy officials. The memo notes that the organization might be described as an "environmental Enron" and could be depicted as having "systematically colluded with wealthy individuals and corporations to conduct land transactions that manipulate the tax code to the benefit of the affluent."[50]

Ten years earlier, Arnold and Gottlieb shrewdly observed that the Nature Conservancy was "more interested in deals than ideals." Indeed.

The Martha's Vineyard real estate deal, for instance, was but a repeat of the Conservancy's earlier creation of the Virginia Coast Reserve. Helping the farmer hide income by paying his wife was only part of the story. Between 1970 and the mid-1980s, the Conservancy, working with surrogate buyers and assisted by donations from the Mary Flagler Cary Charitable Trust, acquired 14 of the 18 barrier islands on the coast of Virginia's Delmarva Peninsula. What came to be called the Virginia Coastal Reserve contains 45,000 acres on a 60-mile stretch of the state's eastern shore. Once it possessed the property, the Conservancy stopped development on the islands except for its own vacation homes and condominiums.

Similarly, the two grants for $40 million awarded by the Richard King Mellon Foundation to the Conservancy in the early 1980s were not born of altruism. Working for the most part behind the scenes, Mellon helped the Conservancy acquire additional property on the Virginia mainland opposite the barrier islands. The buyer was the Allegheny Duck Club, a partnership of Seward Prosser Mellon and Richard P. Mellon, chairman and president of the foundation, and their sister, Constance Mellon Brown. Through surrogates, the Allegheny Duck Club began to buy up 12,000 acres. In December 1985, the Conservancy announced that it had signed a contract with the Club to obtain property along a 100-mile stretch from the Atlantic Ocean to the

Chesapeake Bay. Local residents were confronted by the takeover of their communities by wealthy outsiders.[51]

The upshot? In the 1990s, the Conservancy launched a series of for-profit ventures designed to convince the local population that small businesses and the environment could flourish. The brain-child of Conservancy president John C. Sawhill and acting president W. William Weeks, the "flagship" projects included a sweet potato-chip company, an oyster and clam operation, arts and crafts, "eco-friendly" seaside farms, and the conversion of an abandoned Coast Guard station to an inn. However, the Conservancy-created Eastern Shore Corporation, designated to oversee the ambitious projects, was soon awash in red ink as one after another business failed.[52]

A post-mortem audit report by the Ford Foundation, one of the project's unfortunate investors, was unsparing in its criticism of the Conservancy's management of the business ventures. The Eastern Shore Corporation proceeded with a "flawed concept," "flawed business plan," and "flawed execution." It was "more of an intruder than a catalyst for local action," the report noted, and the Conservancy's attempt to go into business was "the story of a fish out of water."

Stephen McCormick had to explain the Conservancy's well-documented misdeeds to members of the Senate Finance Committee at a hearing in June 2005. He acknowledged that his group "got a little outside our own headlights," but assured the committee, "our mission compels us to come up with additional core competencies."[53] This was as close to a *mea culpa* as the senators would get.

Founded in 1951, the Nature Conservancy is descended from two groups, the Ecological Society of America (1917) and its off-shoot, the Ecological Union (1946). During its first two decades the Conservancy did practice private conservation on sites across the country. It did not accept government money and it did not sell its properties to government. The Conservancy was determined to "stay private and buy preserves with private funds."

But that began to change in the early 1970s under the guiding hand of Patrick Noonan, who remain Conservancy president until 1980. He shrewdly used Mellon money and the growing public awareness of the environmental cause to create a multi-billion dollar real estate empire. Increasingly, the Conservancy bought private land under the pretext of preservation and then "flipped" it to empire-building government agencies. A 1994 GAO report, "Land Acquisitions by Nonprofit Organizations," uncovered a case in which the Conservancy sold land that had been donated to it to the U.S. Forest Service for over $1 million.

After expenses, the profit was calculated at $877,000. Ron Arnold has rightly called the Nature Conservancy "a conduit for the nationalization of private land" and journalist Warren Brookes once observed that so-called land trusts like the Nature Conservancy were "rapidly becoming nothing more than government advance men and land agents, aggressively purchasing private property not to preserve, but simply to resell to agencies with whom it develops symbiotic relationships."[54]

In 1996 the Conservancy pocketed nearly $38 million in sales of private land to federal, state and local governments. In 2000 it purchased the giant 100,000-acre Baca Ranch in Colorado and sold the property to the U.S. Park Service to help create the Great Sand Dunes National Park. According to the *Washington Post*, the Conservancy by the early 2000s was taking in over $100 million annually from government consulting fees and other payments.[55]

The Nature Conservancy, like the rest of the environmental movement, has come a long way. From humble beginnings as a traditional conservation organization, it has evolved into a high-rolling, inside-dealing, land-flipping mockery of itself. It is now a fitting symbol for the movement overall. Wealth and power are the breeding ground for misdeeds, particularly when those who wield it are convinced of the righteousness of their cause. Endowed with the financial resources and ideological commitment that have enabled it to take over and transform a host of institutions, the movement leaves its impact on all it touches.

Chapter 5

THE GREEN COUNTER-ESTABLISHMENT: HOW IT HOLDS POWER

"Fanaticism consists in redoubling your efforts when you have forgotten your aim."[1]

GEORGE SANTAYANA

The Nature Conservancy, the Sierra Club, the Audubon Society, and the National Wildlife Federation are examples of traditional conservation organizations that underwent a radical transformation during the rise of modern environmentalism. On the other hand, Greenpeace, NRDC, the Environmental Working Group, the Center for Biological Diversity, and the Rainforest Action Network are examples of groups that came of age after the first Earth Day. What both groups have in common is that they recognize the importance of money—and lots of it—to achieve their ends. Whether through land deals, foundation grants, government funding, individual contributions or membership dues, the big environmental groups have found a way to stay big and rich.

The movement has put in place the "alternative power structure" that Joshua Mailman and his colleagues a quarter-century ago shrewdly identified as the necessary prerequisite for the Left's ability to do battle with the capitalist system it seeks to transform. This parallel universe of interlocking relationships and mutually reinforcing political agendas, so compellingly depicted by Jarol Manheim and Ron Arnold, is not just about money, however. Money can grease the skids, buy advertising, hire staff, print books, fund demonstrations, and finance studies. But to transform society, you have to change the way people think. Or, to speak in the language of latter-day students of Hegel, Marx and Gramsci, you have to alter consciousness. The neo-Marxist Antonio Gramsci understood this better than anyone. Whether the leaders and the foot soldiers of the environmental movement know it or not, they are executing Gramsci's battle plan superbly.

According to Gramsci, a dominant group in a modern society does not exercise control solely by coercion and brute force; it has what Gramsci called "hegemony." The concept of hegemony, as explained by philosopher Steven Yates, means "the pervasive and mostly tacit use of a system of values that supports and reinforces the interests of the dominant group. The repressed groups may not even know they are repressed, in Gramsci's view, because they have internalized the system of values that justifies their repression. They have internalized a 'false consciousness' and become unwitting participants in their own domination."

Gramsci argued that because people in modern capitalist societies are captive to a false consciousness, the only way to overcome it is to create a "counter-hegemony" of new values. These new values, which today include environmentalism, would undermine and delegitimize the prevailing ideas and institutions of the capitalist hegemony. Yates elaborates:

"And because hegemonic values permeate the whole of society and are embodied in the warp and woof of daily life, daily life becomes part of the ideological background. All the institutions we take for granted—schools, churches, the media, businesses, as well as art, literature, philosophy, and so on— become places where the "counter-hegemonic" values can be seeded and allowed to take root. They become domains to be infiltrated, and brought into the service of the movement."[2]

The environmental movement has succeeded in building an alternative power structure that has enabled it to infiltrate and transform existing institutions and where its counter-hegemonic values have taken root. The green counter-hegemony takes many forms. We saw it, for example, in the predisposition among some in the media and in the scientific community to attribute problems afflicting certain frog species in California and Minnesota to human-induced pollution.

It was also evident in the way many opinion-makers were certain that the severe Atlantic hurricane seasons of 2004 and 2005 were caused by anthropogenic global warming. "Such warmer waters fuel the formation and ferocity of hurricanes," the *Baltimore Sun* assured its readers in an editorial the day after Katrina struck the U.S. Gulf coast. "Warmer oceans are an inseparable by-product of global warming, and it's foolish to ignore the link to the burning of fossil fuels."

In its post-Katrina coverage, the *Washington Post* left unchallenged a statement by Kevin Trenberth of the nonprofit National Center for Atmospheric Research (NCAR). "There's a clear signature of global warming in [Katrina]," Trenberth said. "While it's not the dominant factor, in some things it becomes the straw that breaks the camel's back." What "clear signal"? Which "straw"? These are left unexplained. The *Post* also neglected to point out that Trenberth's organization, NCAR, is a purveyor of global warming alarmism.[3]

While no one expects an editorial writer to be well-versed in the subject of hurricanes, the *Suns's* willingness to make such blanket cause-and-effect statements with no supporting data speaks to the mind-set that has taken hold in public opinion—and that demonstrates the power of the green counter-hegemony. In the same vein, the *Post* printed Trenberth's musings without presenting contrasting views. Both papers ignored findings by the National Hurricane Center showing that, over the past 100 years, it was the decade of the 1940s which had the greatest number of hurricanes making landfall in the U.S. Indeed, James J. O'Brien, director of the Center for Ocean Atmospheric Prediction Studies at Florida State University, attributes swings in Atlantic hurricane activity to natural 25-to-40-year cycles driven by fluctuations in ocean circulation. The finer points of climatology aside, the issue here is the almost reflexive reaction on the part of some in the media to see things—like "60 Minutes" saw in Alar—just as environmental activists want them to be seen.[4]

"Nothing is Sacred"

The counter-hegemony also prevails now in many of the nation's houses of worship, where it gives new meaning to the phrase "Nothing is sacred." In late 2002, the Evangelical Environmental Network (EEN) launched a high-profile anti-SUV advertising campaign asking: "What Would Jesus Drive?" "As our Savior and Lord Jesus Christ teaches us," one ad read, "'Love your neighbor as yourself' (Mark: 12:31). Of all the choices we make, as consumers, the cars we drive have the single biggest impact on all of God's creation."

This bit of tastelessness coincided with Arianna Huffington's anti-SUV campaign. The syndicated columnist and Hollywood maven made the outrageous claim that owning a SUV helps the cause of terrorism because it makes America dependent on Middle East oil. Both the Huffington and the EEN campaigns used the formidable fear-mongering skills of Fenton Communications. This is the left-leaning Washington PR firm that, as we have seen, has stirred the pot with scare campaigns targeting children's toys, plastic medical devices, Alar, and endocrine disrupters—just to name a few. Indeed, in the "What Would Jesus Drive?" campaign, a Fenton news release boasted: "Here's how we did it." Fenton estimated that it turned EEN's $70,000 investment into $3 to $4 million in free publicity, including 1,900 articles and extensive coverage on network television news shows.[5]

Is it far-fetched to link environmentalist doomsaying to a biblical Day of Reckoning, or to tie the green fixation on healthy "ecosystems" to the Bible's injunction to care for God's creation? Not for a movement that pushes the envelope in rhetorical excess. Moreover, some aspects of Catholic social thought and the Protestant "social gospel" lend themselves to the environmentalist cause. Many politically-active members of the clergy are eager to embrace it.

On June 15, 2001, the nation's Catholic bishops unanimously approved a statement urging as a "moral imperative" taking action to end global warming. "At its core, global climate change is not about economic theory nor political platforms, nor about partisan advantage or interest group pressures," said the bishops' statement. "It is about the future of God's creation, and the one human family." Several days before, the Greater Boston Coalition on the Environment and Jewish Life released a letter signed by 19 local leaders, which said that the Bush administration's energy plan "does not yet meet biblical standards for stewardship and justice." It called on Jewish communities to "raise awareness of how fossil fuel use contributes to global warming." Earlier in the month, a coalition of Protestant and Orthodox Christian leaders released a letter in New York City warning that "by depleting energy sources, causing global warming, fouling the air with pollution, and poisoning the land with radioactive waste, a policy of increased reliance on fossil fuels and nuclear power jeopardizes health and well-being for life on Earth."[6]

These three statements, released shortly after President Bush's rejection of the Kyoto Protocol, show how many churches and synagogues have positioned themselves in environmental debate. Their outlook is an outgrowth of the National Religious Partnership for the Environment (NRPE), founded in 1993, an alliance of the U.S. Conference of Catholic Bishops and the National Council of Churches, along with EEN (an affiliate of Evangelicals for Social Action) and the Coalition on the Environment and Jewish Life. NRPE activities have been coordinated from the group's inception by its longtime executive director, Paul Gorman, a former vice president for public affairs and advocacy at the Episcopal Cathedral of St. John the Divine in New York. Described by the Acton Institute for the Study of Religion and Liberty as a "mecca for new age, ecological thought since the 1970s," the Cathedral provided a wealth of experience and contacts for Gorman to take to NRPE.[7]

NRPE's first major undertaking was a three-year, $4.5 million campaign to distribute "education and action kits" to over 100,000 U.S. congregations. Funded by grants from the Washington-based National Environmental Trust (NET), the project also distributed prayers to worshipers. These were drawn not from the Old or New Testaments but from materials based on the Gaia Hypothesis. Gaia is a maternal earth goddess in Greek mythology, and the Gaia Hypothesis regards earth as a superorganism, both living and divine. Contrived by British atmospheric scientist James Lovelock and Lynn Margulis (wife of the late astronomer Carl Sagan), the hypothesis helps to suffuse environmentalism with a quasi-religious aura of pagan nature worship.

One NRPE prayer that was distributed to congregations resolved that "We must say, do and be everything possible to realize the goal of the environmental Sabbath: an ecological society...We cannot let our mother die. We must love and replenish her." Another prayer, taken from the Iroquois, delivers a similar same message: "We return thanks to our mother, the earth which sustains us. We return thanks to all the herbs, which furnish medicines for the cure of our diseases. We return thanks to our corn and her sisters, the beans and the squashes."

Whatever its impact may be on worshippers, NRPE is very successful as an organization. In May 1999, it unveiled a ten-year, $16 million initiative to "assure that the next generation of religious leaders in America advance care for God's creation as a central priority of organized religion." The initiative proposed to distribute "creation care study resources" to tens of thousands of congregations; train clergy and lay leaders on environmental policy issues; convince "institutionally well-positioned younger clergy and lay leaders to embrace creation care as a life-time vocation"; expand public policy and legislative action networks to mobilize over 30,000 activists and at least 75,000 congregations; enlist "national religious agencies addressing economic justice concerns" into the environmental fold, and prepare environmental materials for Sunday schools and religious day schools. The initiative's political agenda included a state-by-state global warming campaign to urge Senate action on climate change, starting with ratification of the Kyoto Protocol.

With generous grants from the Pew Charitable Trusts and the Blue Moon Fund, NRPE is financially prepared to make its influence felt, particularly in circles identified with the religious Left. But one member of the NRPE alliance, the Evangelical Environmental Network would have a trickier task in getting its flock to embrace a green agenda. How would the group that introduced the "What Would Jesus Drive" campaign deal with an evangelical audience not likely to look fondly on Gaia-inspired environmentalist rhetoric? EEN would have to do more than substitute Jesus for the Earth Mother if it hoped to get evangelicals on board.[8]

EEN executive director Rev. James Ball, who led the effort to paint evangelicals green, admitted that the initiative would not be easy, He told the *Washington Post* in February 2005: "Environmental groups are always going to be viewed in a wary fashion. They just don't have a good enough feel for the evangelical community. There are land mines from the past, and they will hit them without knowing it." That was made clear during the 2004 election. According to the Pew Research Center, nearly four out of five white evangelicals voted for President Bush over avowed environmentalist John Kerry. Evangelicals accounted for more than a third of all votes cast for Bush.[9]

Not long after Kerry's defeat, environmental group leaders met to figure out how to communicate with evangelicals. "There is a lot of suspicion," Larry Schweiger, president of the National Wildlife Fund, told the *Post*. "There are a lot of questions about our real intentions." Schweiger's concerns were well founded. "While evangelicals are open to being good stewards of God's creation," commented John C. Green, director of the Ray. C. Bliss Institute for Applied Politics at the University of Akron, "they believe people should only worship God. This may sound like splitting hairs. But evangelicals don't see it that way. Their stereotype of environmentalists would be Druids who worship trees."

And yet despite the cultural and religious barriers, environmentalists are making significant inroads into the evangelical community. In October 2004, the 30-million member National Association of Evangelicals (NAE) adopted an "Evangelical Call to Civic Responsibility." Its statement on the environment emphasized a Christian duty to care for the planet and government's major role in supporting it.

"We affirm that God-given dominion is a sacred responsibility to steward the earth and not a license to abuse the creation of which we are a part," said the statement, which was distributed to 50,000 churches nationwide. "Because clean air, pure water, and adequate resources are crucial to public health and civic order, government has the obligation to protect its citizens from the effects of environmental degradation." The signatories included such well-known evangelical leaders as James Dobson of Focus on the Family and Charles Colson of Prison Fellowship Ministries. That fall, the influential evangelical magazine *Christianity Today* entered the debate on global warming. "Christians should make it clear to government and businesses that we are willing to adapt our lifestyles and support steps toward changes that protect our environment, it said." The magazine endorsed the McCain-Lieberman bill to impose binding restrictions on U.S. emissions of man-made greenhouse gases.

This infatuation for all things green provoked a backlash within the evangelical community. At a March 2005 Capitol Hill meeting of the National Association of Evangelicals (NAE), attendees debated whether the evangelicals' political platform should go beyond such issues as opposition to abortion and support for traditional marriages. Fissures surfaced. Arguing against a "one or two-item political approach" was the Rev. Ronald J. Sider, president of Evangelicals for Social Responsibility, the EEN parent organization. Opposition to greening the NAE was led by the late Diane Knippers, president of the Institute on Religion and Democracy, who said: "The religious left is political smoke and mirrors." Added Tom Minnery, vice president of Focus on the Family, "Do not make this about global warming."[10]

But they did. Over the next year, Ball's EEN and its allies lobbied NAE's president, the Rev. Ted Haggard, to extend the idea of "creation care" to include support for measures to reduce emissions of greenhouse gases. However, in February 2006 NAE announced that because it could not reach a consensus on climate change, the group would take no stand on global warming. In a letter to Haggard, more than 20 evangelical leaders had urged NAE not to adopt "any official position" on global climate change because "Bible-believing evangelicals...disagree about the cause, severity and solutions to the global warming issue."[11]

Calvin DeWitt, a University of Wisconsin professor of environmental studies and an evangelical, called the NAE decision "a retreat and a defeat." "A year ago, it looked as though evangelicals would become a strong, collective voice for what we call 'creation care' and others may call environmentalism," DeWitt told the *Washington Post*. "This will have negative consequences for the ability of evangelicals to influence the White House, unfortunately and sadly."

But E. Calvin Beisner, professor of social ethics at Knox Theological Seminary in Fort Lauderdale, Florida, spoke for many more evangelicals. According to the *Post*, Beisner helped draft the letter to Haggard. He warned that the NAE was about to "assume as true certain things we think still are debatable, such as that global warming is not only real but also almost certainly going to be catastrophically harmful; second, that it is being driven to a significant extent by human activity; and, third that some regime, some international treaty for mandatory reductions in CO_2 emissions, could make a significant enough drop in global emissions to justify the costs to human economy."

EEN's attempt to attract socially conservative evangelicals to the banner of environmentalism was a feat of daring. Still, the effort has fallen short. Many NAE leaders have refused to let their faith serve another's purpose, which was the point of Diane Knippers' warning against "smoke and mirrors." There was after all nothing even remotely subtle about EEN's "What Would Jesus Drive?" campaign. EEN and its environmentalist allies had tipped their hand too early in the game to have a chance at winning this particular pot. For now, the leading evangelical organization in America will not join the green "parallel universe." They are not going to be part of Gramsci's "counter-hegemony."[12]

Green Power Structure

There will be inevitable setbacks in the never-ending trial-and-error game of seeking to spread environmentalist influence into hitherto unoccupied territory. But ever resourceful, both financially and politically, green advocacy groups remain determined to open up new avenues of influence. In late March 2006, for example, Environmental Defense (ED) teamed up with the Advertising Council and the high-powered New York PR firm of Ogilvy & Mather to launch a national public service advertising campaign to "motivate Americans to participate in activities that will help combat global warming." The ads are created pro bono by Ogilvy & Mather and distributed nationwide. "According to Environmental Defense," the Ad Council press release states, "our nation's most distinguished science community agrees that global warming is an urgent problem, we are causing it, and we have time to avoid the most dangerous consequences, which could happen in our children's lifetime." "We've launched this campaign as a wake-up call," adds Fred Krupp, president of Environmental Defense. "This is the most serious environmental challenge of our time. It is more urgent and its dangers more fundamental than most Americans realize."[13]

It would be tempting to dismiss such comments as just more alarmist rhetoric from a movement accustomed to using calculated exaggerations to make its case. But getting the Ad Council to disseminate global warming propaganda through ostensibly non-political public service announcements over TV, radio, and the Internet was an impressive bit of showmanship by Environmental Defense. What's more, ED enticed Republican pollster Whit Ayers and former George H.W. Bush White House deputy communications director Tucker Eskew to lend their reputations to the campaign, giving it a bipartisan flavor.[14]

Environmental Defense, once known as the Environmental Defense Fund, first made a name for itself in the late 1960s and early 1970s in calling for a ban on DDT. Four decades later, it continues to generate environmental scares, even if its tone is more muffled than Greenpeace or NRDC. What has changed, however, is ED's finances. From its upscale Park Avenue address in Manhattan, to its annual 2003 income of $50,289,354 (according to its latest available federal tax forms) to the $358,172 in salary and benefits pocketed by ED president Fred Krupp, ED is riding high in the saddle. It also helps to have had Teresa Heinz Kerry serve on its board of trustees for over 20 years and to enjoy grants from such foundations as Heinz, Mott, Blue Moon, MacArthur, Turner, Cummings, and the Rockefeller Brothers Fund. ED epitomizes the green elite, whose comfortable surroundings bear little resemblance to the natural world over which it regularly issues the most dire pronouncements

ED's upscale ways have not endeared it to less-well-heeled groups. Says Tim Hermach, executive director of Oregon's radical Native Forest Council: "Environmental Defense is a pseudo-environmental, pro-corporate Democratic Party front group that has abandoned its grassroots base for compromised Beltway political power, while we're out here taking the principled stands such as Zero-Cut for old-growth forests."[15]

Of course, jealousy, envy, competition for money and power, conflict between purists and pragmatists—these are the hallmarks of every political movement, and environmentalism is no exception. But Hermach's comments are more than the railings of a "have-not" against a "have." They make it clear that the big environmental groups have become a part of the establishment they seek to transform. ED's Manhattan neighbor the Natural Resources Defense Council rakes in even more money: $57,303,067 in 2003. And these two high-fliers are not even the wealthiest. The annual incomes of the nation's biggest environmental groups, according to the latest available IRS tax forms, are staggering:

- The Nature Conservancy, $732,402,173 (2003)
- World Wildlife Fund, $112,001,561 (2004)
- National Wildlife Federation, $100,534,318 (2004)
- Sierra Club, $91,843,757 (2004)
- National Audubon Society, $76,595,365 (2003)
- Conservation Fund, $67,546,599 (2004)
- Natural Resources Defense Council, $57,303,087 (2004)
- Environmental Defense, $43,661,043 (2003)
- Conservation International Foundation, $43,659,355 (2003)
- The Wilderness Society, $27,234,601 (2003)
- Defenders of Wildlife, $25,729,780 (2003)
- Earthjustice, $21,090,378 (2004)
- World Resources Institute, $16,179,169 (2003)
- Greenpeace, $15,913,343 (2004)
- National Environmental Trust, $13,352,810 (2004)
- Union of Concerned Scientists, $12,130,811 (2003)
- Resources for the Future, $9,189,422 (2003)
- League of Conservation Voters, $8,369,006 (2004)

Some of this impressive wealth has made its way into the pockets of the leaders of key environmental groups. How well do they do? Here's a sampling of what the best-paid environmental leaders earn in salary plus benefits, according to IRS Form 990. The list confirms what many environmental advocates have been saying for years: It pays to be green.

- Steven McCormick, president & CEO, The Nature Conservancy, $380,067 (2003)
- Fred Krupp, president, Environmental Defense, $358,172 (2003)
- John Flicker, president, National Audubon Society, $362,237 (2003)
- Kathryn Fuller, president and director, World Wildlife Fund, $310,781 (2003)
- Jonathan Lash, president, World Resources Institute, $302,186 (2003)
- Peter Seligmann, chairman & CEO, Conservation International Federation, $336,353 (2003)
- John Adams, president, Natural Resources Defense Council, $353,220 (2004)
- Rodger Schlickeisen, president & CEO, Defenders of Wildlife, $281,473 (2003)
- John Selzer, president & CEO, The Conservation Fund, $268,977 (2004)
- Carl Pope, executive director, Sierra Club, $241,224 (2004)
- William Meadows, president, The Wilderness Society, $236,675 (2003)

- Vawter Parker, executive director, Earthjustice, $234,869 (2004)
- Phillip Clapp, president, National Environmental Trust, $190,462 (2004)
- Kenneth Cook, president, Environmental Working Group, $160,122 (2004)
- Leslie Carothers, president, Environmental Law Institute, $156,350 (2004)
- Stephanie Pollack, vice president, Conservation Law Foundation, $153,995 (2003)
- Paul Hansen, executive director, Izaak Walton League of America, $151,958 (2003)
- Larry Schweiger, president, National Wildlife Federation, $151,610 (2003)
- Kevin Knobloch, president, Union of Concerned Scientists, $149,671 (2003)
- Brent Blackwelder, president, Friends of the Earth, $139,250 (2004)
- John Passacantando, executive director, Greenpeace, $16,749 (2004) [16]

The Corporate Connection

While their compensation packages pale in comparison with those of Fortune 500 CEOs, those at the top of the green NGO ladder enjoy the perks of power, and they use it to give their seal of approval to corporations that toe the green line. Politically-correct companies are expected to follow a code of conduct based on environmentalist-inspired notions of sustainable development and corporate social responsibility (CSR). Companies that embrace CSR or otherwise flaunt their green *bona fides* are not, however, necessarily selfless environmental stewards or sterling corporate citizens. Sometimes they earn their green credentials in less than honorable ways. Here are three recent examples:

Enron: Once-mighty Enron Corp. has come to symbolize corporate greed and irresponsibility. Its spectacular collapse in 2002 is commonly lumped with such odious contemporaries as GlobalCrossing, WorldCom, Adelphi, and Tyco. But Enron's self-serving commitment to combating global warming should stand alongside its notorious accounting schemes as an example of its fraudulent claims.

Toward the end of the Clinton administration Enron began to claim that it would help counter changes to the planet's climate—and increase its bottom line—by emissions trading, a scheme that involves selling the right to emit greenhouse gases. On December 12, 1997, one day after the Kyoto Protocol was adopted, an internal Enron memo predicted that the company would profit handsomely from a global warming treaty. Enron, the memo noted, had "excellent credentials" with many environmental groups and they were referring to the company in "glowing terms." The Kyoto Protocol, the memo asserted, would "do more to promote Enron's business" than any other initiative, and the treaty's emissions trading provisions would be "good for Enron stock."

Confident that emissions trading would open up a bright future for his company, Enron president Ken Lay met with President Bill Clinton and Vice President Al Gore to express his support for the administration's climate policy. "Enron hoped to cash in on Kyoto by masterminding a worldwide trading network in which major industries could buy and sell credits to emit carbon dioxide," observes Bill O'Keefe, president of the George C. Marshall Institute. But Enron's descent into bankruptcy and ignominy put an end to its dreams of global warming profits even as it ruined the finances of its employees and shareholders.[17]

BP: When Ken Lay went to that White House meeting with Clinton and Gore, he was joined by Sir John Browne, CEO of energy giant BP. "Sir John," an internal Enron memo points out, "thinks there will soon be government regulation of greenhouse gases. And companies that have anticipated regulation will not only know how to use it to their advantage; they will also, as Browne puts it, 'gain a seat at the table, a chance to influence future rules.'" One could hardy find a better description of what economists call "rent-seeking"—pursuing profit by using political influence and taking advantage of regulations that skew the market. BP, which has enormous natural gas reserves, saw an opportunity to rig Kyoto-like regulatory schemes in its favor. Because natural gas emits less carbon dioxide than coal or oil when it burns, BP stands to benefit handsomely from any Kyoto-driven switch to natural gas.

Enron's collapse has removed it from the global warming game, but BP is still eager to play. Even though the Kyoto Protocol proves itself increasingly unworkable, BP is pouring millions into high-visibility advertising campaigns on television and in newspapers touting the virtues of the company's commitment to reducing the effects of carbon dioxide. "It's time to turn up the heat on global warming," reads the headline on a full-page ad in the *Wall Street Journal*. "We were the first major energy company to take steps to reduce greenhouse gas emissions," proclaims another full-page *WSJ* ad. "BP supports energy education throughout the country," it continues, "from a traveling classroom that teaches alternative energy, to the Solar Decathlon in Washington, D.C." "Reducing our footprint: Here's where we stand," begins another ad. It closes with the company's logo and the words "BP beyond petroleum."[18]

And yet BP's footprint is still very much with us. In late 2005, the Environmental Protection Agency launched a criminal investigation of BP's management of pipelines in Alaska's North Slope. EPA later expanded its inquiry to include the spill of an estimated 134,000 to 267,000 gallons of crude oil from a BP-operated pipeline in Prudhoe Bay. According to Alaska state conservation officials, the pipeline ruptured from internal corrosion, causing what is considered the largest spill ever in the energy-rich North Slope. Officials at Alaska's Department of Environmental Conservation announced they would seek fines of up to $2 million from BP for damage caused by the spill.

The Alaska spill isn't the only recent blemish on BP's environmental record. In 2005, 15 workers were killed and over 170 injured in an explosion at the company's Texas City plant, which earned BP a $21.3 million fine from federal workplace safety regulators. *The Wall Street Journal* reported that the case had been passed on to the Justice Department for possible criminal investigation. Current and former BP employees accused the company of skimping on maintenance and ignoring repeated warnings of trouble at the Texas and Alaska facilities. BP has denied the charges. However, in April 2006 BP's environmental credentials were further called into question by the Occupational Health and Safety Administration, which fined the company $2.4 million for safety violations at its Oregon, Ohio refinery. OSHA said the violations were similar to those uncovered in the Texas City explosion.[19]

BP's culpability in the cases cited here will have to be determined by further investigations and possibly by the courts. The oil and gas business is inherently risky, and no one should accuse BP or any other energy company of intentionally disregarding environmental or safety concerns. One cannot help but wonder, however, if the tens of millions BP poured into self-congratulatory testimonials to its global warming achievements might not have been better spent on workplace safety and maintenance at facilities it managed in Alaska, Texas and Ohio.

Goldman Sachs: In November 2005, the global investment banking and securities giant Goldman Sachs Group, Inc. joined Citigroup, J.P. Morgan, Bank of America, and the World Bank in capitulating to a radical activist environmental group. These financial behemoths caved in to the demands of the Rainforest Action Network (2004 income: $2.9 million). Goldman Sachs adopted sweeping environmental policies to guide its lending practices in developing countries. Following the demands of RAN, it agreed that human-induced greenhouse gases cause catastrophic climate changes that must immediately be reduced; that the self-appointed representatives of indigenous peoples must approve all its development projects; and that logging must be conducted according to procedures developed by eco-activists.

Within months after it adopted the new lending guidelines, Goldman Sachs revealed that it would donate 680,000 acres of land it owns in Tierra del Fuego, Chile to the New York-based Wildlife Conservation Society. The Chilean land deal provides a revealing glimpse of the cozy relationships between corporate heavy-weights and well-connected green advocacy groups. Goldman Sachs CEO Hank Paulson, since named Treasury Secretary by President Bush, was chairman of the board of the Nature Conservancy, and Paulson's wife is a former Conservancy board member. The Nature Conservancy, the world's wealthiest environmental group, has long-standing ties to the Wildlife Conservation Society, having worked with it on projects outside the United States. One of the trustees of the Wildlife Conservation Society (2004 total revenue: $195,598,851) is H. Merritt Paulson, the son of Hank Paulson. Goldman Sachs officials have rushed to the defense of Paulson and brushed aside questions about conflict of interest. But they are at a loss to explain why the Nature Conservancy, no stranger to land deals, was paid a $144,000 "consulting fee" for its role in the transaction.

Two New York City-based powerhouses—one a global investment banking firm, the other a blue-stocking environmental group with over $700 million in assets—with family ties in common are disposing of 680,000 acres of land in far-away rural Chile and it's considered rude to ask questions? The deal was completed without the advice and consent of the inhabitants of Tierra del Fuego who, in Paul Driessen's words, are "about to have a no-development conservation easement forced on them." "Nor," he adds, "did anyone assess the vast area's potential value for timber, oil or metals, so that locals and [Goldman Sachs] shareholders would at least know the true cost of the giveaway."[20]

Enron and BP are examples of rent-seeking companies eager to assist global environmental officials and green NGOs in creating a regulatory structure they can exploit. The Goldman Sachs land giveaway—a variation on the theme of insider trading—shows how those who bask in the glow of "corporate social responsibility" take care of their own at the expense of the less well-connected. All three examples attest to the extraordinary ability of well-situated elites to use the green power structure to their advantage.

Settling Accounts

The green power structure rewards those who play by its rules and punishes those who challenge its new orthodoxy. The most celebrated recent example of how heretics are persecuted is the treatment of Danish statistician Bjorn Lomborg, whose 2001 book, *The Skeptical Environmentalist*, outraged green activists and their allies in the media and academia. Lomborg is a young, left-of-center vegetarian and former member of Greenpeace—not the kind of critic environmental activists typically encounter. He took a look at what he has called "The Litany" of environmentalist claims. Using data compiled by the UN, World Bank, OECD, and numerous environmental and health agencies, and buttressing his research with 2,930 footnotes and over 70 pages of bibliography, Lomborg has concluded that environmentalist alarmism is not supported by the readily available evidence.

"We're not running out of energy or natural resources," he explains. "There is ever more food, and fewer people are starving. In 1900, the average life expectancy was 30 years; today it is 67. We have reduced poverty more in the past 50 years than we did in the preceding 500. Air pollution in the industrialized world has declined—in London the air has never been cleaner since medieval times."[21]

Although he accepts the notion of human-induced global warming, Lomborg has no use for the Kyoto Protocol. "[A]ll current models show that the Kyoto Protocol would have little impact on climate—at a cost of $150 billion to $350 billion annually," he writes. "With global warming disproportionately affecting Third World countries, we have to ask if Kyoto is the best way to help them. For the amount Kyoto would cost the U.S. per year, we could provide everyone in the world with access to basic health, education, water and sanitation. Isn't this a better way to serve the world?"

The answer from the environmental establishment has been a resounding "no." The Washington-based World Resources Institute posted a media alert on its website stating: "WRI is urging journalists to exercise caution in reporting or reviewing the new book, *The Skeptical Environmentalist*." *Grist* magazine, Tompaine.com, and the Union of Concerned Scientists were among the many groups who also attacked Lomborg. *Scientific American* devoted eleven pages of its January 2002 issue to an attack on Lomborg under the Orwellian title of "Science

Defends Itself Against 'The Skeptical Environmentalist.'" Lomborg's critics, which included the splendidly named Danish Committee on Scientific Dishonesty, cloaked their arguments in a veil of science but were at a loss to refute the data he meticulously researched for the book.

By denying the scientific basis of the green's litany of doom, Lomborg revealed for anyone to see what *Genome* author Matt Ridley called "a narrow but lucrative industry of environmental fund-raising that has a vested interest in claims of alarmism."[22]

The Danish statistician is not the only researcher to come under fire for reaching conclusions contrary to environmentalist wisdom. "Scientists who dissent from alarmism have seen their grant funds disappear, their work derided, and themselves derided as industry stooges, scientific hacks or worse," notes Richard Lindzen, Alfred P. Sloan Professor of Atmospheric Sciences at MIT. Lindzen notes that Henk Tennekes, the research director of the Royal Dutch Meteorological Society, was dismissed after he questioned the scientific underpinnings of global warming. "Aksel Winn-Nielsen, former director of the UN's World Meteorological Organization," Lindzen adds, "was tarred by Bert Bolin, first head of the IPCC [Intergovernmental Panel on Climate Change], as a tool of the coal industry for questioning climate alarmism."[23]

Ostracism awaits dissident scientists in other fields as well. Rob Roy Ramey, a wildlife biologist, was curator of vertebrate zoology at the Denver Museum of Nature and Science (DNMS) until October 2005, when he was forced to resign in the wake of a controversy over a mouse. The rodent in question is called the Preble's meadow jumping mouse. Since 1998 the creature has been listed as a threatened sub-species under the Endangered Species Act and 31,000 acres of government and private land in Colorado and Wyoming have been put off-limits to development to protect its habitat.

The Preble's mouse bears a striking resemblance to other North American meadow mice. With funds from the U.S. Fish & Wildlife Service and the state of Wyoming, Ramey led a team of scientists to determine whether it was genetically a distinct sub-species. In December 2003 the team released its conclusion that the Preble's mouse "is not a valid sub-species based on physical characteristics and genetics" and it published a report in 2005 in *Animal Conservation*, a peer-reviewed journal of the Zoological Society of London. That led Wyoming officials and the group Coloradans for Water Conservation and Development to ask the federal government to remove the Preble's mouse from the endangered species list.

Two environmental groups, Earthjustice and the Center for Native

Ecosystems accused Ramey of "doing everything possible to hijack the science" and branding him the "leader of a high-profile campaign to remove protection for the Preble's mouse." The assault on Ramey, carried out by what *Rocky Mountain News* columnist Vincent Carroll calls the "Preble's posse," continued with *ad hominem* attacks on the biologist in e-mails sent to Ramey's superiors at the Denver museum. Preble's posse also included activists with the Trust for Public Land, local officials at the Denver office of the Fish and Wildlife Service, and consultants who stood to make money advising residents, businesses, and local governments on mouse-related land-use issues.[24]

"I've been nearly stampeded by a herd of agitated elephants in Africa and suspended from some of the highest cliffs in North America," Ramey told the *Wall Street Journal's* Stephen Moore, "but nothing prepared me for the viciousness of the attacks from the environmentalist lobby." An e-mail from one Carron Meaney, a self-described "research associate" at the museum, warned "there are a lot of people who question your approach and have concerns about working with the museum in the future. I love the DMNS, and am very concerned to watch the alienation your behavior has wrought between the museum and the biology community." Less reticent opponents called Ramey "dishonest," a "whore for industry," and "a shill for the Bush administration." Ramey left the museum, a consequence of the inflamed, well-orchestrated reaction to his research. In the words of the *Rocky Mountain News* columnist Vincent Carroll, the furor "had less to do with science than with the political agenda of environmentalists and their allies in federal and state agencies who are determined to use the Endangered Species Act to influence land-use decisions up and down the Front Range."[25]

The vilification of Lomborg and Ramey stands in sharp contrast to the widely reported "muzzling" of scientists allegedly carried out by the Bush administration. We met James Hansen, director of NASA's Goddard Institute for Space Studies, in our discussion of the origins of the debate over global warming. Hansen, who popularized the issue in testimony before Congress in 1988, can legitimately be called "the father of global warming." While Hansen's scientific credentials are beyond question, his dedication to the cause with which he has come to be identified has led him to rhetorical excesses. The man who once admitted to devising "extreme scenarios" about global warming to get the attention of "decision-makers," has also gotten the attention of the media. Describing working conditions for government scientists in disagreement with the Bush administration's climate policies, Hansen told a New York audience in February 2006: "It seems more like Nazi

174

Germany or the Soviet Union than the United States." He told CBS's "60 Minutes" the following month that "in my more than three decades in the government, I've never witnessed such restrictions on the ability of scientists to communicate with the public." Hansen's allegations have also been featured in the *Washington Post, New York Times,* and, in a fawning portrait in its May 2006 "Special Green Issue" of *Vanity Fair.*[26]

Despite environmentalist claims of a "consensus" on global warming, climate science is contentious. Like other fields of scientific inquiry, there are clashes between scientists in and out of government, and there are conflicts between career government scientists and political appointees. At stake are not just scientific reputations and political agendas but also much-sought-after grant money to fund further research. These disputes are beneficial to the extent that they shed light on the subject and are conducted with civility. And in this regard, it is worth noting that *Washington Post* reporter Juliet Eilperin has written that while there were tensions between government scientists and Bush administration officials, "none of the scientists said political appointees had influenced their research on climate change or disciplined them for questioning the administration. Indeed, several researchers have received bigger budgets in recent years because President Bush has focused on studying global warming rather than curbing greenhouse gases."[27]

Hansen's determination to turn the science of climate change into a political cause celebre has moved him into the center of the green establishment. He received a $250,000 Heinz Award from the Heinz Foundation in 2001, then endorsed Teresa Heinz Kerry's husband, John, for president in 2004, and served as a consultant to former Vice President Al Gore in putting together Gore's 2006 traveling slide show/power-point presentation on climate change. Hansen's ties to Gore and Kerry are a matter of public record. But when CBS's "60 Minutes" reporter Scott Pelley interviewed Hansen for the network's March 19, 2006 segment on climate scientists and the Bush administration, Pelley failed to mention Hansen's political links and referred to him as an "independent."

Environmental advocacy groups have been eager to echo Hansen's accusations. For instance, NRDC senior attorney Robert F. Kennedy Jr. ludicrously says Bush and his appointees "are engaged in a campaign to suppress science that is arguably unmatched in the Western world since the Inquisition." Kennedy, whose knowledge of Western history since the late Middle Ages apparently does not extend to the Third Reich, is simply expressing a disdain for the give and take of scientific debate that is by no means limited to green activists.

Fiona Harvey, environmental correspondent for the *Financial Times* of London, has this to say about balance when reporting on climate change: "In the United States you have lots of news stories that, in the name of balance, give equal credence to the skeptics. We don't do that here—not because we're not balanced but because we think it's unbalanced to give equal validity to a fringe few with no science behind them."[28]

Harvey's comments are a reflection of the enduring influence environmentalism has had in shaping public and published opinion. Whether the subject is climatology, animal biology, nanotechnology, biotechnology, biochemistry or any other field of inquiry, the notion that science is settled and that dissenting viewpoints expressed by those out of favor with elite opinion can be dismissed as musings of the "fringe," is dangerous. It is dangerous because it is at odds with how the world's wealthiest societies—those with the healthiest inhabitants and environments—got to be that way. In their magisterial study, *How the West Grew Rich: The Economic Transformation of the Industrial World*, Nathan Rosenberg and L.E. Birdzell, Jr. point out that:

"Western innovation owes much to interaction between economic and scientific spheres. Underlying the geometric growth in the output of Western economies has been a geometric growth in scientific knowledge, linked to a variety of institutions that transmute the growth in scientific knowledge into growth in material welfare. This growth in scientific knowledge has shaped, nurtured, and fueled Western economic growth. It offers a key to understanding the growth process."[29]

The operative word here is "growth"—both in scientific knowledge and material welfare. But what if growth is seen as the root of all that threatens the well-being of the "planet"? "Limits to Growth" was not just a fashionable slogan of the now-forgotten Club of Rome, the idea has guided leading environmentalist advocacy groups to this day. The precautionary principle, it will be recalled, was conjured up to ensure that the growth in scientific knowledge didn't interfere with green elites imposing their will on the rest of the world. Limiting growth is the ideological glue that holds together environmentalism's alternative universe, its counter-hegemony. The green power structure— the interlocking networks of power and influence that promote environmentalist goals—now has a prominent and well-padded seat at the table of public policy. It will not be dislodged easily.

Epilogue

Half of the harm that is done in this world
Is due to people who want to feel important.
They don't mean to do harm—but the harm does not
interest them.
Or they do not see it, or they justify it.
Because they are absorbed in the endless struggle
To think well of themselves.

T.S. ELIOT[1]

"A chance discovery on a routine field trip in England's Suffolk seacoast led to evidence that humans reached northern Europe 700,000 years ago, about 200,000 years earlier then previously thought." With these words, *Washington Post* staff reporter Guy Gugliotta informed his readers in December 2005 of findings by a team of scientists looking for evidence of human habitation on Suffolk's fossil-rich lowlands bordering the North Sea. Evidence of primitive tool-making came from the recovery of 32 hand-worked black flint flakes found in seashore sediments. The team of scientists believes that distant ancestors of humans, probably a variant of the species known as *Homo heidelbergensis*, crossed the Alps hundreds of thousands of years ago before eventually settling in northern Europe.

Reporting in the journal *Nature*, as summarized in the *Post*, the team said early settlers "apparently took advantage of climatic conditions during a relatively warm 'interglacial' period to dwell in fertile lowlands that formed part of a land bridge connecting what is now the island of Britain with the rest of Europe."

"It was warmer than it is today, a big delta with a fan of rivers," paleoanthropologist Christopher Stringer of London's Natural History Museum told the *Post*. "It had a dry, Mediterranean climate, exotic beasts and lots of resources."[2]

A few weeks earlier, *Nature* reported that tracks made by a giant water scorpion some 330 million years ago had been discovered in sandstone in Scotland. The creature, estimated to have been just over five feet long and three and one-half feet wide, is thought to have abandoned its natural habitat in a nearby lake to try its luck on dry land. Paleontologist Martin A. White, who found the tracks, suggested that the giant scorpions were attempting to make the transition from a water-borne existence to one spent on land. It didn't work out. Too slow to pursue prey and elude predators, the water scorpion eventually failed as a land-dweller, and the species went extinct about 280 million years ago.[3]

And then there is the small fir forest standing in eastern Iowa. The balsam fir, *Abies balsamea,* is a popular ornamental and Christmas tree that grows predominantly in Canada. Yet hundreds of miles to the south, the balsam fir stands tall in Iowa. The little forest is a relic of the last Ice Age which ended around 11,000 years ago. As the climate warmed, balsam firs migrated northward, save for those that managed to hang on in what is now a patch of the U.S. Midwest. Having adapted to changed circumstances, the Iowa fir forest thrives in splendid isolation from its more numerous brethren to the north.

The fir forest in Iowa is what is known as a "disjunct" population, and such occurrences are not as rare as one might think. The U.S. Department of Agriculture, which has mapped the distribution of all major tree species in North America, finds that for almost every species, there are separate disjunct populations living far away from their main climatic distribution. Nature is nothing if not disorderly.[4]

Human ancestors taking advantage of a change in climate and migrating over land to what is now the island of Britain, a long-forgotten scorpion changing its habitat and eventually going extinct, an Ice-Age fir forest defying the odds and surviving in a warmer climate—these and similar occurrences, well documented in the scientific literature, reveal the earth, and the universe of which it is a part, as constantly in flux. Geologists have known about continental drift for well over a century; the same holds true for paleontologists with respect to the rise and fall of species. Yet these and many other fundamental elements of earth science are almost completely absent from the environmental movement's vision of the planet it has set out to save. Its clear preference is for theories that stress natural ecological equilibrium undisturbed by man, even though such notions have undergone a steady debunking in the scientific literature for the last two decades. As Michael Crichton points out:

In the thirty-five-odd years since the environmental movement came into

178

existence, science has undergone a major revolution. This revolution has brought new understanding of nonlinear dynamics, complex systems, chaos theory, catastrophe theory. It has transformed the way we think about evolution and ecology. Yet these no-longer-new ideas have hardly penetrated the thinking of environmental activists, which seems oddly fixed in the concepts and theories of the 1970s.[5]

Environmental activists are as capable as anyone of acquainting themselves with the far-reaching changes that have taken place in scientific thinking in recent decades. Instead, they have sought refuge—and political power—in biocentrism, a postmodern form of nature worship, and in the precautionary principle, a doctrine which celebrates the triumph of conjecture over evidence. More often than not, science is used to provide political cover, as in the alleged scientific "consensus" on global warming.

"For some people, environmentalism is collectivism in drag," observes columnist George Will. "Such people use environmental causes and rhetoric not for the purpose of environmental improvements. Rather, for them, changing the society's politics is the end, and environmental policies are mere means to that end."[6]

Of course, the environment will improve, but improvement will come courtesy of the forces the environmental movement is determined to discredit. In one of its "Modern Marvels" programs, the *History Channel* recounts how a building material like concrete has improved our lot since the time of ancient Rome. In the present day, the program shows what happened to Denver's old Stapleton airport after the facility closed in 1994.

What to do with the vast network of concrete runways? Not too long ago, they would have been dug up, broken into pieces, loaded onto trucks, and dumped into a landfill miles from the old airport. Not today. Instead, the concrete is sent to a newly constructed facility on site where it is chemically treated to create—recycled concrete. It's ready to pour and to be used for street curbing, sidewalks, and the foundations of new homes, retail outlets, and office parks where the old airport once stood.

The terrible damage and loss of life caused by hurricanes, tsunamis, tornados and other natural disasters has led innovative minds in the construction industry to come up with building materials that can better withstand the whims of nature. Across the country, builders and suppliers are developing new products and technologies to construct homes that are strengthened well beyond existing building codes. They are developing windows to withstand 130-mile winds, and paint-like coatings to block water from penetrating concrete walls after severe storms. A Florida firm is developing a high-tech fiberglass composite to make the frame and shell of a house. According to the *Wall Street Journal*, "the composite, which is similar to the material used to make the military's stealth bomber, is lightweight and, according to company officials, can withstand winds far stronger than those of the most powerful hurricanes."[7]

Manmade chemicals, some of which may even be "toxic" at certain levels, are responsible for the redevelopment of the old Denver airport and the emergence of these new building materials. But since Rachel Carson's *Silent Spring* and the birth of modern environmentalism over four decades ago, manmade chemicals have been under constant attack by the environmental movement and under intense regulatory scrutiny by environmental agencies. Rachel Carson was a false prophet, and her disciples have done themselves no honor with their shrill rhetoric and never-ending scare tactics.

The Club of Rome, one of the driving forces behind the idea of "sustainable development," published a statement by Alexander King and Bertrand Schneider in 1991 which observed:

In search for a new enemy to unite us, we came up with the idea of pollution, the threat of global warming, water shortages, famine, and the like would fit the bill...All these dangers are caused by human intervention...The real enemy, then, is humanity itself.

Paul Watson, a co-founder of Greenpeace in the United States, has referred to human beings as the "AIDS of the Earth." And a Greenpeace leaflet, produced for recruiting purposes in the United Kingdom, has this to say about the human species:

Modern Man has made a rubbish tip of Paradise. He has multiplied his numbers to plague proportions, caused the extinction of 500 species of animals, ransacked the planet for fuels and now stands like a brutish infant, gloating over his meteoric rise to ascendancy, on the brink of a war to end all wars and of effectively destroying this oasis of life in the solar system."[8]

Such outbursts have become so commonplace that, at long last, some green activists have begun to criticize them. Paul W. Hansen, executive director of the Izaak Walton League of America took to the pages of the *Washington Post* in March 2005 to bemoan a "lack of civility in the rhetoric and tactics used by some groups..." But there is little reason to believe that calls for toning down the rhetoric will bear fruit. The vituperative attacks on Bjorn Lomborg by environmentalists and their allies in the media and academia do not indicate that the movement is ready to engage in civil discourse with its serious critics. Lomborg, after all, has done little more than show that environmental data do not support environmentalist rhetoric.[9]

"Though this be madness, yet there is method in i't," Shakespeare's Polonius tells Hamlet. Fanning the flames of fear may, indeed, seem like madness. But for environmental activists and others who stand to benefit from alarmism, it's simply good for business. As Richard Lindzen points out:

> Ambiguous scientific statements about climate are hyped by those with a vested interest in alarm, thus raising the political stakes for policy makers who provide funds for more scientific research to feed more alarm to increase the political stakes. After all, who puts money into science—whether for AIDS, or space, or climate—where there is nothing really alarming?"[10]

Lindzen's remarks about climate science apply equally to endangered species, manmade chemicals, agricultural biotechnology, and all the other areas of environmental advocacy that have brought green NGOs money, influence, and power. Sadly, alarmism works. In 2004, the American Cancer Society reported that 68 percent of the public believed that the risk of dying from cancer was increasing and that 40 percent believed that living in a polluted city puts one at greater risk for lung cancer than does smoking a pack of cigarettes a day.[11]

G.K. Chesterton once remarked: "The old tyrants invoked the past. The new tyrants will invoke the future." The future invoked by the environmental movement is one of the impending ecological collapse, preventable only by imposing what's called "global governance" on us all.

Meanwhile, environmentalism is being overtaken by the environment. According to the EPA, between 1970 and 2003, gross domestic product increased 176 percent, vehicle miles traveled increased 155 percent, consumption increased 45 percent, and U.S. population grew by 39 percent. During the same time period, total emissions of the six major air pollutants decreased by 51 percent. In July 2005, the Centers for Disease Control and Prevention reported that Americans had lower levels of lead, pesticides, nicotine, and other potentially harmful substances in their blood than they did a decade earlier. And in February 2006, the American Cancer Society reported the first annual decrease in cancer deaths in the U.S. since 1930. Death rates fell for lung, breast, prostate, and colorectal cancer.[12]

But what are statistics or, for that matter, what is the truth, when there is a planet to save? Promoting his movie, *"An Inconvenient Truth,"* former Vice President Al Gore had this to say in May 2006 about stretching the truth on the subject of global warming: "I believe it is appropriate to have an overrepresentation of factual presentation on how dangerous it is, as a predicate to open up the audience." True to form, Gore told an audience of movie enthusiasts in Cannes, France that same month that we were in a "planetary emergency."[13]

There is nothing glamorous about creating new building materials, figuring out how to recycle concrete, devising ways to make fuel burn more economically, or even developing new cures for diseases. Those who do these things usually do not seek the limelight. They often toil for years, make mistakes, lose their way, and try again. Eventually, some succeed in improving our lot by old-fashioned ingenuity and perseverance. Film footage of Nobel Prize winners in the fields of medicine, biology, physics or chemistry invariably show somewhat awkward figures, unaccustomed to, and uncomfortable with, the publicity that is thrust upon them. They can't wait for the last reporter's question to be asked and for the klieg lights to be turned off. The laboratory beckons. Their world is as far removed from that of the globe-trotting environmental savior as one can imagine. It's also a better one.

Appendix
The Key Players
(In Alphabetical Order)

American Lung Association
61 Broadway
6th Floor
New York NY 10006
212-315-8700 (phone)
212-265-5642 (fax)
www.ala.org

Membership
9,500

Tax Status
501(c)(3)

Year Founded
1904

2004 Revenue (IRS Form 990)
$22,619,434

Executive Director
Janet Wolmer

Stated Objectives
"The American Lung Association (ALA) is the oldest voluntary health organization in the United States, with a national office and constituent and affiliate organization around the country. Founded in 1904 to fight tuberculosis, ALA today fights lung disease in all forms, with special emphasis on asthma, tobacco control and environmental health. ALA is funded by contributions from the public, along with gifts and grants from corporations, foundations and government agencies. ALA achieves its many successes through the work of thousands of committed volunteers and staff."

Major Donations Received 2000-2004
- California Endowment, $891,681
- Energy Foundation, $387,000
- Merck Cpmpany Fund, $240,000
- Community Foundation for the National Capital Region, $213,640
- BP Foundation, $110,000
- Houston Endowment, $100,000
- Beldon Fund, $75,000
- Wood-Claeyssems Foundation, $75,000
- Aetna Foundation, $50,000

Center for Biological Diversity
PO Box 710
Tucson, AZ 85702
520-623-5252 (phone)
520-623-9797 (fax)
www.biologicaldiversity.org

Tax Status
501(c)(3)

Year Founded
1992

2004 Revenue (IRS Form 990)
$2,205,962

Policy Director
Kieran Suckling

Stated Objectives
"Protecting endangered species and wild places through science, policy education, and environmental law."

Major Donations Received 2000-2004
- Wilburforce Foundation, $252,000
- Foundation for Deep Ecology, $140,000
- Turner Foundation, $100,000
- Argosy Foundation, $75,000
- Wendy P. McCaw Foundation, $70,000
- Deep Creek Foundation, $50,000

Conservation Fund

1800 N. Kent Street, Suite 1120
Arlington, VA 22209-2156
703-525-5300 (phone)
703-525-4610 (fax)
www.conservationfund.org

Tax Status
501(c)(3)

Year Founded
1985

2004 Revenue (IRS 990)
$67,546,599

President and CEO
Lawrence A. Selzer

Stated Objectives
"The Conservation Fund forges partnerships to protect America's legacy of land and water resources. Through land acquisition, sustainable programs, and leadership training, the Fund and its partners demonstrate effective conservation solutions emphasizing the integration of economic and environmental goals."

Major Donations Received 2000-2003
- David and Lucile Packard Foundation, $8,118,400
- Charles Stewart Mott Foundation, $8,086,000
- Doris Duke Foundation, $5,540,000
- Richard King Mellon Foundation, $3,100,000
- Richard & Rhoda Goldman Foundation, $1,813,100
- Ford Foundation, $1,400,000
- Turner Foundation, $813,000
- Virginia Environmental Endowment, $250,000
- John D. and Catherine T. MacArthur Foundation, $237,000
- Gates Family Foundation, $200,000
- Ford Motor Company Fund, $158,000
- Foundation for Deep Ecology, $147,500
- Surdna Foundation, $100,000
- ALCOA Foundation, $70,000
- Fannie Mae Foundation, $50,000

Conservation International Foundation

1919 M Street N.W., Suite 600
Washington, D.C. 20036
202-912-1000 (phone)
www.conservation.org

Tax Status
501(c)(3)

Year Founded
1987

2003 Revenue (IRS Form 990)
$43,659,355

Senior Director
Timothy B. Werner

Stated Objectives
"Conservation International (CI) is a global, field-based nonprofit organization that protects biodiversity. CI is headquartered in Washington, DC. with over 800 professional staff in offices around the world."

Major Donations Received 2000-2003
- John D. and Catherine T. MacArthur Foundation, $60,370,000
- Blue Moon Fund, $700,000
- Charles Stewart Mott Foundation, $400,000

Conservation Law Foundation

62 Summer Street
Boston, MA 02110
617-350-0990 (phone)
617-350-4030 (fax)
www.clf.org

Tax Status
501(c)(3)
Year Founded
1966

2003 Revenue (IRS Form 990)
$3,772,844

President
Philip Warburg

Stated Objectives
Uses "years of experience with communications, regulation, and cooperative problem-solving" to "integrate into our work environment business transaction, which we call ventures."

Major Donations Received 2000-2003
- Rockefeller Foundation, $770,000
- Pew Charitable Trusts, $576,000
- Surdna Foundation, $450,000
- Energy Foundation, $435,000
- Boston Foundation, $357,000
- Ford Foundation, $300,000
- Oak Foundation USA, $140,000
- New York Charitable Trust, $110,000
- John Merck Fund, $100,000
- Sherman Foundation, $90,000
- Fannie Mae Foundation, $50,000

Defenders of Wildlife
1101 14th Street, N.W., Suite # 1400
Washington, D.C. 22205
202-682-9400 (phone)
202-682-1331 (fax)
www.defenders.org

Membership
455,000

Tax Status
501(c)(3)

Year Founded
1947

2003 Revenue (IRS Form 990)
$25,729,780

President
Rodger Schlickeisen

Stated Objectives

"Defenders of Wildlife is dedicated to the protection of all native wild animals and plants in their natural communities. We focus our programs on what scientists consider two of the most serious environmental threats to the planet: the accelerating rate of extinction of species and the associated loss of biological diversity, and the habitat alteration and destruction. Long known for our leadership on endangered species issues, Defenders of Wildlife also advocates new approaches to wildlife conservation that will help species from becoming endangered. Our programs encourage protection of entire ecosystems and interconnected habitats while protecting predators that serve as indicator species for ecosystem health."

Major Donations Received 2000-2004

- Turner Foundation, $1,605,000
- Doris Duke Charitable Trust, $437,430
- Surdna Foundation, $375,000
- Geraldine R. Dodge Foundation, $60,000
- Beldon Fund, $50,000
- David and Lucile Packard Foundation, $40,000
- Walt Disney Company Fund, $19,500

EarthJustice Legal Defense Fund

426 17th Street
6th Floor
Oakland, CA 94612-2820
510-550-6700 (phone)
510-550-6740 (fax)
www.earthjustice.org

Tax Status
501(c)(3)

Year Founded
1971

2004 Revenue (IRS Form 990)
$21,090,378

Executive Director
Vawter Parker

Stated Objective

"Earthjustice is a non-profit public interest law firm, dedicated to protecting the magnificent places, wildlife, and natural resources of this earth and to defending the right of all people to a healthy environment. We bring about far-reaching change by enforcing and strengthening environmental laws on behalf of hundreds of organizations and communities."

Major Donations Received 2000-2004

- Pew Charitable Trusts, $20,471,000
- Alaska Conservation Foundation, $768,666
- Richard & Rhoda Goldman Fund, $545,000
- David and Lucile Packard Foundation, $449,999
- Charles Stewart Mott Foundation, $350,000
- Turner Foundation, $315,000
- Beldon Fund, $300,000
- Blue Moon Fund, $300,000
- Nathan Cummings Foundation, $150,000
- Compton Foundation, $100,000
- Wilburforce Foundation, $80,000

Environmental Defense

257 Park Avenue South
New York, NY 10010
212-505-2100 (phone)
212-505-2375 (fax)
www.environmentaldefense.org

Tax Status

501(c)(3)

Year Founded

1967

2003 Revenue (IRS Form 990)

$50,289,354

President

Fred Krupp

Stated Objective

"Environmental Defense brings together experts in science, law and economics to tackle complex environmental issues that affect our oceans, our air, our natural resources, the liveability of our man-made environment , and the species with whom we share our world."

Major Donations Received 2000-2004

- Starr Foundation, $6,000,000
- Doris Duke Charitable Trust, $5,000,000
- David and Lucile Packard Foundation, $3,687,500
- Energy Foundation, $2,312,923
- William and Flora Hewlett Foundation, $1,350,000
- Joyce Foundation, $1,280,000
- Charles Stewart Mott Foundation, $650,000
- Richard & Rhoda Goldman Fund, $500,000
- Beldon Fund, $575,000
- San Francisco Foundation, $412,500
- Nathan Cummings Foundation, $400,000
- John D. and Catherine T. MacArthur Foundation, $360,000
- Pew Charitable Trusts, $300,000
- Turner Foundation, $253,875
- Henry Luce Foundation, $250,000
- Blue Moon Fund, #200,000

Environmental Law Institute

2000 L Street, N.W., Suite 620
Washington, D.C. 20036
202-939-3874 (phone)
202-939-3868 (fax)
www.eli.org

Membership
4,000

Tax Status
501(c((3)

Year Founded
1970

2004 Revenue (IRS Form 990)
$4,740,165

President
Leslie Carothers

Stated Objectives

"To achieve environmental protection by improving law, policy, and management. ELI researches pressing problems, educates professionals and citizens about the nature of these issues, and convenes all sectors in forging solutions."

Major Donations Received 2000-2004

- John D. and Catherine T. MacArthur Foundation, $680,000
- Ford Foundation, $637,000
- David and Lucile Packard Foundation, $415,000
- Rockefeller Foundation, $403,933
- William and Flora Hewlett Foundation, $325,000
- Andrew Mellon Foundation, $200,000
- Richard King Mellon Foundation, $200,000
- Blue Moon Fund, $160,000
- GE Foundation, $150,000
- Joyce Foundation, $70,000
- Turner Foundation, $70,000

Environmental Working Group

1436 U Street, N.W.
Washington, DC 20009
202-667-6982 (phone)
202-232-2592 (fax)
www.ewg.org

Tax Status
501(c)(3)

Year Founded
1993

2004 Revenue (IRS Form 990)
$2,811,403

President
Kenneth Cook

Stated Objective

"The Environmental Working Group is a not-for-profit environmental research organization dedicated to improving public health and the environment by reducing pollution in air, water and food."

Major Donations Received 2000-2003

- Joyce Foundation, $1,820,000
- Marisla Foundation, $755,000
- Blue Moon Fund, $495,000
- Beldon Fund, $400,000
- William and Flora Hewlett Foundation, $300,000
- Turner Foundation, $150,000
- Richard & Rhoda Goldman Fund, $100,000
- Ford Foundation, $100,000
- Surdna Foundation, $75,000
- San Francisco Foundation, $70,000
- New York Charitable Trust, $75,000

Friends of the Earth

1025 Vermont Avenue, N.W., Suite 300
Washington, D.C. 20005-6303
202-783-7400 (phone)
202-783-0444 (fax)
www.FoE.org

Tax Status
501(c)(3)

Year Founded
1967

2003 Revenue (IRS Form 990)
$3,807,497

President
Brent Blackwelder

Stated Objective
"Friends of the Earth is dedicated to protecting the planet from environmental degradation; preserving biological, cultural and ethnic diversity; and empowering citizens to have an influential voice in decisions affecting the quality of their environment—and their lives."

Major Donations Received 2000-2004

- Charles Stewart Mott Foundation, $1,710,000
- Blue Moon Fund, $650,000
- Pew Charitable Trusts, $600,000
- Ford Foundation, $505,000

- Wallace Global Fund, $314,000
- Richard & Rhoda Goldman Fund, $250,000
- Beldon Fund, $150,000
- Turner Foundation, $150,000
- Foundation for Deep Ecology, $77,500

Greenpeace, Inc.
702 H Street, N.W.
Washington, D.C. 20001
202-462-1177 (phone)
202-(fax)
www.greenpeace.org

Tax Status
501(c)(4)

Year Founded
1971

2004 Revenue (IRS Form 990)
$16,163,800

Executive Director
John W. Passacantando

Stated Objectives
"Greenpeace works to expose global environmental issues and promote solutions essential to protecting and preserving the environment through education, lobbying, advocacy and peaceful direct action."

Major Donations Received 2000-2003
- Turner Foundation, $1,050,000
- Rockefeller Brothers Fund, $780,000
- Blue Moon Fund, $390,000
- John Merck Fund, $120,000
- Brainard Foundation, $100,000

Izaak Walton League of America

707 Conservation Lane
Gaithersburg, MD 20878-2983
301-548-0150 (phone)
301-548-0146 (fax)
www.iwla.org

Tax Status
501(c)(3)

Year Founded
1922

2003 Revenue (IRS Form 990)
$3,486,915

Executive Director
Paul Hansen

Stated Objectives
"[T]o conserve, maintain, protect and restore the soil, forest, water and other natural resources of the United States of America and other lands; to promote means and opportunities for the education of the public with respect to such resources and the enjoyment and wholesome utilization thereof."

Major Donations Received 2000-2004
- David and Lucile Packard Foundation, $4,355,957
- Charles Stewart Mott Foundation, $1,250,000
- Doris Duke Charitable Trust, $1,000,000
- ALCOA Foundation, $800,000
- Ford Foundation, $788,000
- Rockefeller Foundation, $717,138
- Spencer T. and Ann Olin Foundation, $554,679
- Energy Foundation, $559,000
- Pew Charitable Trusts, $500,000

League of Conservation Voters

1920 L Street, N.W., Suite 800
Washington, D.C. 20036
202-785-0730 (phone)
202-835-0491 (fax)

Membership
40,000

Tax Status
501(c)(4)

Year Founded
1970

2004 Revenue (IRS Form 990)
$8,369,006

President
Gene Karpinski

Stated Objectives
"The League of Conservation Voters (LCV) is the political voice of the national environmental movement and the only organization devoted full-time to shaping a pro-environment Congress. We run tough and effective campaigns to defeat anti-environment candidates, and support those leaders who stand up for a clean, healthy future for America. Through our National Environmental Scorecard we hold Congress accountable for their actions on the environment. Through regional offices, we build coalitions, promote grassroots power, and train the next generation of environmental leaders."

Major Donations 2000-2003
• Turner Foundation, $6,657,126
• Blue Moon Fund, $300,000
• Wyss Foundation, $200,000
• Brainard Foundation, $110,000

National Audubon Society

700 Broadway
New York, NY 10003
212-979-3000 (phone)
212-979-3188 (fax)
www.audubon.org

Membership
554,000 (518 Chapters)

Tax Status
501(c)(3)

Year Founded
1886

2003 Revenue (IRS Form 990)
$76,595,365

President
John Flicker

Stated Objectives
"Audubon's mission is to conserve and restore natural ecosystems, focusing on birds and other wildlife for the benefits of humanity and the earth's biological diversity."

Major Donations Received 2000-2003
- David and Lucile Packard Foundation, $6,764,450
- Ford Motor Company Fund, $4,500,000
- Richard King Mellon Foundation, $610,000
- John D. and Catherine T. MacArthur Foundation, $450,000
- Richard & Rhoda Goldman Fund, $305,000
- Mary Flagler Cary Charitable Trust, $109,000
- Turner Foundation, $80,000
- John Merck Fund, $35,000

National Environmental Trust

1200 18th Street, N.W., Fifth Floor
Washington, D.C. 20036
202-887-8000 (phone)
202-887-8877 (fax)
www.net.org

Tax Status
501(c)(3)

Year Founded
1994

2004 Revenue (IRS Form 990)
$13,352,810

President
Phillip Clapp

Stated Objectives
"NET's public education campaigns present the latest scientific studies and public opinion research so that Americans from all walks of life can understand complex environmental issues."

Major Donations Received 2000-2004
- Pew Charitable Trusts, $20,500,000
- David and Lucile Packard Foundation, $1,210,000
- Energy Foundation, $1,200,000
- Blue Moon Fund, $1,200,000
- Rockefeller Brothers Fund, $950,000
- William and Flora Hewlett Foundation, $750,000
- Beldon Fund, $250,000
- Turner Foundation, $150,000
- New York Community Trust, $150,000
- Surdna Foundation, $150,000
- Tides Foundation, $60,000

National Wildlife Federation

11100 Wildlife Center Drive
Reston, VA 20190-5362
703-438-6000 (phone)
703-438-6075 (fax)
www.nwf.org

Membership
4,4000,000

Tax Status
501(c)(3)

Year Founded
1936

2004 Revenue (IRS Form 990)
$100,534,318

President
Larry Schweiger

Stated Objectives
"The mission of the National Wildlife Federation is to educate, inspire
and assist individuals and organizations of diverse cultures to conserve
wildlife and other natural resources and to protect the Earth's environment in order to achieve a peaceful, equitable and sustainable future."
World Resources Institute

Natural Resources Defense Council

40 West 20th Street
New York, NY 10011
212-727-2700 (phone)
212-727-1773 (fax)
www.nrdc.org

Tax Status
501(c)(3)

Year Founded
1970

2004 Revenue (IRS Form 990)
$57,303,087

President
John Adams

Stated Objectives
"The Natural Resources Defense Council's purpose is to safeguard the Earth; its people, its plants and animals and the natural systems on which all life depends. We work to restore the integrity of the elements that sustain life -- air, land and water -- and to defend endangered natural places. We seek to establish sustainability and good stewardship of the Earth as central ethical imperatives of human society. NRDC affirms the integral place of human beings in the environment. We strive to protect nature in ways that advance the long-term welfare of present and future generations. We work to foster the fundamental right of all people to have a voice in decisions that affect their environment. We seek to break down the pattern of disproportionate environmental burdens borne by people of color and other who face social or economic inequities. Ultimately, NRDC strives to help create a new way of life for humankind, one that can be sustained indefinitely without fouling or depleting the resources that support all life on Earth."

Major Donations Received 2000-2004
- Energy Foundation, $3,678,348
- Turner Foundation, $1,426,687
- William and Flora Hewlett Foundation, $1,100,000
- Blue Moon Fund, $775,000
- Surdna Foundation, $625,000
- David and Lucile Packard Foundation, $525,000
- New York Community Trust, $320,000
- Park Foundation, $300,000
- Geraldine R. Dodge Foundation, $300,000
- Henry Luce Foundation, $270,000
- Joyce Foundation, $250,000
- Peninsula Community Foundation, $195,000
- John Merck Fund, $185,000
- Ford Foundation, $150,000
- Pew Charitable Trusts, $150,000

Nature Conservancy

4245 N. Fairfax Drive, Suite 100
Arlington, VA 22203-1606
703-841-5300 (phone)
703--841-1283 (fax)
www.tnc.org

Membership
1,000,000

Tax Status
501(c)(3)

Year Founded
1951

2003 Revenue (IRS Form 990)
$732,402,173

President
Steven McCormick

Stated Objectives
"To preserves the plants, animals and natural communities that represent the diversity of life on Earth by protecting the lands and waters they need to survive."

Major Donations Received 2000-2004
- Charles Stewart Mott Foundation, $5,007,000
- David and Lucile Packard Foundation, $1,350,000
- Turner Foundation, $600,000
- ALCOA Foundation, $550,000
- John D. and Catherine T. MacArthur Foundation, $485,000
- Procter & Gamble Fund, $265,000
- Blue Moon Fund, $254,000
- Heinz Endowments, $100,000
- Bank of America Foundation, $80,000

Rainforest Action Network

221 Pine Street, Suite 500
San Francisco, CA 94104
415-398-4404 (phone)
415-398-2732 (fax)
www.ran.org

Tax Status
501(c)(3)

Year Founded
1985

2003 Revenue (IRS Form 990)
$1,000,672

President
Randall Hayes

Stated Objectives
"We believe a sustainable world can be achieved in our lifetime and that aggressive action must be taken immediately to leave a safe and secure world for our children."

Major Donations Received 2000-2003
- Rockefeller Foundation, $400,000
- Ford Foundation, $290,000
- Richard & Rhoda Goldman Fund, $250,000
- Tides Foundation, $201,815
- Turner Foundation, $80,000
- Compton Foundation, $70,400
- Wallace Global Fund, $65,000
- Foundation for Deep Ecology, $55,000
- Blue Moon Fund, $50,000

Resources for the Future

1616 P Street, N.W.
Washington, DC 20036-1400
202-328-5000 (phone)
202-939-3460 (fax)
www.rff.org

Tax Status
501(c)(3)

Year Founded
1952

2003 Revenue (IRS Form 990)
$9,189,422

President
Philip R. Sharp

Stated Objectives
"RFF is a nonprofit and nonpartisan thing tank located in Washington, DC that conducts independent research—rooted primarily in economics and other social sciences—on environmental and other natural resources issues."

Major Donations Received 2000-2003
- Andrew Mellon Foundation, $1,630,000
- Rockefeller Foundation, $459,594
- Energy Foundation, $125,000
- William and Flora Hewlett Foundation, $100,000
- John Merck Fund, $25,000
- ExxonMobil Foundation, $25,000

Sierra Club

85 Second Street, 2nd Floor
San Francisco, CA 94105-3441
415-977-5500 (phone)
415 977-5799 (fax)
www.sierraclub.org

Membership
700,000

Tax Status
501(c)(4)

Year Founded
1892

2004 Revenue (IRS Form 990)
$91,843,757

Executive Director
Carl Pope

Stated Objectives
"More than a century ago, conservationist John Muir challenged Americans to 'do something for wilderness and make the mountains glad.' Today, the Sierra Club is still meeting that challenge to explore, enjoy, and protect the planet.

The Sierra Club believes that citizen action can alter and redefine local, national, and global environmental priorities. And the Sierra Club's experienced, respected, and committed fellowship of community volunteers will lead the way.

Our powerful grassroots member base, our widespread public support, our influential media connections, and our long-established relationships with local and national decision-makers make us uniquely effective in influencing public policy and achieving environmental progress. The Sierra Club defines the issues, puts them in the public eye, and then mobilizes the support necessary to compel decision-makers to take action."

Major Donations Received 1998-2004
- Pew Charitable Trusts, $1,689,000
- Charles Stewart Mott Foundation, $1,234,000
- Brainard Foundation, $988,500
- Turner Foundation, $715,000
- Rockefeller Brothers Fund, $710,000
- Nathan Cummings Foundation, $315,000
- John Merck Fund, $60,000

Union of Concerned Scientists

Two Brattle Square
Cambridge, MA 02238-9105
617-547-5552 (phone)
617-864-9405 (fax)
www.ucsusa.org

Membership
50,000

Tax Status
501(c)(3)

Year Founded
1969

2003 Revenue (IRS Form 990)
$12,130,811

President
Kevin Knobloch

Stated Objectives
"The Union of Concerned scientists is a nonprofit partnership of scientists and citizens combining rigorous scientific analysis, innovative policy development and effective citizen advocacy to achieve practical environmental solutions.

Established in 1969, we seek to ensure that all people have clean air, energy and transportation, as well as food that is produced in a safe and sustainable manner. We strive for a future that is free from the threats of global warming and nuclear war, and a planet that supports a rich diversity of life. Sound science guides our efforts to secure changes in government policy, corporate practices and consumer choices that will protect and improve the health of our environment globally, nationally and in our communities throughout the United States. In short, UCS seeks a great change in humanity's stewardship of the earth."

Major Donations Received 2000-2004
- Pew Charitable Trusts, $2,999,000
- William and Flora Hewlett Foundation, $750,000
- Ford Foundation, $670,000
- Blue Moon Fund, $481,500
- Henry Luce Foundation, $400,000
- Energy Foundation, $350,000

- Joyce Foundation, $325.000
- John Merck Fund, $195,000
- David and Lucile Packard Foundation, $127,000
- New York Charitable Trust, $125,000
- Turner Foundation, $50,000

Wilderness Society

1615 M Street, N.W.
Washington, D.C. 20036
1-800-843-9353 (phone)
202-429-3757 (fax)
www.wilderness.org

Membership
313,000

Tax Status
501(c)(3)

Year Founded
1935

2003 Revenue (IRS Form 990)
$27,234,601

President
William Meadows

Stated Objectives
"Deliver to future generations an unspoiled legacy of wild places, with all the precious values they hold.   Biological diversity; clean air and water;towering forests; rushing water, and sage=sweet, silent deserts

We bring to bear our scientific expertise, analysis and bold advocacy at the highest levels to save, protect and restore America's wilderness areas."

Major Donations Received 1999-2004
- Pew Charitable Trusts, $2,596,000
- Rockefeller Brothers Fund, $520,000
- Brainard Foundation, $450,000
- Nathan Cummings Foundation, $275,000
- David and Lucile Packard Foundation, $275,000
- William and Flora Hewlett Foundation, $272,000

- Town Creek Foundation, $250,000
- Turner Foundation, $200,000
- Surdna Foundation, $200,000
- Compton Foundation, $110,000

World Resources Institute
10 G Street, N.E.
Washington, D.C. 20002
202-729-7600 (phone)
202-729-7610 (fax)
www.wri.org

Tax Status
501(c)(3)

Year Founded
1982

Stated Objectives
"The World Resource Institute's mission is to move human society to live in ways that protect Earth's environment and its capacity to provide for the needs and aspirations of current and future generations.

Because people are inspired by ideas, empowered by knowledge, and moved to change by greater understanding, WRI provides— and helps other organizations provide—objective information and practical proposals for policy and institutional change that will foster environmentally sound, socially equitable development."

Major Donations Received 2000-2002
- William and Lucile Packard Foundation, $4,395,977
- Charles Stewart Mott Foundation, $1,250,000
- Ford Foundation, $1,040,000
- Doris Duke Charitable Trust, $1,000,000
- ALCOA Foundation, $750,000
- Spencer T. and Ann W. Olin Foundation, $554,679
- Pew Charitable Trusts, $500,000
- Rockefeller Foundation, $292,000
- Richard & Rhoda Goldman Foundation, $230,000
- Energy Foundation, $200,000
- John D. Catherine T. MacArthur Foundation, $375,000

World Wildlife Fund/Conservation Foundation

1250 24th Street, N.W.
Washington, D.C. 20037
202-293-4800 (phone)
202-293-2239 (fax)
www.worldwildlife.org

Membership
1,200,000

Tax Status
501(c)(3)

Year Founded
1961

2003 Revenue (IRS Form 990)
$112,001,561

President and Director
Kathryn Fuller

Stated Objectives
"Known worldwide by its panda logo, World Wildlife Fund (WWF) is dedicated to protecting the world's wildlife and wildlands. The largest privately supported international conservation organization in the world, WWF has more than 1 million members in the U.S. alone. Since its inception in 1961, WWF has invested in over 13,100 projects in 157 countries.

WWF directs its conservation efforts toward three goals: protecting endangered species, saving endangered species and addressing global threats. From working to save the giant panda, tiger, and rhino to helping establish and manage parks and reserves worldwide. WWF has been a conservation leader for 40 years."

Major Donations Received 2000-2003
- David and Lucile Packard Foundation, $12,715,400
- New York Charitable Trust, $1,145,000
- Pew Charitable Trusts, $1,000,000
- Eastman Kodak Charitable Trust, $990,000
- ALCOA Foundation, $750,000
- Ford Foundation, $600,000
- Richard & Rhoda Goldman Fund, $500,000
- Henry Luce Foundation, $450,000

- W.K. Kellog Foundation, $304,374
- Blue Moon Fund, $180,000
- Charles Stewart Mott Foundation, $171,000
- Energy Foundation, $175,857
- Joyce Foundation, $150,000
- Turner Foundation, $100,000

Worldwatch Institute
1776 Massachusetts Avenue, N.W.
Washington, DC 20036
202-452-1999 (phone)
202-296-7365 (fax)
www.worldwatch.org

Tax Status
501(c)(3)

Year Founded
1974

2004 Revenue (IRS Form 990)
$2,612,042

Founder
Lester Brown

Stated Objectives
"The Worldwatch Institute is an independent research organization that works for an environmentally sustainable and socially just society, in which the needs of all people are met without threatening the health of the natural environment or the well-being of future generations. By providing compelling, accessible, and fact-based analysis of critical global issues, Worldwatch informs people around the world about the complex interactions between people, nature, and economies. Worldwatch focuses on the underlying causes of and practical solutions to the world's problems, in order to inspire people to demand new policies, investment patters and lifestyle choices."

Major Donations 2000-2003
- William and Flora Hewlett Foundations, $1,550,000
- David and Lucile Packard Foundation, $650,000
- Blue Moon Fund, $360,000
- Turner Foundation, $315,000

- Charles Stewart Mott Foundation, $300,000
- Richard & Rhoda Goldman Foundation, $200,000
- Wallace Global Fund, $90,000

- All data cited in this section are drawn from IRS Form 990s posted on www.guidestar.org; www.capitalresearch.org; and www.activistcash.org.

Notes

Introduction

1. Quoted in Michael Crichton, *State of Fear* (New York: Harper Collins, 2004), p.580.
2. Michael Shellenberger and Ted Nordhaus, "The Death of Environmentalism: Global Warming Politics in a Post-Environmental World," *Grist,* Jan. 13, 2005, p. 6
   <http://www.grist.org/news/maindish/2005/01/13/doe-reprint
3. Felicity Barringer, "Paper Sets Off Debate on Environmentalism's Future," *New York Times*, Feb. 6, 2005.
4. Carl Pope, "And Now Something Completely Different: An In-Depth Response to the 'Death of Environmentalism,'" *Grist,* Jan. 13, 2005, 1
   <http://www.grist.org/news/maindish/2005/01/13/pope-reprint/
5. Angela Logomasini, e-mail to the author, Feb. 8, 2005.
6. See George Will, "Global Warming? Hot Air," *Washington Post,* Dec. 23, 2004, p. A23.

Chapter One

1. Quoted in Jarol B. Manheim, *Biz-War and the Out-of-Power Elite: The Progressive Left's Attack on the Corporation* (Mahwah, N.J.: Lawrence Erlbaum Associates, 2004), p.15.
2. Steven Milloy, "Turning Children Against," *New York Sun,* Jan. 27, 2005. <http://www.csrwatch.com/turningchildren.htm>, and Allan Murray, "Scandals Leave Big Banks Vulnerable," *Wall Street Journal,* April 13, 2005), p. A2.
3. Manheim, p. 5.
4. Manheim, pp. 16-17.
5. Quoted in David Henderson, *The Role of Business in the Modern World: Progress, Pressures and Prospects for the Market Economy* (Washington, D.C.: Competitive Enterprise Institute, 2004), p. 95.
6. Henderson, p. 96.
7. Quoted in Jonathan Adler, *Environmentalism at the Crossroads: Green Activism in America* (Washington, D.C.: Capital Research Center, 1995), p. 50.

8. Stephen Schimdheiny of the Business Council on Sustainable Development in *Changing Course: A Global Business Perspective on Development and the Environment* (Cambridge, Mass.: MIT Press, 1992), p. 6.

9. Manheim, p. 86.

10. Quoted in David Henderson, *Misguided Virtue: False Notions of CSR* (London: Institute of Economic Affairs, 2001), p. 12.

11. Steven Milloy, "The Subliminal Corporate Takeover," *New York Sun,* March 3, 2005
    <http://www.csrwatch.com/Corporate_Takeover.htm>.

12. Henderson, *Role of Business,* p. 18.

13. Milloy "Subliminal Corporate Takeover."

14. Henderson, *Misguided Virtue,* p. 15.

15. Henderson, *Role of Business,* p. 108.

16. Henderson, *Misguided Virtue,* p. 16.

17. Quoted in Henderson, *Misguided Virtue,* p. 42.

18. Quoted in Henderson, *Misguided Virtue,* p. 12.

19. Jim Carlton, "J.P. Morgan Adopts Green Lending Policies," *Wall Street Journal,* April 25, 2005, p. B1.

20. Carlton. P. B1.

21. Manheim, pp. 36-37. See Manheim, pp. 26-42 for a fascinating discussion of Mailman's wide-ranging fund-raising activities for the Left.

22. Interview with Steven Milloy, April 29, 2005. Milloy is managing partner of Action Fund Management, LLC, an advisor to the Free Enterprise Action Fund.

23. Quoted in Manheim, p. 90.

24. Manheim, p. 97.

25. Carlton, p, B1.

26. Christopher Rowland, "Greening of the Boardroom: Socially Responsible Investors Get Results on Global Warming," *Boston Globe,* March 31, 2005 <http://www.bostonglobe.com/business/ articles/2005/03/31/greening_of_the_boardroom.>.

27. Steven Milloy, "Warning to CEOs: Global Warming is in Junk Mail," *New York Sun,* Feb. 17, 2005,
    http://www.csrwatch.com/Warning_for_CEOs.htm.>.

28. Milloy, "Warning."

29. Henderson, *Misguided Virtue,* p. 16.

30. Quoted in Arthur M. Laffer, Andrew Coors and Wayne Winegarden, "Does Corporate Social Responsibility Enhance Business Profitability?" Laffer Associates 2004, p. 1.

31. Laffer, Coors and Winegarden, p. 6.
32. Manheim, p. 3.
33. Carlton, p. B1; Murray, p. A2.

Chapter Two

1. Quoted in Thomas R. DeGregori, *Bountiful Harvest: Technology, Food Safety, and the Environment* (Washington, D.C.: Cato Institute, 2002), p. 59.
2. Dick Taverne, T*he March of Unreason: Science, Democracy and the New Fundamentalism* (Oxford: Oxford University Press, 2005), p. 26.
3. Quoted in James M. Sheehan, *Global Greens: Inside the International Environmental Establishment* (Washington, D.C.: Capital Research Center, 1998), p. 11.
4. Sheehan, p. 5.
5. Jeremy Rabkin and James Sheehan, *Global Greens, Global Governance.* IEA Environment Working Paper No.4 (London: Institute for Economic Affairs, 1999), p. 39.
6. Sheehan, p. 23.
7. Indur M. Goklany, *The Precautionary Principle: A Critical Appraisal of Environmental Risk Assessment* (Washington, D.C.: Cato Institute, 2001), p. 23; Taverne, p. 29.
8. G. Gorden Edwards, "DDT: A Case Study in Scientific Fraud," *Journal of American Physicians and Surgeons* (vol. 9, no. 3, Fall 2004), p. 86; Tina Rosenberg, "What the World Needs Now is DDT," *New York Times Magazine*, April 11, 2004, p. 11; Malcolm Gladwell, "The Mosquito Killer," *The New Yorker,* July 2, 2001, p. 42.
9. Ron Arnold and Alan Gottlieb, *Trashing the Economy: How Runaway Environmentalism is Wrecking America* (Belleview, Washington: Merrill Press, 1993), p. 290.
10. Goklany, p. 15.
11. Quoted in Edwards, p. 83.
12. Gladwell, p. 44.
13. Quoted in Edwards, p. 86.
14. Rosenberg, p. 12.
15. Taverne, p. 185.
16. Quoted in DeGregori, p. 135.
17. Rosenberg, p. 13.
18. Paul Driessen, *Eco-Imperialism: Green Power, Black Death* (Belleview, Washington: Free Enterprise Press, 2003), p. 66.

19. Quoted in Edwards, p. 86.

20. Aaron Wildavsky, *But Is It True? A Citizen's Guide to Environmental Health and Safety Issues* (Cambridge: Harvard University Press, 1993), pp. 55-80.

21. Quoted in Driessen, p. 73.

22. Goklany, p. 16.

23. Quoted in James Hoare, "Greenpeace, WWF Repudiate Anti-DDT Agenda." *Environment & Climate News* (vol. 8, no. 3: April 2005), P. 19.

24. Hoare, p. 19.

25. Elizabeth M. Whelan, "Phony Science and Real Risks: The Human Costs of Hyperbole About Environmental Threats," in *The Wages of Fear: The Costs to Society of Attacks on the Products of Human Ingenuity* (Arlington, Virginia: Lexington Institute, 2002), pp. 4-6.

26. Goklany, p. 4.

27. Bonner R. Cohen, "The Safety Nazis: The Precautionaries Shun the Burden of Truth," *The American Spectator* June 2001, p. 32.

28. Goklany, pp. 4-5.

29. Cohen, "Safety Nazis," p. 34.

30. Goklany, p. 6.

31. Quoted in Bonner R. Cohen, "Precautionary Principle Flouts Science," *Spokane Spokesman-Review*, July 15, 2001.

32. Quoted in DeGregori, p. 121.

33. DeGregori, p. 122.

34. John D. Graham, "The Perils of the Precautionary Principle: Lessons From the American and European Experience," *Heritage Lecture #818* (Washington, DC: Heritage Foundation), Jan. 15, 2004, http://www.heritage.org/Research/Regulation/h818.cfm.

35. Henry Miller and Gregory Conko, "Children, Fear and Biotechnology," in Deland R. Juberg, *Are Children More Vulnerable to Environmental Chemicals? Scientific and Regulatory Issues in Perspective* (New York: American Council on Science and Health, 2003), p. 179.

36. Henry I. Miller, "Some Still Can't Digest Idea of Biotech Food," Investor's Business Daily April 15, 2004.

37. Miller and Conko, p. 179.

38. Miller and Conko, p. 179-180.

39. Taverne, p. 96.

40. Henry Miller and Greg Conko, "Biotech's Antagonists," *Techcentralstation,* May 4, 2004
www.techcentralstation.com/050404D.html.>/

41. DeGregori, p. 120-121.
42. Taverne, p. 80.
43. Jonathan Rauch, "Will Frankenfood Save the Planet?" *Atlantic Monthly*, Oct. 2003.
44. Robert James Bidinotto, "Death by Environmentalism," *The Objectivist Newsletter*, April 19, 2004.
45. DeGregori, p. 121.
46. Wildavsky, p. 430.
47. Rauch, p. 3.
48. Rauch, p. 3.
49. Driessen, pp. 59-60; Susan Dudly and Eileen Norcross, "States of Fear," *Regulation*, Spring 2005, p. 60.
50. Henry I. Miller and Gregory Conko, "NGO War on Biotechnology," *Journal of Commercial Biotechnology* (vol. 11, no 3, April 2005), p. 216.
51. David Burke, "The Frankenfood Myth: How Protests and Politics Threaten the Biotechnology Revolution," *Journal of Commercial Biotechnology* (Vol. 11, No. 2, Jan. 2005), p. 191.
52. Miller and Conko, "NGO War," p. 214.
53. Henry Miller and Gregory Conko, "Misnamed Activists Are Thorns in Rose of Agbiotech Foods," *Investor's Business Daily*, March 4, 2005, p. A16.
54. Quoted in Miller and Conko, "NGO War," p. 218-219.
55. Driessen, p. 56.
56. DeGregori, p. 102.
57. Quoted in Taverne, pp. 84-85.
58. Dudley and Norcross, p. 59.
59. Quoted in Taverne, p. 96.
60. Rauch, p. 8.
61. Paul Johnson, "What Europe Really Needs," *Wall Street Journal* June 17, 2005, p. A14.
62. Quoted in Driessen, p. 51.
63. Quoted in DeGregori, p. 122.
64. Dudley and Norcross, p. 59.
65. Bonner R. Cohen, "Natural Resources Defense Council: Weapons in the Environmentalists' Arsenal: Lawsuits, Blacklists and Publicity," *Organization Trends* (Washington, D.C.: Capital Research Center, August 2005), p. 1.
66. Carlo Stagnaro, "The Political Economy of Climate Change," in Kendra Okonski (ed.) *Adapt or Die: The Science, Politics and Economics of Climate Change* (London: Profile Books, 2003), p. 201.

67. Philip Slott, "Global Climate Change Has Always Occurred," *Savannah Morning News,* Jan. 8, 2000, p. 9A.

68. Patrick J. Michaels and Robert C. Balling, *The Satanic Gasses: Clearing the Air on Global Warming* (Washington: Cato Institute, 2000), p. 14.

69. Wildavsky, pp. 334-336; Sheehan, pp. 33-37.

70. Wildavsky, p. 338.

71. Sheehan, p. 36.

72. Quoted in Thomas J. Bray (Ed.) *Unconventional Wisdom: The Best of Warren Brookes* (San Francisco: Pacific Research Institute for Public Policy, 1997), p. 211.

73. Oppenheimer, Leggett and Sierra Clubs quotes from Jonathan Adler, p. 55.

74. See Wildavsky, pp. 370 and 387 for Schneider on global cooling.

75. Gore quoted in Easterbrook, p. 278.

76. Michaels and Balling, pp. 16-17.

77. Wildavsky, p. 345.

78. Richard A. Lindzen, "Global Warming: The Origins and Nature of Alleged Scientific Consensus," in John A. Baden, *Environmental Gore: A Constructive Response to "Earth in the Balance"* (San Francisco: Pacific Research Institute for Public Policy, 1994), p. 128.

79. Lindzen, p. 135.

80. Justin Blum, "Exxon Mobil Chief to Leave," *Washington Post,* August 5, 2005, p. D3.

81. James Schlesinger, "Science Unsettled on Global Warming," *Washington Post,* Nov. 15, 2003, p.A19.

82. "Die Klimakatastrophe Kommt," (Climate Disaster is Coming), *Suddeutsche Zeitung* (Munich), July 23, 2001.

83. James Schlesinger, "The Theology of Global Warming," *Wall Street Journal,* Aug. 8, 2005, p. A10.

84. Sheehan, pp. 38-40 on NGO influence.

85. Pranay Gupte and Bonner R. Cohen, "Gore's Crusaders," *Forbes,* Feb. 22, 1999, 74-76; Ron Arnold, *Undue Influence: Wealthy Foundation, Grant-Driven Environmental Groups, and Zealous Bureaucrats That Control Your Future* (Bellvue, Wash.: Free Enterprise Press, 1999), pp. 198-208.

86. See Michaels and Balling, p. 19.

87. Quoted in Sheehan, p. 42.

88. The author attended the conference as a correspondent for *Earth Times.*

89. Quoted in Sheehan, p. 47.

90. Personal recollection of the author from the Kyoto conference.
91. Gore quoted in Sheehan, p. 46.
92. Quoted in Bruce Yandle and Stuart Buck, "Bootleggers, Baptists and the Global Warming Battle," in Okonski, p. 173.
93. Robert J. Samuelson, "Greenhouse Hypocrisy," *Washington Post,* June 29, 2005, A21.
94. James L. Johnston, "EU Emissions Trading Off Slow Start," *Environment & Climate News* July 2005, p. 10.
95. James Glassman, "Way Beyond Kyoto," *Washington Times,* August 3, 2005, p. A12.
96. Quoted in Lindzen, p. 132.
97. Goklany, p. 79.
98. Barbara Helfferich, "Cutting Global Warming," *Washington Post,* July 7, 2005, p. A16.
99. Quoted in John Vidal, "Europe Fails to Cut Greenhouse Gas Emissions," *The Guardian,* June 18, 2005.
100. Shankar Vedantam, "Kyoto Credits System Aids the Rich, Some Say," *Washington Post,* March 12, 2005, p.A12.
101. Johnston, p.10; Vedantam, p. A15.
102. Statement by the President, The White House, Office of the Press Secretary, July 27, 2005.
103. President Bush and the Asian-Pacific Partnership for Clean Development, The White House, Office of the Press Secretary July 27, 2005.
104. "Australia Claims Part Credit for Beyond Kyoto," *Reuters,* July 28, 2005.
105. Nicholas Kralev," U.S. Completes 6-Nation Deal on Emissions," *Washington Times,* July 28, 2005, p. A10.
106. Michelle Nichols, "Beyond Kyoto Greenhouse Pact Being Formed," *Reuters,* July 27, 2005.
107. James G. Lakely, "China Chirac Claims Victory Over U.S. Kyoto," *Washington Times,* July 8, 2005, p. A4; Robert D. Novak, "Bush's Climate Victory," *Washington Post,* July 14, 2005, p. A25.
108. Michaels and Balling, p. 15.
109. Joe Barton, Chairman, U.S. House of Representatives Committee on Energy and Commerce, letter to Dr. Rajendra K. Pachauri, chairman, Intergovernmental Panel on Climate Change, June 23, 2005, p. 1.
110. Antonio Regalado, "In Climate Debate, the Hockey Stick Leads to a Face-Off," *Wall Street Journal,* Feb. 14, 2005, p. A1.
111. Schlesinger, "Theology," p. A10.

112. Barton, p. 1-2.
113. S. Fred Singer, TWTW, July 23, 2005 <http://sepp.org>.
114. Quoted in Kralev, p. A10.
115. Juliet Eilperin, "Senate Rejects Emissions Limits," *Washington Post,* August 24, 2005, p. A3.
116. Juliet Eilperin, "Three States Seek Emissions Pact," *Washington Post,* August 25, 2005, p. A2; Anthony dePalma, "9 States in Plan to Cut Emissions by Power Plants," *New York Times,* August 24, 2005, p. A7.
117. "States Toughen Emissions Rules," *Washington Times,* August 22, 2005, p. C11.
118. USEPA, "Control of Emissions From New Highway Vehicles," 08. Fed. Reg. 52922, 62929, Sept. 8, 2003.
119. U.S.C. 49, Sec. 32919 (a).
120. Eilperin, "Three States," p. A2.
121. Jeff Kueter, "Funding Flow for Climate Change Research and Related Activities," (Washington D.C.: George Marshall Institute) Feb. 2002, p. 2.
122. Quoted in "Understanding Mercury Deposition in the U.S.," EPW Fact of the Day, U.S. Senate Environment and Public Works Committee, August 5, 2005; Friends of the Earth advertisement in *USA Today,* March 16, 2004; NRDC advertisement in *New York Times,* March 26, 2004.
123. Bonner R. Cohen, "The Environmental Working Group: Peddlers of Fear," *Organization Trends* (Capital Research Center) Jan. 2004; www.ewg.org/issues/mercury/20031209/index.php.>.
124. U.S. House of Representatives, Committee on Resources, Richard W. Pombo and Jim Gibbons, *Mercury in Perspective: Fact and Fiction About the Debate Over Mercury,* Feb. 16, 2005, p. 7.
125. Pranay Gupte and Bonner R. Cohen, "Master of Mission Creep," *Forbes,* Oct. 20, 1997, pp. 170-173.
126. *Mercury in Perspective,* p.11.
127. Henry Miller, "EPA Issues Cap and Trade Mercury Rule," *Environment & Climate News,* May 2005, p. 1.
128. US EPA, *Regulatory Finding on the Emission of Hazardous Air Pollutants From Electric Utility Steam Generating Units,* EPA 65 FR 79825 (Dec. 28, 2000).
129. *Mercury in Perspective,* p. 15.
130. Louis Sullivan, "Mercury in Tuna: A Tenuous Connection," letter to the editor *Wall Street Journal,* Aug. 12, 2005, p. A9.
131. Nat Mund, "Mercury and Tuna," letter to the editor *Wall Street*

Journal, Aug. 12, 2005, p. A9.
132. Quoted in Darmen Samualsohn, "Court Rejects Enviros' Plea to Halt EPA Rule," *Greenwire,* Aug. 4, 2005.
133. Quoted in Debra Saunders, "Blair Takes Heat for Global-Warming Remarks," *San Francisco Chronicle,* Oct. 2, 2005.
134. Juliet Eilperin, "U.S. Won't Join in Binding Climate Talks," *Washington Post,* Dec. 11, 2005, pp. A1, 27.
135. Morgan quoted in Eilperin, "U.S. Won't Join," A27; Claussen quoted in Michael Fumento, "Ditch Kyoto," *Washington Times,* Dec. 12, 2005, p. A16.
136. Revkin quoted in Tom Randall, "World Turns President Bush's Way in Climate Change: Cutting CO2 Useless, Harmful," *Winningreen,* Dec. 6, 2005, p. 1.
137. Angela Logomasini and Henry I. Miller, "REACH: Exceeding Its Grasp," *Regulation* (Washington: Cato Institute, Fall 2005), p. 11.
138. Henry I. Miller and Gregory Conko, "The UN at 60," *techcentralstation,* July 5, 2005, www.techcentralstation.com/070505E.html.> and Angela Logomasini, "Europe's Global REACH: Costly for the World; Suicidal for Europe," www.cei.org/environment/eurpesglobal reach.html.>.
139. Duane Parde, American Legislative Exchange Council letter to John Shoaff, U.S. Environmental Protection Agency, Sept. 6, 2005, p. 1-2.
140. Angela Logomasini, "Earth Sense in the Balance," *CEI Envirowire* (Washington: Competitive Enterprise Institute, Sept. 23, 2005), p. 1.
141. Logomasini, "Europe's Global REACH," 2; 257. Sally McNamara, "REACH: The EU's Proposed Chemicals Regime," *Atlantic Connection* (Washington: American Legislative Exchange Council, VIII, July 2005). P. 4.
142. Quoted in Driessen, p. 109.
143. John O'Sullivan, "Beware the Tranzis," *Washington Times*, Aug. 12, 2005, p. A17; Chirac quoted in Driessen, p. 110.
144. Degregori, p. 202.
145. Slott, p. 13A.
146. Joyce Howard Price, "U.S. Takes New View on DDT in Africa," *Washington Times*, May 3, 2006, p, A1.

Chapter Three

1. John Adams, "Defence of the Constitutions of Government of the United States," *Works* (1787) 6:8-9 in "The Founders' Constitution," chapter 16 ("Property"), http://press-pubs.uchicago.edu /founders >http://press-pubs.uchicago.edu/founders/tocs/v1ch16.html<

2. John Carlton, "Rancher Turns the Tables," *Wall Street Journal,* August 19, 2005, p. B1.

3. http://www.biodiversity.org/swcbd/aboutus/index.

4. Arnold, *Undue Influence,* p. 17.

5. Philip J. Maslar and David Hogberg, "Deep Ecology and Depthless Thinking: How the Foundation for Deep Ecology Supports Radical Environmentalists," *Foundation Watch* (Capital Research Center, Oct. 2005), p. 5.

6. Quoted in Arnold, p. 263.

7. Quoted in Maslar and Hogberg, p. 2.

8. Quoted in Bonner R. Cohen, "The Green Landgrabbers: It's Not Just the Feds Who Are After Your Land," *Foundation Watch* (Capital Research Center, November 2001), p. 5.

9. Maslar and Hogberg, 3; Cohen, "Green Landgrabbers," p. 5.

10. Allan K. Fitzsimmons, "The Illusion of Ecosystem Management," *PERC Reports* (Political Economy Research Center, December 1999), p. 1.

11. Alston Chase, *In a Dark Wood: The Fight Over Forests and the Rising Tyranny of Ecology* (Houghton Mifflin, New York, 1995), p. 7.

12. Quoted in Fitzsimmons, p. 4.

13. Charles Mann and Mark Plummer, *Noah's Choice: The Future of Endangered Species* (New York: Alfred A. Knopf, 1995), pp. 89-90.

14. Chase, p. 114.

15. Chase, p. 118.

16. Mann and Plummer, pp. 24-25.

17. Mann and Plummer, p. 17.

18. Chase, pp. 80-81.

19. R.J. Smith, "Helping Endangered Species Survive," in Bonner R. Cohen, Steven J. Milloy and Steven J. Zrake, *American Values: An Environmental Vision* (Environmental Policy Network, Washington, DC, 1996), p. 62; Chase, p. 150.

20. Smith, pp. 62-63; Chase, 150.

21. Mann and Plummer, p. 149.

22. Quoted in Ron Arnold and Alan Gottlieb, *Trashing the Economy:*

How Runaway Environmentalism is Wrecking America (Bellevue, Wash.: Free Enterprise Press, 1993), p. 231.

23. Arnold and Gottlieb, p. 230; Chase, p. 115.
24. Arnold and Gottlieb, p. 234; Arnold, pp. 55-56; Chase, p. 283.
25. Chase, p. 260.
26. Chase, p. 313.
27. Robert H. Nelson, "Western Myths and Realities," *Regulation* (Cato Institute, Summer 2002), p. 41.
28. Kimberley Strassel, "Owls of Protest," *Wall Street Journal,* Oct. 19, 2005, p. A12.
29. "Owl Story Takes a New Twist," *Washington Times,* June 22, 2004, p. A9; Strassel, p. A12.
30. Arnold, pp. 221-234.
31. Quoted in Chase. p, 360.
32. Chase, p. 9.
33. Nicholas Lemann, "No People Allowed," *New Yorker,* Nov. 22, 1999, p. 106
34. Smith, "Helping Species," p. 63; Jonathan Adler, "Bad for Land, Bad for Critters," *Wall Street Journal,* Dec. 31, 2003, p. A8.
35. Smith, pp. 64-66.
36. "People Suck" (editorial), *Wall Street Journal,* May 16, 2001, p. A22.
37. Quoted in Blain Harden, "A Wildlife Sanctuary Withers," *Washington Post,* April 4, 2004, p. A2.
38. Chase, pp. 274-275.
39. Gretchen Randall, "Taxpayers Fund Center for Biological Diversity," *Winningreen,* June 1, 2005.
40. Audrey Hudson, "306 Acres End Habitat Battle for Shrimp," *Washington Times,* April 20, 2005, p. A6.
41. R.J. Smith, "The Endangered Species Act: Shoot, Shovel and Shut Up," in *Big Government and Bad Science: Ten Case Studies in Regulatory Abuse* (Lexington Institute November 1999), p. 13.
42. <http://www.resourcescommittee.house.go/press/releases/2005/0517ESAreport.htm>; "Endangering Species" (editorial), *Wall Street Journal,* July 1, 2005, p. A8.
43. Juliet Eilperin, "Rewrite of Endangered Species Act Approved," *Washington Post,* Sept. 23, 2005, p. A2.
44. Audrey Hudson, "Report Pegs Cost of Species Protection in Billions," *Washington Times,* April 15, 2004, p. A8.
45. Joan Lowy, "GOP Takes Aim at Endangered Species Act," *Washington Times,* Nov. 27, 2004, p. A3.
46. Eilperin, "Rewrite," p. A2.

47. Bonner R. Cohen, "Federal Land Squeezing Budgets," *Arizona Republic,* Jan. 4, 2003; Chris Cannon, "Freeing Up Federal Lands," *Washington Times,* March 8, 2005, p. A10.

48. Shepherd Pittman, "The Last of True America," (interview with Chilton Williamson) *Washington Times,* Oct. 15, 2005, p. A2.

49. Arnold, pp. 235-245.

50. Tom Nelson, "Forest Health Care Crisis," *Washington Times,* Aug. 2, 2003, p. A17; "Hope for Healthy Forests" (editorial), *Washington Times,* Oct. 1, 2003, p. A14.

51. Thomas Bonnicksen, "There is an Answer to Our Wildfire Problem," *San Diego Union-Tribune,* Aug. 14, 2002.

52. Patrick Moore, "Nature vs. Politics," *Wall Street Journal,* June 18, 2003, p. A19.

53. Robert H. Nelson, "Abolish the Forest Service," *Forbes,* Sept. 18, 2002, p. 194.

54. Bonner R. Cohen, "Mandating Roadless Areas Leads to Harm," *Florida Times-Union,* June 26, 2002.

55. "The Fire Next Time" (editorial), *Wall Street Journal,* June 21, 2002, p. A8; For a portrait of McGinty, see Arnold, pp. 219-223.

56. "An Analytical Review of the Development of the President's Roadless Area Initiative," A Preliminary Staff Report of the Subcommittee on Forests and Forest Health, Feb. 18, 2000, p. 1.

57. "Analytical Review," p.1.

58. "Analytical Review," p. 1.

59. "Analytical Review," p. 5.

60. "Analytical Review," p. 2.

61. Juliet Eilperin, "Roadless Rules for Forests Set Aside," *Washington Post,* July 13, 2004, pp. A1, A5; Audrey Hudson, "Bush Drops Roadless Forest Rule," *Washington Times,* June 13, 2004, p. A9.

62. Quoted in Hudson, "Bush Drops Roadless," p. A9 and Eilperin, "Roadless Rules," p. A5.

63. Tom Nelson, "Forest Health Care Crisis," p. A17; "Hope for Healthy Forests," p. A17.

64. Roberrt J. Smith, "A New Beginning for Our Forests," *San Diego Union-Tribune,* November 30, 2004.

65. "Forest Policy Fans Political Fires in West," *Wall Street Journal,* June 17, 2004, p. A4.

66. Thomas Bonnicksen, "Preventing Tomorrow's Fires," *Washington Times,* Jan. 3, 2004, p. A13.

67. Chad Hanson, "Should Congress Ban Road-Building in Forests?" *Cape Cod Times,* July 8, 2002.

Chapter Four

1. Hu Shih (1891-1962) spoke out for liberal ideas in modern China. Quoted in DeGregori, p. 203.

2. Alex Avery, "Rachel Carson Syndrome: Jumping to Pesticide Conclusions in the Global Frog Crisis," <http://www.cgfi.org/materials/key_pubs/frogs_pesticides_2005>.

3. Theo Colborn, Dianne Gumanoski, and John Peterson Myers, *Our Stolen Future; Are We Threatening our Fertility, Intelligence, and Survival?—A Detective Story* (New York: Dutton, 1996); Arnold. *Undue Influence*, p. 106.

4. Bjorn Lomborg, *The Skeptical Environmentalist,* (Cambridge University Press, 2001), p. 238-243:; Ruth Kava and Daland Juberg, "The Latest Example of Alleged Chemical Threats: Endocrine Modulators," in Juberg, *Are Children More Vulnerable to Environmental Chemicals?* (American Council on Science and Health, 2002), pp. 79-92; DeGregori, p. 67.

5. See Steven Milloy and Michael Gough, *Silencing Science* (Washington: Cato Institute, 1998) 49-50; Lomborg 241-242; Arnold *Undue Influence,* p. 107-108.

6. DeGregori, p. 65.

7. Manheim, p. 192; Bonner R. Cohen, "Scaring Up Money With False Attacks on Science," *Sunday Republican* (Waterbury, Conn.), Sept. 24, 2000; Arnold, *Undue Influence*, p. 97, 107.

8. Bonner R. Cohen, "The Role of the Media," in Juberg, pp. 144-145.

9. "The Heat Is On," *National Geographic,* Sept. 2004; Patrick Michaels, "National Geographic Melting Down?," *Washington Times* Sept. 7, 2004, p. A15.

10. Daniel Glick, "The Big Thaw," *National Geographic* Sept. 2004, p. 14.; "Deforestation Causing Dry Climate," *Nature,* Nov. 24, 2003. <http://www.usenet.com/newsgroups/talk/environment/msg05757.html>.

11. "Dry Air the Kilimanjaro Culprit," *International Journal of Climatology,* March 15, 2004 <http://www.umass.edu/climate/tanzania/pubs/kaser_etal_2004ijc.pdf>'; *Journal of Geophysical Research,* Aug. 25, 2004. <http://www.umass.edu/climate/tanzania/pubs/moelg_hardy_2004jgr.pdf>

12. Bill Allen, "From the Editor," *National Geographic,* Sept. 2004.

13. Manheim, p. 124.

14. Arnold *Undue Influence,* pp. 86-87 and Martin Morse Wooster, *The Great Philanthropists and the Problem of 'Donor Intent,* (Washington, DC: Capital Research Center, 1998) pp.44-53.

15. Manheim, pp. 26-35.
16. Quoted in Arnold, *Undue Influence*, p. 78.
17. Patrick Reilly, "The Tides Foundation and Center: Unusual Philanthropies Funnel Money to Activist Groups," *Foundation Watch* (Washington: Capital Research Center, Jan. 1998), p. 4.
18. Gretchen Randall and Tom Randall, "The Tides Foundation: Liberal Crossroads of Money and Ideas," *Foundation Watch* (Washington: Capital Research Center, Dec. 2003), p. 1; Reilly, p. 3.
19. "Tides Center," Capital Research Database Profile <http://www.capitalresearch.org/utils/print_profile.>.
20. Arnold, *Undue Influence*, p. 69.
21. Cohen, "Green Landgrabbers," p. 2.
22. Ron Arnold, "The Pew Charitable Trusts: Global Warming Power Nexus," *Foundation Watch* (Washington: Capital Research Center, May 2004), p. 1; Arnold, *Undue Influence,* pp. 88-89.
23. "Pew Charitable Trusts," Capital Research Center Grantmaker Profile <http:..www.capitalresearch.org?utils/print_gm.asp>; Manheim, pp. 40-51.
24. See Capital Research Center Grantmaker Profile <http://www.capitalresearch.org for this and all subsequent funding sources.
25. Neil Hrab, "A Look at the MacArthur Foundation," *Foundation Watch* (Washington: Capital Research Center, Aug. 2003), p. 1.
26. Arnold and Gottlieb, pp. 147-148, 602-604.
27. Arnold, *Undue Influence,* p. 70.
28. Driessen, pp. 55-56.
29. Arnold, *Undue Influence,* pp.35, 71-72, 233-235.
30. Ron Arnold, "The Heinz Foundations and the Kerry Campaign: One Has Money, the Other Needs Money," *Foundation Watch* (Washington: Capital Research Center, April 2004), pp. 1-2.
31. Arnold, *Undue Influence,* p.110,. Randall, "Tides Foundation," p. 2.
32. Quoted in Thomas B. Edsall and James Grimaldi, "New Routes for Money to Sway Voters: 501(c)(3) Groups Escape Disclosure Rules," *Washington Post,* Sept. 27, 2004, p.A1.
33. Sally Torbert, "Ted Turner: Down But Not Out," *Foundation Watch* (Washington: Capital Research Center, Nov. 2004), p. 1.
34. See Jennifer Locetta and David Hogberg, "De-energizing the Market: The Energy Foundation," *Foundation Watch* (Washington: Capital Research Center, Jan. 2006)
35. U.S. Senate Environment and Public Works Committee, *Grants Management at the Environmental Protection Agency: A New*

Culture Required to Cure a History of Problems (Washington, Sept. 2004), p. 3.

36. GAO and Heist testimony quoted in *Grants Management,* pp. 8-11.
37. U.S. Environmental Protection Agency Office of Inspector General, *Audit Report Consumer Federation of America—Cost Claimed Under Cooperative Agreements,* CX825612-01, CX825837-01, CX824939-01, and X827938-01 Report No. 2004-4-00014, March 1, 2004, p. 6.
38. U.S. Environmental Protection Agency Grants Awards Database *All Awards to Non-Profits ,* <http://www.yosemite.epa.gov/oarm/igms_egf.nsf?Reports?Mon-Profit+Grants?OpenView>.
39. CEHN and NRDC grants discussed in *Grants Management,* pp. 17-19.
40. David Healy, "NRDC: Biting the Taxpayers Who Feed Them," *Organization Trends* (Washington: Capital Research Center, Sept. 2004), p. 2.
41. See David Schoenbrod, *Saving Our Environment From Washington: How Congress Grabs Power, Shirks Responsibility, and Shortchanges the People* (New Haven: Yale University Press, 2005), pp. 59-67; Alan H. Carpien and Daniel L. Fort, "Overseeing EPA," in *American Values,* pp. 47-60.
42. *All Awards to Non-Profits* See note 38.
43. Quoted in David B. Ottaway and Joe Stephens, "Nonprofit Land Bank Amasses Billions," *Washington Post,* May 4, 2003, p. A22.
44. Joe Stephens and David B. Ottaway, "Conservancy Abandons Disputed Practices," *Washington Post,* June, 14, 2003, pp. A1,10; Ottaway and Stephens "Nonprofit Land Bank," p. A22.
45. Joe Stephens and David B. Ottaway, "IRS to Audit Nature Conservancy From Inside," *Washington Post,* Jan. 17, 2004, p. A12.
46. Joe Stephens and David B. Ottaway, "How a Bid to Save a Species Came to Grief," *Washington Post,* May 5, 2003, pp. A1,10-11.
47. Quoted in Joe Stephens, "IRS Starts Team on Easement Abuses," *Washington Post,* June 9, 2005, p. A6.
48. David B. Ottaway and Joe Stephens, "Landing a Big One: Preservation, Private Development," *Washington Post,* May 6, 2003, p. A9.
49. Joe Stephens and David B. Ottaway, "420,000 a Year and No-Strings Fund," *Washington Post,* May 4, 2003, p. A21.
50. Joe Stephens and David B. Ottaway, "Image Is a Sensitive Issue," *Washington Post,* May 4, 2003, p. A23.

51. Arnold and Gottlieb, pp. 83-85 for a discussion of VCR and Mellon events.
52. David B. Ottaway and Joe Stephens, "On Eastern Shore, For-Profit 'Flagship' Hits Shoals," *Washington Post,* May 5, 2003, p. A11.
53. Quoted in Brad Wolverton, "Senators Question Tax Breaks Given by Donors to Conservation Groups," *The Chronicle of Philanthropy,* June 8, 2005, p. 3.
54. See Arnold and Gottlieb, pp. 82-88, Arnold, *Undue Influence,* p. 163; Brookes quoted in Thomas Bray (ed.), *Unconventional Wisdoms: The Best of Warren Brookes,* (San Francisco: Pacific Research Institute, 1997), p. 285.
55. Arnold, *Undue Influence,* p. 163; Ottoway and Stephens, "Nonprofit Land Bank," *Washington Post,* p. A22

Chapter Five

1. George Santayana, *The Life of Reason* [vol.1] "Introduction."
2. Stephen Yates, "Understanding the Culture War: Gramscians, Tocquevillians, and Others," LewRockwell.com, ww.lewrockwell.com/yates/yates24.html.
3. The *Sun* and *Post* are quoted in Steven Milloy, "Katrina Exposes Media's Global Warming Bias," *Environment & Climate News,* Nov. 2005, p. 10.
4. Dennis Byrnne, "Leading Hurricane Experts Downplay Global Warming," *Environment & Climate News*, Oct. 2005, p. 9. Byrne adds: "In an interview with Environment & Climate News, O'Brien said the more likely cause of hurricane frequency might be found in variations in the Atlantic Ocean Conveyer, the movement of the warm Gulf Stream whose waters, taken from the South Atlantic, replace the cooler, sinking water in the North Atlantic. O'Brien said historic records show that when the conveyer is strong, there is an increase in the number and intensity of Atlantic hurricanes; when it is weak, so are the hurricane seasons. For a hurricane to grow stronger, it must keep moving over water warmer than 80 degrees F, which leads some people to link global warming and the storms. But, he said, there's no evidence to show that such areas of warm water are increasing in size."
5. Mark Truby, "PR Firm Doesn't Shy From Provocative Ads," *Courier-Journal* (Louisville, Ky.), Jan. 29, 2003. See also John Gizzi, "David Fenton: Media Maestro of the Left," *Organization Trends* (Washington: Capital Research Center, Dec. 2004) p. 4.

6. Michael Paulson, "Bishops Say Fighting Global Warming Is a Moral Duty," *Boston Globe*, June 16, 2001, p. A10.

7. "The National Religious Partnership for the Environment," *Environmental Stewardship Review* (Grand Rapids, Mich.: Acton Institute for the Study of Religion and Liberty, 1999), p. 6.

8. NRPE received grants totaling $272,000 and $230,000 from the Blue Moon Fund and the Pew Charitable Trusts, respectively, in the years 2000-2004.

9. Quoted in Blaine Harden, "The Greening of Evangelicals: Christian Right Turns, Sometimes Warily, to Environmentalism," *Washington Post*, Feb. 6, 2005, p. A1.

10. Laurie Goodstein, "Evangelicals Consider Expanding Political and Social Goals," *New York Times*, March 12, 2005.

11. Alan Cooperman, "Evangelicals Will Not Take Stand on Global Warming," *Washington Post,* Feb. 2, 2006, p. A8.

12. Leftist evangelicals have by no means given up the fight. They have launched the "Evangelical Climate Initiative," whose website contains a statement on the perils of global warming signed by dozens of ministers and officials of evangelical colleges. See <http://www.christianclimate.org/statement>.

13. "The Advertising Council and Environmental Defense Launch National PSA Campaign to Combat Global Warming," (press release, March 23, 2006),
<http://www.adcouncil.org/newsDetail.aspx?id=79>.

14. Juliet Eilperin, "GOP Joins Fight on Warming," *Washington Post*, March 23, 2006, p. A5.

15. See Ron Arnold, "The Politics of Environmental Defense: Will John Kerry Listen to ED Trustee Teresa Heinz Kerry?," *Foundation Watch* (Washington: Capital Research Center, Aug. 2004).

16. Data taken from IRS Form 990 is available on the invaluable "Guidestar" website, <http://www.guidestar.org.

17. On Enron memo contents, see Paul Driessen, *Eco-Imperialism*, pp. 100-101, 105.

18. *Wall Street Journal* Aug. 18, 2005, p. A12; July 21, 2005, p. A12; Aug. 25, 2005, p. A10.

19. Jim Carlton, "BP Faces Federal Criminal Probe of Alaskan Pipelines," *Wall Street Journal*, April 6, 2006, p. A3; Jim Carlton, "BP Finds New Pipeline Rupture Caused by Corrosion in Alaska," *Wall Street Journal,* April 17, 2006, p. A3; Amy Joyce, "BP Fined Over Safety Issues at Ohio Refinery," *Washington Post*, April 26, 2006, p. D2.

20. Paul Driessen, "Time to Clean House at Goldman Sachs," <http://www.americandaily.com/article/12680>; "Free Enterprise Update: Goldman Meeting Hijacked by Free Enterprisers," (press release: Free Enterprise Fund, April 3, 2006) <http://www.freeenterpriser.com>; Judith H. Dobrzynski, "Green-nosing," *Wall Street Journal*, April 4, 2006, p. A22. For a defense of the Goldman Sachs land deal, see letters to the editor by Paul Newman and John H. Bryan, *Wall Street Journal*, April 10, 2006, p. A19. See also "The Conservation Capitalist: Hank Paulson: Chairman and CEO, the Goldman Sachs Group," *Vanity Fair*, May 2006, p. 182.
21. Bjorn Lomborg, "Something is Rotten in the State of Denmark," *Wall Street Journal*, Jan. 23, 2003.
22. James K. Glassman, "Green With Rage: Why Environmentalists Throw Pies Against Bjorn Lomborg," *The Weekly Standard*, Feb. 25, 2002, p. 14.
23. Richard Lindzen, "Climate of Fear," *Wall Street Journal*, April 12, 2006.
24. See Stephen Moore, "Of Mice and Men," *Wall Street Journal*, March 23, 2006, p. A17; David Holthouse, "Building a Better Mousetrap: Biologist Rob Ramey Isn't Afraid of Taking Risks—But Taking on Environmentalists May be His Riskiest Move," *Denver Westword* Jan. 20, 2005; Rob Roy Ramey II, Hsiu-Ping Liu, Clinton W. Epps, Lance M. Carpenter and John D. Wehausen, "Genetic Relatedness of the Preble's Meadow Jumping Mouse (Zapus hudsonnius preblei) to Nearby Subspecies of Z. hudsonius as Inferred in Variations in Cranial Morphology, Mitochondrial DNA and Microsatellite DNA: Implications for Taxomony and Conservation," *Animal Conservation* (2005) 8, pp. 329-346.
25. Interview with Dr. Rob Roy Ramey April 19, 2006; Vincent Carroll, "On Point: The Mouse That Roard," *Rocky Mountain News*, April 5, 2006, <http://www.rockymountainnews.com>; Vincent Carroll, "On Point: Species Act Abused," *Rocky Mountain News*, April 6, 2006 <http://www.rockymountainnews.com>.
26. New York quote in Juliet Eilperin, "Censorship is Alleged at NOAA," *Washington Post*, Feb. 11, 2006, p. A7; "60 Minutes" quote in Marc Morano, "Scientist Alleging Bush Censorship Helped Gore, Kerry," *CNSNews.com*, March 23, 2006; Robert D. Novak, "Spinning Global Warming," *Washington Post*, April 3, 2006, p. A19; see also James Walcott, "Hall of Fame: Vanity Fair Nominates Dr. James E. Hansen," *Vanity Fair* May 2006, p. 106.
27. Juliet Eilperin, "Climate Researchers Feeling Heat From White House," *Washington Post*, April 6, 2006, p. A27.

28. Quoted in Mark Hertsgaard, "While Washington Slept," *Vanity Fair,* May 2006, p. 241.

29. Nathan Rosenberg and L.E. Birdzell, *How the West Grew Rich: The Economic Transformation of the Industrial World* (New York: Basic Books, 1986), p. 333.

Epilogue

1. T. S. Eliot, "The Cocktail Party," [1950] (Harcourt, Brace, 1964), p.103

2. Guy Gugliotta, "Tools Found in Britain Show Much Earlier Human Existence," *Washington Post*, Dec. 15, 2005, p. A24.

3. Gugliotta, "On the Trail of a Giant Scorpion," *Washington Post,* Dec. 12, 2005, p. A8.

4. Patrick Michaels, "Massive Extinction of Logic," *Washington Times,* Jan. 15, 2004, p. A17.

5. Crichton, *State of Fear,* p. 571.

6. George F. Will, "Our Fake Drilling Debate, *Washington Post,* Dec. 15, 2005, p. A33.

7. Leo Francis, Kembra J. Dunham and Alex Frangos, "New 'Fortified' Homes Aim to Withstand Nature's Assaults," *Wall Street Journal,* Nov. 23, 2005, p. B1.

8. King and Schneider, Watson and the leaflet quoted in Phillip W. De Vous, "The Moral Case for Human Ingenuity: Protecting Human Dignity and Promoting Public Health and Safety," in *The Wages of Fear: The Costs to Society of Attacks on the Products of Human Ingenuity,* (Arllington, VA: Lexington Institute, August 2002), www.cgfi.org/materials/key_pubs/wagesoffear/pdf., p. 15.

9. Paul W. Hansen, "Greens in Gridlock," *Washington Post,* March 11, 2005, p. A23.

10. Richard Lindzen, "Climate of Fear," *Wall Street Journal,* April, 12, 2006.

11. David Schoenbrod, *Saving Our Environment from Washington,* p. 61

12. See "Inhofe Sites Environmental Progress for Earth Day '05," (press release) U.S. Senate Environment and Public Works Committee, April 22, 2005; "In Americans, Lower Levels of Chemicals," *Washington Post,* July 22, 2005, p. A3; "Cancer Rates Fall 1st Time Since 1930," *Washington Times,* Feb. 9, 2006, p. A7.

13. Quoted in Patrick Michaels, "Gore's Inconvenient Lie," *Washington Times,* May 24, 2006, p. A17; quoted in "Inside Politics", *Washington Times,* May 23, 2006, p. A6.

Index

231

Izaak Walton League,
139, 142, 146, 148, 151,
168, 180, 194
J.C. Penney, 129
J.P. Morgan Chase, 5, 6, 11,
13-16, 170
Jablow, Judy, 111
Jaffe, Greg, 41
Jenkins, Holman, 33
John Merck Fund, 142, 187, 193,
196, 199, 202, 203, 205
Johnson, Paul, 43
Journal of Biogeography, 47
Journal of Geophysical Research,
123, 124
Joyce Foundation, 136, 148, 190,
191, 192, 199, 205, 208
Joyce-Mertz-Gilmore Foundation,
147
Kalam, A.P.J., 43
Karpinski, Gene, 110, 195
Kennedy Jr., Robert F., 175
Kennedy, Anne, 110
Kerry, Sen. John, 140, 163
Keystone Center, 146
King, Alexander, 180
Kirby, William, 134
Knippers, Diane, 164
Knobloch, Kevin, 168, 204
Knudson, Tom, 131
Kostyack, John, 103
Kristof, Nicholas, 29
Krupp, Fred, 165, 166, 167, 189
Krutch, Joseph Wood, 89
L.L. Bean, 136
Laffer, Arthur, 18
Langfitt, Thomas, 126
Lash, Jonathan, 55, 167
Lawrence, Niel, 110
Lay, Ken, 169

League of Conservation Voters,
3, 70, 71, 130, 137, 138, 140,
141, 143, 145, 167, 195
Leavitt, Michael, 106
Leggett, Jerry, 51
Lehman Brothers, 122
Lehman, Jane Bagley, 128
Leopold, Aldo, 89
Letterman, David, 154
Levin, Simon, 90
Lieberman, Sen. Joseph, 66
Lindblom, Lance, 132
Lindzen, Richard, 52, 173, 181
Lippman, Steve, 13
Living Earth Foundation, 130
Lobbying Disclosure Act, 150
Locker, Michael, 7
Logomasini, Angela,
2, 3, 77, 78, 79
Lomborg, Bjorn, 172, 181
Longabaugh, Mark, 141
Los Angeles Times, 87, 115
Lovejoy, Frank, 144
Lovelock, James, 162
Lyons, Jim, 110
MacArthur Foundation,
John D. and Catherine T., 122,
131, 133, 147, 185, 186, 190,
191, 196, 200
MacArthur, John, 134
Mailman, Joshua, 14, 127, 130, 158
Maloney, Rep. Carolyn, 87
Manheim, Jarol,
6, 7, 8, 10, 15, 19, 124,
125, 127, 143, 158
Mann, Charles C., 91
Mann, Michael, 64
Margulis, Lynn, 162
Marisla Foundation, 192
Mary Flagler Cary
Charitable Trust, 155, 196